HV
91
.P38
1998

$27.00

D1572958

WITHDRAWN

MEDIA CENTER
ELIZABETHTOWN COMMUNITY COLLEGE
600 COLLEGE STREET ROAD
ELIZABETHTOWN, KY 42701

OVERCOMING WELFARE

James L. Payne

OVERCOMING WELFARE

Expecting More from the Poor—and from Ourselves

Basic Books
A Member of Perseus Books, L.L.C.

Copyright © 1998 by James L. Payne.

Published by Basic Books, a Member of Perseus Books, L.L.C.

All rights reserved.

Printed in the United States of America.

No part of this book may be used or reproduced in any manner whatsoever without written
permission except in the case of brief quotations embodied in critical articles and reviews.
For information address Basic Books, 10 East 53rd Street, New York, NY 10022.

FIRST EDITION.

Designed by Jenny Dossin

Library of Congress Cataloging-in-Publication Data

Payne, James L.

Overcoming welfare : expecting more from the poor—and from ourselves /
James L. Payne. — 1st ed.

p.   cm.

Includes bibliographical references and index.

ISBN 0-465-06924-X

1. Public welfare—United States.

2. Poor—Government policy—United States.

3. Welfare recipients—United States.

4. United States—Social policy—1993–

I. Title.

HV91.P38   1998

362.5'8'0973—dc21

98–5360

CIP

1   3   5   7   9   10   8   6   4   2

98   00   01   99

Contents

PART IV

Paths for the Future

Acknowledgments

This book grew from my experience as a temporary manual laborer for Industrial Labor Services in Dallas, Texas. Eric Veblen, who was the assistant manager of ILS, had for years been urging me to consider the policy implications of this humble business that gave work and shelter to members of the underclass. In the fall of 1994, I put on my jeans, flew to Dallas, and went to the ILS shelter and hiring hall on South Ervay Street. I found that this commercial, profit-making firm was clearly helping the homeless in a more constructive way than most charity-based shelters and employment programs. The key to its success, I realized, was that it incorporated the idea of exchange—expecting something in return for assistance given.

In the following years, I pursued this concept of "expectant giving" to see how it might bear on the problems of the national welfare system. I interviewed welfare officials in my hometown of Sandpoint, Idaho, and then began taking trips to other states to study their welfare arrangements. In 1996 a Bradley Fellowship at the Heritage Foundation in Washington made it possible for me to observe the making of federal welfare policy and to use the Library of Congress, with its treasure of writings by nineteenth-century charity leaders.

The research for this book has been aided by many people. First, I would like to thank the several hundred workers and volunteers in assistance programs who gave me interviews and allowed me to observe their programs. Even most government officials were generally cooperative. A handful did clam up or try to prevent me from finding out anything significant, but most were willing to talk frankly, and at some risk to their careers, about the defects of current programs.

I am also grateful to the publications that gave me an opportunity to present findings and develop my arguments as the research progressed. These include *Policy Review*, *The American Enterprise*, *The Public Interest*, *Insight*, and *Philanthropy, Culture, and Society*.

Finally, I would like to thank the many people who read this work at various stages and gave helpful suggestions for improvement: Adam Meyerson, Heather Mac Donald, Charles Glock, Craig Rennebohm, Mark Reiner, Ed Donaldson, John Bosma, Pat Fagan, David Mason, Ken Weinstein, Dorothy Boerner, David Miller, Colleen Miller, Joyce Poirot, Dorothy Simcox, Ellen Solomon, Bobbie Brown, Jack White, and editors Tim Duggan and Arthur Magida. No list of acknowledgments would be complete without including my wife Judy, for her patient attention as I tested out the ideas of this book on her more times than either of us could count.

Sandpoint, Idaho
January 1998

Introduction
Managing a Policy Beyond Our Comprehension

At the height of the welfare reform debate in the summer of 1996, I obtained a copy of the final Senate version of the measure, S. 1956. As an observer of welfare policies, I felt obliged to find out what this legislation actually contained. I was dismayed to discover that it was the size of a city telephone directory, 1,027 pages long.

The cover page made the ritual declaration that the bill had been "read twice" before being placed on the Senate calendar, but clearly that was no more than a statement of a legislative ideal. No one could have read this measure even once. Perhaps certain staff members on the nineteen different committees and subcommittees that contributed to it had read the subsection they were responsible for, but the idea that any senator actually read the document he or she voted on was implausible.

Not that reading it would have been much help in understanding it. For one thing, the language was breathtakingly complicated, a Boolean algebra of legalese, with exceptions to exceptions and amendments to amendments. Even if readers finally disentangled what appeared to be intended, they still had to guess what would actually become of the intention after it suffered the normal mutilation of bureaucracy, pressure groups, inattention, and folly.

To take one example, the legislation provided, in section 824, that able-bodied single adults could not receive food stamps for more than three months unless they obtained part-time jobs or entered a workfare program. It seemed a simple clause to ensure that food stamps were only a "hand up" for those without a good excuse for not getting back to work. However, in another clause the act provided an exemption for regions with relatively high unemployment. Almost before the ink was dry, state welfare officials began making use of this provision, twisting economic data to make their problems look as bad as possible and pleading with a sympathetic Department of Agriculture to exempt them. Within months, forty states had applied for an exemption; in many of these states, more than half of the able-bodied single adults covered by the act were exempted and allowed to continue on food stamps. As a result of these exemptions, the expected budget "savings" from this provision had shrunk by 20 percent halfway through the first year of the reform.[1]

The obscurity of legislation is only one aspect of a larger complexity. Morally and intellectually, welfare is the nation's most convoluted policy subject. Policies of social assistance deal with the whole person, with what he does with his entire life, with whether he is, and remains, happy and productive. No other policy attempts this kind of comprehensive concern. A law against speeding simply tries to get drivers to slow down; it doesn't ask whether they have enough to eat, live in satisfactory housing, are fulfilled in their work, or enjoy a stable family life. The same is true of laws on labor, on tariffs, on pollution, and so on. All of these treat specific behaviors. In welfare, on the other hand, practically *everything* about the person matters.

The result is that we get drawn into a towering complexity, trying to figure out who deserves what, and what the effect of intervention will be on the recipient's future life and prosperity. This ambiguity is daunting but perhaps manageable when individuals help individuals, friends, or family members they know well. But when a group of people try to help another group of people, the confusion mounts exponentially.

The helpers disagree among themselves about how the needy should behave. Exactly what do 270 million Americans want an indigent unwed teen mother to do? Some think she should go to work, others say she should get married, others say she should stay home and raise her children. If she gets pregnant again, some say she should be put away in an institution, others that she should have an abortion, and others that she should put the baby up for adoption. Still others say she should keep her baby and be supported by taxpayers. Americans are similarly divided on what behavior to expect from those in other assistance categories: what to demand of the unemployed, the school dropout, the disabled.

And then, of course, there is the complexity of the target population. We do not have just one indigent unwed teen mother, but millions, each of whom has somewhat different problems and somewhat different prospects. In all of the other categories of need, we confront this same staggering complexity: millions of different cases, each needing individual treatment. In our efforts to devise welfare policies, we are, in truth, attempting to legislate for cases beyond our comprehension.

A First Principle

▼

Collective systems of social assistance—systems that are jointly funded and jointly directed—are dangerously complex. They tempt us to be so distracted by particulars, by the one small corner we happen to be looking at, that we lose sight of overall strategy. If we are not to flounder in indecision and drift further toward social disaster, we need some basic principles that will steer us in a useful direction.

The central mistake we have been making in welfare policy is to assume that we need to *give* to the needy. It's an understandable error: if people are suffering because they lack some material good, it's natural to think that if we give it to them, we will solve their problem.

If the past half-century of trillion-dollar welfare spending has taught us anything, it is that the problems of the needy are not, at bottom, economic ones. If the dysfunctions of poverty could be cured by giving people money, or things that money can buy, they would have been cured many times over. The problems of those we call needy lie mainly outside the material realm. For some, the limitations are mental or physical; for many others, the problems are psychological or moral, having to do with willpower, pride, and character, with bad habits and irresponsible decisions. Giving material aid does not address these difficulties. It is like giving a stone to a man who needs bread.

We need to reverse our thinking about the needy. Paradoxical as it sounds, what the poor actually need is *to be asked to give*, not to be given to. It is through their contributions, their rising to challenges and achievements, that they overcome weaknesses and disabilities. Assistance systems need to be oriented toward what I call "expectant giving," arrangements that expect or require a constructive response or contribution from the person being assisted. By this standard, the best aid program is not the one that gives away the most to the needy, but the one that is successful in eliciting the greatest contribution from them.

In recent years, welfare reforms at both the state and national levels have begun to incorporate this idea of expecting something from those being assisted. However, it has entered policy unconsciously for the most part. Most of the welfare programs still ignore it and remain fully in the something-for-nothing mold. Even when expectant giving has been added to a program, its application has been halting and contentious because policy makers lack a clear picture of its underlying rationale. This book aims to provide this picture, to set out the underlying perspectives and theory that animate the current efforts at welfare reform. After surveying past welfare policies to explain why the valuable principle of expectant giving has so often been ignored, we shall identify what must be done to apply it in the future.

Correcting the failings of our current welfare system is rather like trying to forge a path out of a jungle. Action is necessary, of course, but action alone, uninformed by an overall purpose, is likely to worsen our plight. The past few years of welfare reform represent a useful start in reshaping social assistance policies. But to maintain and extend this success, we shall need a guide that shows where we must head and why. It is my hope that this book will provide a compass for our efforts.

PART I

Giving Right, Giving Wrong

The Policy Nobody Wants

Though welfare receives a great deal of attention these days, it cannot, properly speaking, be called a topic of "conversation." Americans don't converse about welfare, asking questions and delving into points of view. Their opinions about it are much too strong; they just say what they think. And what they say, with remarkable uniformity, is that the existing policies are wrong, wrong, wrong. "People take advantage of it," says a Denver woman in a focus group. "Sitting home, watching TV, going to amusement parks. They're using our tax money." A Birmingham man says, "Welfare cripples people. They're looking for a handout—that shouldn't be. They become dependent."[1] Opinion polls show a public deeply skeptical about welfare programs. In an April 1995 survey by the National Opinion Research Center, 66 percent of respondents thought the nation was spending "too much" on welfare; only 9 percent said we were spending "too little."[2]

Defenders of the welfare system fear that this opposition reflects the onset of a sinister, antisocial mood, that Americans are becoming a nation of selfish pleasure seekers who no longer care about their neighbors. When welfare reform in 1996 limited certain benefits, liberals saw a black cloud. "America has lost its will to lift up the poor," wrote a columnist in the *Chronicle of Philanthropy*. "That is the underlying message of the new welfare law."[3]

The truth appears to be much simpler. Americans are upset with welfare spending because it is obviously not working. Political elites and welfare experts were given large sums of money to treat social problems. Sweeping promises were made about what this would accomplish. In 1964 President Lyndon Johnson held out the prospect of a "total victory" in a "national war on poverty" and urged the adoption of a number of additional welfare programs. "For the first time in our history," Johnson declared, "it is possible to conquer poverty." Sargent Shriver, the administration's leading antipoverty warrior, told Congress that the nation had "both the resources and the know-how to eliminate grinding poverty in the United States."[4]

For many years, the country went along with officials and their rhetoric. The intentions seemed noble, and legislators and administrators claimed to know what they were doing. Then, around the late 1970s, the mood began to shift. Instead of listening to promises, the public began to look at performance. Americans began to see that the nation had escalating social problems—homelessness, drug abuse, illiteracy, illegitimacy, crime—even while spending to treat these ills had grown by leaps and bounds. It was like paying a very high bill for a new roof and waking up to find the rain soaking through your mattress.

Naturally, Americans are upset. Perhaps more significantly, those who work with the poor are upset. Bill Lock is a Black church leader and self-help organizer in Milwaukee. He gives a modern reformer's view of government's war on poverty:

In fighting this war we have created an industry that feeds on itself, like a mad general who has lost thousands of soldiers but continues to say, "I can still win if you send me more troops." This is what our government's effort to fight poverty is like today. It is an endless cycle of programs, projects, and personnel, often supported by people with strong motives, but without a clear and sensible vision of what needs to be done.

My community has not been untouched in this war. I live in central Milwaukee and my zip code has a large population of the shell-shocked. This is the result of being bombarded by programs that have reduced survival skills and the spirit of individual initiative.[5]

Instead of reducing poverty, government assistance programs seem to have been multiplying it. That is why we are disappointed. Americans disapprove of the welfare system not because they lack compassion but because they have it.

Hand up or Handout?

▼

The United States is a democracy where policies are supposed to be supported by popular majorities. How did we end up with welfare programs almost everyone dislikes? In broad terms, the dissatisfaction with welfare can be explained by a persistent confusion between two methods of trying to help the needy. One method is recognized as genuinely helpful and constructive; the other is understood to be harmful and corrupting. The nation wanted, and was promised, the helpful policy. But the policy actually carried out was the harmful one.

The helpful policy is popularly known as the "hand up." Its aim is to help people get back on their feet, or to "help people help themselves." In this book, we call it "expectant giving"—giving with a definite expectation that the needy person will do something constructive in exchange for the help rendered. The classic example of this approach is giving someone work so that he can earn what he needs.

The destructive policy is the "handout," also known as "giving something for nothing." It does not demand constructive behavior from the recipient. I call this "sympathetic giving"; its size is governed by the degree of sympathy or pity we feel for the recipient. The classic example is giving a beggar money because he is (or appears to be) crippled. The beggar is not expected to *do* anything to overcome his disability; indeed, the more helpless and unfortunate he seems, the bigger the gift.

It is easy to see that a policy of expectant giving, of giving the needy a "hand up," is the healthy one. This kind of helping bolsters the energy, self-esteem, and usefulness of people in unfortunate circumstances. The dangers of sympathetic giving are equally apparent. Handouts reinforce dysfunctional behavior and attitudes and undermine the pride and self-confidence of recipients.

Sympathetic giving is the policy nobody wants. Yet, amazingly, this is the policy we keep getting. All the major welfare programs have been variations on sympathetic giving. They give cash and material resources to people on the basis of their misfortune and expect no significant effort in return. One sign of how far we have traveled in this direction is the lack of programs that *lend* to the needy. If we really believed that our aid was a "hand up," then aid programs would involve loans that the needy could pay back once they were on their feet. Today's programs lack such a feature. We consider the notion fanciful that the poor should ever pay back even a penny of the cost of their food stamps or job training or drug rehabilitation or housing vouchers or medical care. It's our way of saying that we don't really expect anything from them.

The massive system of giveaways was never recommended by any national leader. To the contrary, everyone firmly warned against it, starting with the nineteenth-century charity theorists who worked closely with the poor. They knew that sympathetic giving was destructive, that it "pauperized" the very poor it was supposed to assist.

The twentieth-century politicians who built the welfare system agreed with them. Consider the New Deal. Many of today's handout programs, including Aid to Families with Dependent Children (AFDC), were creations of the Roosevelt administration. Yet Franklin Roosevelt deplored the idea of something-for-nothing giving in the strongest terms. Here is how he put it in his 1935 State of the Union address:

> The lessons of history, confirmed by the evidence immediately before me show conclusively that continued dependence upon relief induces a spiritual and moral disintegration fundamentally destructive to the national fiber. To dole out relief in this way is to administer a narcotic, a subtle destroyer of the human spirit. It is inimical to the dictates of sound policy.[6]

Lyndon Johnson, who greatly expanded handout programs in his 1964 war on poverty, shared this disapproval of giveaway programs. "The war on poverty is not a struggle simply to support people, to make them dependent on the generosity of others," he said. "It is a struggle to give people a chance. It is an effort to allow them to develop and use their capacities."[7]

One of the most demoralizing welfare programs today is the federal disability system, which now has more than eleven million beneficiaries mired in virtually permanent dependency on it. Instead of prodding them to overcome their disabilities—such as the loss of a limb, or stress, or insomnia—and live useful and happy lives, the system pays them for their suffering and uselessness. The Nixon administration set up this discouraging program in 1972 when it urged Congress to enact the supplemental security income (SSI) program in 1972. Yet in the special message to Congress on welfare reform in which he urged the creation of SSI, Richard Nixon denounced dependency. "The welfare life-style continues to dehumanize those who are caught in it," he said, "and threatens now to create yet another 'welfare generation.'"[8]

All politicians have paid lip service to the idea of expecting self-help from the needy, and all have condemned the something-for-nothing approach. In this stance, they have simply reflected the American consensus that giveaway programs are to be avoided. That is why the policy outcome has been so puzzling: under the banner of "a hand up, not a handout," the nation marched to establish a gigantic system of . . . handouts.

Why We Stumble

▼

What, then, can we expect of future attempts to fix welfare programs? The year 1996 saw another federal welfare reform, and we are bound to see many more. Policy makers will tell us not to worry: the new programs will not degenerate into more demoralizing handouts, and caseloads in some programs are falling. But we ought to be cautious. Leaders have promised an end to handouts many times before, and we have seen caseloads dip numerous times, only to see record growth a few years later. If a man tries to go up a flight of stairs five times and falls down every time, it's not reasonable to hope that on his sixth try he will be successful. It makes more sense to conclude that there's something wrong with the climber. When Franklin Roosevelt created the AFDC program, he had no evidence that government could help the needy in a sensitive, disciplined way. All he had was a politician's naive confidence that somehow the future would not resemble the past. Past welfare programs, as he himself said, had led to "spiritual and moral disintegration." Common sense would have predicted that, in due course, AFDC would also play its part in moral and social decline—as everyone now concedes it has.

It is time to go beyond ahistorical optimism about government welfare programs. Welfare is not like a machine, a simple toy that one can fix by tightening some screws here and there. The welfare programs we deplore are the outgrowths of our own errors of reason and perception. Until we identify and transcend these fatal biases, welfare programs will never come right. We oversimplify by saying that welfare is something we need to reform; it is rooted in a flawed mindset that needs to be overcome.

As we unravel the flaws in thinking that have led to the current crisis, we must first analyze concepts of giving. One reason we keep stumbling into giveaway programs is that we confuse different types of giving, and further, we confuse giving with helping. For example, many policy makers denounce "giveaways," saying that they sap motivation, industry, and self-esteem. But in the next breath, they endorse giveaways for those who seem "deserving," such as the laid-off worker or the veteran. If handouts sap motivation and undermine self-esteem, isn't this approach unsound for everyone, even highly deserving individuals? In chapter 2, we review the confusions that cloud our thinking about giving and develop a framework for analyzing social assistance policies.

In seeking explanations for the handout character of modern welfare programs, one of the first factors we notice is the role of government. Government welfare programs have an inherent tendency to lapse into something-for-nothing giving. This may seem a commonplace observation, a self-evident conclusion from the historical record, but because hope springs eternal where government is concerned, it is necessary to examine it in detail. Chapters 5 and 6 review the fiscal, bureaucratic, and institutional pressures inherent in government that push even programs with the best of intentions into the handout mode. This analysis reveals a fundamental inconsistency in the modern approach: we insist on using government to help the poor, yet government's way of helping is the much-deplored handout. A frank recognition of this dilemma leads, it seems, to the conclusion that welfare reform cannot succeed if it does not include a strategy for removing government from social assistance in the long run.

Ideology also pushes welfare programs into the handout mode. For generations, many philosophers and reformers have embraced the doctrine of income redistribution, believing that government should take from the rich and give to the poor. A handout policy follows almost automatically from this approach. If the poor are morally "entitled" to government payments, it is wrong to demand that they do anything in return for them. Thus, the policy of income redistribution has seriously harmed the cause of sound assistance policy.

As government established a massive presence in the welfare business, especially with the advent of the New Deal, it began to create constituencies and vested interests that reinforced the handout orientation. Making up one of these groups are social workers. As volunteers or employees of local, private charities, nineteenth-century social workers had a position of independence from which they could observe, and comment on, the dangers of handouts. The country thus gained a bastion of poverty experts who firmly and eloquently denounced sympathetic giving. As government took over welfare activities, social workers became predominantly employees of government giveaway programs, and they had to align their thinking with these programs or leave the field. The result, as we show in chapter 8, is that modern social work has adopted a worldview that justifies sympathetic giving, and social workers have become an energetic lobby defending giveaway programs.

The Paradox of Affluence

▼

Government's role, the ideology of redistribution, and the beliefs of social workers, all go a long way toward accounting for why we keep drifting into handouts even though we don't believe in them. But these factors provide only a partial explanation. A more elementary force is at work: wealth.

Giving to the needy is an extremely simple, primitive reaction to their plight. Human beings are naturally compassionate. When we see a suffering person, our first impulse is to end his suffering by giving him what he lacks. If a person is hungry, we want to give him food. If he is homeless, we want to give him shelter. The first restraint against this tendency is, simply, the state of our finances: our own money may be so scarce that we have to think twice about giving it away. Up until about two centuries ago, the poverty of donors was a natural barrier against any widespread tendency toward sympathetic giving. People lived on the brink of starvation, and almost everyone lacked the bare essentials of life. Even having a fork or a spoon was considered a luxury. So although people might have been disposed to give handouts to the needy, they didn't have all that much to give.

Over the past two hundred years, this condition of general deprivation has been alleviated, at least in the developed countries. In our age of amazing material abundance, we throw away at fast-food restaurants more forks and spoons (of course, they're plastic) than the entire world possessed one thousand years ago. Vast numbers of people have money to spend on luxuries and frivolities, on grooming pets, on cellular phones, on power windows in automobiles, on second homes and third television sets. Indulging shortsighted impulses of sympathy has become easier and easier to do. Giving a few dollars to a beggar no longer entails any significant sacrifice.

The same point applies to government monies. Centuries ago, governments had to squeeze hard to collect enough taxes to carry on their activities. However compassionate rulers often wanted to be, it was impossible for them to transfer large amounts of resources to the poor on a sustained basis. Today's prosperity gives government undreamed-of revenues—and vast sums available for handout programs.

The connection between wealth and sympathetic giving underlies the great paradox of our age—poverty amid plenty. It would have seemed that growing productivity would banish poverty, that the coming of affluence would mark the end of neediness. It obviously doesn't work that way. The problems of poverty—unemployment, homelessness, addiction, abandoned children—increase *along with* the growth in income. What has happened is that *increased wealth increases the flow of handouts, which lure the needy into dependent and dysfunctional lifestyles.*

Learning how to give wisely to the poor is therefore vitally important today. Those with little wealth—in biblical times or in medieval times—could afford to have shallow, shortsighted theories about how to help the poor. With their few pennies, they could do little damage with the wrong approach. Today we have an avalanche of dollars at our command, and they can kill as well as cure. So we must be especially clear about constructive approaches to helping the needy.

Innovative Reformers

▼

Fortunately, we live in a society of energetic, independent-minded people who are not generally cowed by authority. Even though government has committed massive resources to failed programs of sympathetic giving, it has not eclipsed all alternatives. Innovators and entrepreneurs have developed their own approaches to the problems of the needy. Through practical experiment and patient evolution, they have begun to rediscover the principles of giving that were so widely appreciated in the nineteenth century. This puts us in the happy position of being able to balance our survey of unsound giving with a review of positive developments in the charity field.

At the center of all of these useful approaches is the idea of expectant giving. The giver asks, in effect, what do I seek in return? The exchange may take different forms, of course, but one way or another, a serious quid pro quo characterizes every successful assistance arrangement.

In reviewing these arrangements, we begin with perhaps the most obvious type of exchange: commerce. Though everyone agrees that the best way to help a poor person is to provide him or her with a job, this point seems strangely forgotten when we actually meet job givers. They suddenly become "businesspeople," whom modern political culture paints as the enemy of the poor, a class that must be taxed, regulated, and repressed so that the needy can thrive. Yet commercial firms can be surprisingly effective antipoverty "agencies." Voluntary economic exchange has been the foundation of civilization, and it would be folly to ignore its inherent power to assist everyone, including the poor.

Sometimes, however, the beneficial exchange we would like to establish for a needy person cannot succeed on a purely commercial basis. In such cases, as we see in chapter 10, reformers find themselves practicing "charitable capitalism." They establish their organizations along commercial lines, demanding as much from recipients as they are in a position to give, but relying on some degree of philanthropy to balance the bottom line.

Another form of expectant giving involves the needy in formal agreements that stipulate steps of self-help to be made in exchange for aid. These contracts are especially common in privately funded organizations, whose donors and volunteers want to ensure that their charity efforts are actually translated into uplift. But it takes more than money to make such contracts succeed. They require both firmness in insisting on the terms of the contract and personal encouragement and guidance. What's needed is the kind of "tough love" that committed, informed volunteers are most likely to provide.

Perhaps the most important exchange system for uplift involves *no* material benefits at all: mentoring. Someone with a higher skill, or greater self-confidence or experience, guides a less-prepared individual toward improvement. Because they depend on personal relationships, mentoring arrangements are subtle, difficult to quantify, and often overlooked. But as we see in chapter 12, which surveys how mentors influence lives, they are all around us—in the family, in schools, and in many voluntary groups.

▼

In its efforts to address the problems of the needy, the country is not condemned to an endless round of giveaway policies. Compassionate, innovative reformers have created a vast array of programs that embody expectant giving. These approaches can wisely supplant older government programs, especially as national opinion moves away from those programs. The shift will result in more constructive help for the needy and less dependence on tax dollars. It will also require—and, I believe, stimulate—much more personal involvement in helping our neighbors.

2

Helping Those in Need: Basic Principles

At first glance, helping the poor seems to be the simplest subject imaginable. All you need to know is: give! We teach this to our children almost as soon as they can speak. Unfortunately, this simple idea is inadequate, a half-truth that leads to great frustration if we attempt to apply it without qualification.

At the heart of the difficulty is the fact that all acts of giving are based on assumptions—assumptions about why the recipient is in need and what our aid will mean for his or her life. Assisting the needy involves tentative, probabilistic judgments, which are much more difficult than, say, scientific observations or engineering computations. Let's explore some situations of need and see whether we can develop the outlines of a satisfactory approach.

Our new neighbor Louise knocks on the door. Can she borrow a cup of sugar? Practically all of us would be eager to comply with her request. It's natural to want to assist others, to help them with their problems and play a role in their achievements. Plus, we like to have friends, and this is an opportunity to develop a personal relationship. After a cup of coffee and a chat, Louise leaves with her sugar, and we say good-bye and close the door fully pleased with our act of helping.

For many, a welfare system is nothing more than this kind of giving multiplied many times. To make a better world, all we have to do is to keep repeating these simple acts of kindness. What this view fails to recognize, however, is that such giving represents a special category of assistance: *unpredicted, one-time giving*. It is a mistake to confuse this with ongoing welfare systems.

Let's expand our example to illustrate the difference. On the day after her first visit, Louise again knocks on our door. She hasn't returned the sugar, yet now she asks to borrow another cup. Most of us would put up a courteous front and give Louise another cup of sugar. But when we close the door this time, we do not feel that same warm glow of satisfaction. Instead, we have a sinking feeling. Giving twice is not the same as giving once.

What's the problem? The answer is that the second episode of giving begins to define a pattern—an unfortunate pattern. When we gave the first time, we were hoping to begin a mutually beneficial relationship. A natural second step in the development of that relationship would have been for Louise to make some return gesture— say, returning the cup of sugar, or giving us a few of the cookies she baked. We could look forward to many useful exchanges and the growth of a genuine friendship. But when Louise asks for something more—without having reciprocated the first gift—we begin to worry that she may be, well, a sponger, someone who takes advantage of other people.

Any arrangement that involves repeated giving is different from one-time giving, and the problems involved are not present in the one-time situation. Welfare systems involve repeated giving; indeed, the word *system* conveys this quality. Even begging is an arrangement of repeated giving. The donor may never have given to the beggar before, but his giving is not—from the point of view of the beggar—unexpected. Government welfare programs, even though they may adopt the language of one-time giving ("helping people back on their feet") are inevitably programs of predictable, repeated giving. Even those who have never received benefits can predict the system's response to them by consulting with friends and neighbors—or by reading the newspapers.

The mix-up between one-time and repeated giving leads to much confusion in discussions of welfare policies. We debate the repeated giving of welfare systems using the examples and principles of one-time giving. Our culture encourages this error: the lore and literature about helping the needy looks almost exclusively to instances of one-time giving. Take the parable of the Good Samaritan, which is often cited as the inspiration for welfare programs like food stamps or public housing. These programs involve repeated giving, however. The Samaritan gave assistance on one occasion to a traveler who could not possibly have anticipated such aid: he had been robbed and beaten by thieves on the road to Damascus. The Samaritan did not set up a booth along the highway to give aid on a regular basis to needy travelers.

Closely read, the parable tends to criticize, not endorse, the regular giving that an established welfare program involves. The Samaritan's action is clearly contrasted with the disappointing behavior of two other travelers who passed but failed to help the victim: a priest and a Levite, both recognizable as highly observant Jews who, we may assume, carried out all the regular tithing that Jewish teachings advised. The parable exalts the Samaritan—the non-Jew without a formal ethical code—because he was independent enough to react to an unusual situation and respond with what was needed. It criticizes the observant Jews because they did not break out of their closed mindset.

When a sailboat capsizes on the lake, of course it's right to go help the sailors. When a visitor needs directions to the railway station, of course it's right to tell him the way. Helping in unpredicted situations is socially efficient. By extending a helping hand in a first situation of need, we begin valued friendships or useful business relationships. The homilies and parables are right to urge us to be generous toward strangers in unexpected situations. But these teachings do not tell us how to act if we are asked to give a second time. For that, we need to develop a theory of social assistance systems.

There are three general approaches for dealing with repeated applications for aid, and they can be applied to any situation of need, whether it involves millions of welfare recipients or a next-door neighbor. We can illustrate each one as a response to Louise's repeated requests for cooking supplies.

Assistance System I: Sympathetic Giving

One response is to keep giving her what she needs. This solves her immediate problem and therefore makes her happy, at least in the short run. It also makes you look kind and considerate, at least in the short run. If you refuse her, she may get angry and accuse you of being selfish. To avoid the burden of explaining your refusal, it may be easier just to give her what she wants.

This approach is "sympathetic giving": the gift is prompted by the apparent misfortune of the recipient. Alms-giving is an example of sympathetic giving: you give coins to the beggar because he has some characteristic—a missing limb, torn clothes—that inspires your pity. Most of the standard government "means-tested" aid programs fall into this category. They give aid to those who can prove their unfortunate condition, that is, their low income.

Though kindly in the short term, sympathetic giving has a serious drawback. Any pattern of repeated giving reinforces whatever prompted the gift. In mutually beneficial relationships, whether commercial or social, we make deliberate use of this idea. For example, an employer gives an employee money to reinforce his motivation to come to work each day. Unfortunately, this principle also applies to charity, despite our intentions. We don't *want* the needy to stay needy so that they can keep receiving our gifts, but it's likely to happen. If Louise knows she can depend on us when she runs out of kitchen supplies, she is less likely to plan ahead so that she won't run out in the future. As a result, she is even more likely to run short of supplies!

Thus, we arrive at a great paradox, what I call the "aggravation principle" of sympathetic giving: repeated giving prompted by the misfortune of recipients tends to increase the incidence of the misfortune. The aggravation principle is such an elementary idea that practically everyone accepts its general validity. But many are tempted to overlook it in a moment of thoughtless sympathy.

Assistance System II: Refusal

If you do pay heed to the aggravation principle, what should you do? Repeatedly giving aid increases misfortune in the long run, so perhaps you should give no aid at all, thereby minimizing the overall harm. If Louise is becoming a moocher, you reason, this behavior will hurt her, causing neighbors to resent and avoid her. Shouldn't you try to discourage the habit? Refusing to give will impress on her the importance of being self-sufficient and eventually reduce the number of times she runs out of cooking supplies.

Another problem with sympathetic giving is its corrosive psychological effect. After a time, you may resent how Louise is taking advantage of you. Your resentment may poison a possible friendship; it may lead to an abrupt cutoff of aid. You could wind up with the worst of all possible worlds: first Louise is trained to depend on you, then she is denied the assistance she has come to expect. She becomes angry at you, and you become angry at her. Looking back, you see that it would have been much wiser not to have given to her at all. For these two reasons—avoiding the aggravation effect and avoiding resentment—a policy of refusal is often superior to sympathetic giving. It is a sensitive, thoughtful response to someone in need. It does not look that way at first, of course; it simply seems unhelpful.

Our dilemmas about how to help Louise are writ large in the national debate about welfare policy. The liberals believe in sympathetic giving. They want the needy to be given aid to alleviate immediate hardship and suffering. While liberals are uncomfortable saying that they endorse handouts, they certainly prefer them if the only other choice is refusing aid to the needy.

Conservatives argue that sympathetic giving leads to dependency and thus worsens the lot of the poor. Therefore, a policy of not giving aid would actually be *kinder* in the long run. To activists on the left, who fail to grasp the mechanisms of the aggravation principle, the idea of withholding aid from needy people simply seems cruel and heartless.

Assistance System III: Expectant Giving

While there may be less overall suffering under a policy of refusal than under sympathetic giving, there still is suffering. If you tell the unemployed that they will get no payments for being unemployed, a high proportion of them will be prompted to get a job. In the long run, they will be self-supporting and happier. But a few, for one reason or another, will not get jobs, and they will suffer. If we initiate a program that gives them aid, the problem is that we attract many unemployed workers who would otherwise have found a job. So we seem to be faced with an unhappy dilemma: being kind in the short run but aggravating the problem in the long run, or doing nothing about the suffering around us and letting nature take its course.

Fortunately, there is a way out of this dilemma, one that quite a few charity workers through the years have implemented. To understand it, let's go back to the theory of reinforcement. Sympathetic giving is harmful because it reinforces the unfortunate state of the recipients: you give money to people who are unemployed and you reward unemployment; you give money to people suffering from a disability and you discourage them from overcoming the disability. But we don't have to give aid this way. We can take the principle of reinforcement and turn it in a positive direction, setting up rewards for constructive behavior. This is "expectant giving": giving prompted by a contribution or achievement of the recipient.

Instead of simply giving Louise sugar—or refusing her—you try to devise a way to encourage a healthy response in return for your aid. For example, you say that you would be delighted to give her the sugar if she will give you a cup of flour, which you happen to need because you are nearly out. This produces a positive result regardless of Louise's response. If she refuses to lend to you, then she is obviously not that desperate for the sugar and you can refuse her with a clear conscience. If she meets your request but is displeased by it, she is less likely to make future appeals for aid since she understands that they trigger your counter-requests. If she enjoys sharing, then she will feel good about herself, knowing that she is carrying her own weight and has no reason to feel embarrassed.

Expectant giving always involves some type of exchange, and this makes it more complicated than sympathetic giving. In sympathetic giving, the supplicant wants A and the donor gives A. In expectant giving, the supplicant wants A but has to give B in order to get it. At first glance, expectant giving seems not to be giving at all, because no one is sacrificing. To a considerable degree, this is so—and should be so. Healthy human interactions are exchanges in which both sides benefit. The relationships between employers and employees, between friends, between spouses, are mutually supportive. Social assistance policy should aim to achieve the happy state where no one requires gifts because everyone is able to make exchanges for what they need.

In addition to material exchanges, expectant giving can involve psychological transactions in which "donors" give or withhold friendship, support, or approval as a way to get recipients to improve. Another way of handling Louise—probably the most natural way—would have been to indicate, perhaps by some hesitation in your manner, that you disapprove of her borrowing habit. Your disapproval would represent a certain "cost" to Louise and would help discourage her borrowing ways.

Of course, since Louise doesn't know you, she may not at first care very much about your opinion of her. Your influence would be more effective if you built up a relationship with her and became a trusted friend. Then, in the appropriate way, you would indicate your disapproval of her borrowing. This kind of personalized interaction is at the heart of mentoring, a strategy developed to a high art by nineteenth-century workers in practices like "friendly visiting." Middle-class volunteers would get to know needy families and, after securing their trust, provide advice and guidance. As with all kinds of expectant giving, mentoring can evolve into a balanced relationship, with each person contributing support and instruction to the other.

Child-rearing, when properly done, is a good example of expectant giving of the befriending kind. The parent earns the trust and affection of the child by giving him or her attention and care. Then, when the parent urges the child to correct some fault, the child tries to improve in order to please the parent.

Beyond Blame and Merit

▼

Expectant giving is the key to a healthy social assistance policy. It gives us a simple rule that keeps us headed in a sound direction in this highly confusing realm: always expect a meaningful response from the needy. If you are not in a position to demand a response, then don't give. Our thinking on welfare today does not accommodate this principle. In spite of the lip service paid to the idea of helping through a "hand up," both liberals and conservatives still approach welfare policy with sympathetic giving in mind. One sign of this mentality is the unending debate over where to place the blame for poverty. Supporters of giveaway programs claim that the poor are victims of their circumstances and therefore deserve aid. Opponents blame the poor for their problems, since it is their vices—alcoholism, drug addiction, promiscuity—that keep them down. Supporters of giveaway programs then reply that the vices are caused by poverty in the first place, but opponents refute the point with examples of individuals who have overcome poverty and vice.

Why the heated debate? The answer is that both sides are committed to sympathetic giving, to giving gifts to those who merit our sympathy. The argument focuses on blame because blame affects sympathy. We feel sorry for people whose suffering seems to be no fault of their own, while we feel less disposed to give handouts to those who may have brought their suffering on themselves.

If we applied the principle of expectant giving, this debate would fade away. We would agree, on the one hand, that a welfare system should take note of all kinds of suffering, whatever the cause, but we would also agree that no handouts should be given to anyone. All needy persons would be offered an appropriate exchange, to work toward a condition of less suffering. If a worker lost his job because he repeatedly came to work drunk, he would merit concern. So would a worker who lost his job because his plant closed. The degree of individual blame should not affect our compassion. But the two cases would obviously require different treatment. Offering another job to the laid-off worker might take care of him, while the alcoholic might need to be offered a strenuous rehabilitation program (which he might well refuse). For either man, it would be wrong simply to give money out of pity for the condition of unemployment. That is sympathetic giving, and it would lead recipients—and others—deeper into unemployment.

This point applies to aid programs directed at any group that seems deserving or blameless. For example, the encroachment of European civilization destroyed the way of life of Native Americans. A wrong was done to them that has led to poverty and many social problems. That these problems are undeserved does not make sympathetic giving a sound policy. Handouts that help Native Americans survive without achieving and contributing sap their morale and motivation and compound the tragedy of their situation. If help is to be given, it must be given in ways that encourage, and even demand, accomplishment.

Not Giving Up on the Needy

▼

Though simple in theory, expectant giving is often a difficult idea to apply in practice. Making it work involves challenges and hard choices, and these need to be understood before expectant giving can be confidently accepted as a principle of social assistance.

Expectant giving involves some hardship for recipients.

While expectant giving is kinder than outright refusal, it does not immediately indulge recipients, as sympathetic giving does. If the recipient is unwilling to participate in the exchange being offered, then the donor must refuse to give—and the supplicant will suffer whatever he would have suffered without the aid. For example, some missions for homeless men require visitors to shower. Assuming that the men do not want to shower, this rule sets up a degree of expectant giving: improving behavior in exchange for lodging. If a visitor declines to take a shower, the expectant giver refuses to give the shelter.

This refusal aspect gives expectant giving its other name: tough love. One has to be willing to let the person who needs aid suffer if he refuses to take the path of improvement. If you take the position that the poor must not suffer at all, then you cannot practice expectant giving. This point is especially important for government welfare programs. If pressure groups and public opinion will not tolerate *any* suffering of the aided population, then a government attempt to apply expectant giving will fail and the policy will degenerate into sympathetic giving.

Expectant giving makes considerable intellectual demands on donors.

One response to a beggar is to toss him a dollar bill and walk on. This is sympathetic giving. It takes five seconds of your time—and no thought. If you want to try expectant giving, you have to sit down beside the beggar, strike up a conversation, find out what he needs and what he can do for you in exchange. This response is difficult and time-consuming.

Expectant giving's requirements of attention, imagination, and discrimination apply at all levels. In order to practice expectant giving in a local soup kitchen, for example, volunteers would have to discuss the changes they wanted to see in the lives of the clients and then devise sensitive and effective ways to implement exchanges that might bring about those changes. This would take many hours of puzzlement and debate. It's much easier just to ladle out the soup, bowl after bowl, asking nothing, expecting nothing.

One of the main reasons government programs veer toward sympathetic giving is the difficulty of carrying out the discriminating, thoughtful treatment that expectant giving requires. How, after all, could legislators know what to expect of each individual in a group of ten or twenty million needy people? The easiest solution to this problem is to state the sympathy-provoking characteristic—such as low income—and then give everyone in that category material assistance, demanding nothing in return.

Expectant giving is judgmental.

To offer an exchange, you must know what you want the needy person to accomplish. You might require that the recipient give up drinking, or stop swearing, or get a haircut, or lose weight. Any such demand implies that you value the particular behavior. Thus, expectant giving is not value-free. It tends to be a rather intrusive way of helping—like parenting.

Large organizations, especially government agencies, avoid conflict by taking the position that no belief or lifestyle is superior to any other. This position makes them reluctant to demand particular behaviors in exchange for aid. As a result, they drift toward sympathetic giving—giving aid regardless of the behavior of the recipients. If a person is on drugs, you give money to support his drug habit. If an indigent, unmarried teenager has children, you fund that arrangement. Most people would argue that this is a demoralizing approach to social assistance, but the only way to avoid it is to be judgmental.

Expectant giving cannot be applied in cases of extreme helplessness.
Although expectant giving is generally a superior approach to assisting the needy, it cannot logically be applied when improvement is deemed impossible. For the incapable recipient—for example, people in comas, babies, the mentally incompetent—the only workable assistance is sympathetic giving. Since no constructive response is possible from them, expectant giving would be like trying to squeeze blood from a stone. Extremely incapacitated people must rely either on resources they have saved up or on sympathetic giving—that is, handouts.

What constitutes a disability so severe that it merits sympathetic giving? On this point, there is a wide gap between proponents of the two approaches. Those who endorse sympathetic giving adopt a broad definition of helplessness. They justify handouts by saying that recipients are incapable of a meaningful response. After half a century of government something-for-nothing programs, the idea of what constitutes helplessness has been vastly expanded. For example, in the 1996 reform of the food stamp program, which attempted to introduce a work requirement for some recipients, one group of people specifically exempted from having to work in exchange for benefits were any poor people over the age of fifty. In other words, policy makers now consider that being over age fifty renders people so "disabled" that they should never be expected to work.

The welfare establishment's view of the poor as helpless was clearly enunciated by Peter Edleman in a 1997 cover story in the *Atlantic*. Edleman was an assistant secretary at the Department of Health and Human Services who resigned in protest against the 1996 welfare reform, which imposed work requirements for some recipients in some programs. "Much of what we do in the name of welfare is more appropriately a subject for disability policy," he declared. To Edleman's way of thinking, welfare isn't supposed to get people on their feet: "It is what we do for people who can't make it after a genuine attempt has been mounted to help the maximum possible number of people to make it."[1]

Notice the pessimism. Calling welfare recipients "functionally disabled" people who "can't make it" undermines their morale and motivation—and helps ensure that they will never make it on their own. It is rather shocking that such a highly influential reformer with the interests of the poor at heart should have drifted into this detrimental stance. But the "disability" perspective follows from the philosophy of sympathetic giving: when you give handouts, you are strongly tempted to justify them by perceiving the recipients as incapable of helping themselves.

Expectant giving focuses on abilities, not disabilities.

Expectant giving is an optimistic, growth-affirming approach that emphasizes what people *can* do instead of what they can't. Expectant givers don't like to label anyone "disabled," as being incapable of achievement. They agree with Tennyson's Ulysses, the old seafarer (over age fifty!) about to set off on another voyage. Even though "made weak by time and fate," Ulysses spurns comfortable retirement, convinced that the purpose of life is "to strive, to seek, to find, and not to yield."

Practically everyone is capable of contributing or achieving to some degree. It is up to sensitive, insightful expectant givers to determine, in each case, what kind of contribution is possible and how to elicit it. Helen Keller's remarkable life reminds us of what even a seriously disabled human being can accomplish. She was born deaf and blind, seemingly totally cut off from the world except for what she could perceive through her sense of touch. With determination and a committed teacher, she learned to read and write, becoming an inspiration to millions.

In 1983 in Sacramento, California, a group of reformers started a homeless shelter called Loaves and Fishes. It is based on a philosophy of pure sympathetic giving. As a staff member told me when I visited in 1995, "We have no requirements, no expectations. We don't expect people to be in treatment programs or attend certain meetings in order to be fed and to receive services here." The staff works hard to give homeless people material things to make their lives easier: morning coffee and a full-course noon meal every day, free medical care, a library and reading room, free locker storage, free kennel service and free veterinary care for dogs, free pet food, free ice, a bank of free telephones, free hot shower (only if you want it, of course). The staff is careful not to judge or criticize the lifestyles of those being helped, who are called "guests." No advice or exhortation to improve behavior is seen anywhere. There are no mottoes over doorways, no Bible verses on bulletin boards, no posters urging people to get off drugs.

Not surprisingly, the aggravation principle has come into play: the number of clients keeps growing, even through good economic times. Feeding nearly one thousand people a day, Loaves and Fishes is attempting its third expansion—a prospect opposed by many local residents who fear the growth of homelessness that Loaves and Fishes encourages.

How do the staff and volunteers at Loaves and Fishes justify their sympathetic giving? Mainly by defining their clients as utterly helpless. As one worker put it to me, "No one would come here if they had any alternative."

I took a walk around the shelter's Friendship Park, where the homeless spend the day. The services and opportunities were impressive. At six card tables, men were playing bridge and whist; others were playing on the basketball court or at horseshoes, while still others relaxed on the benches in the shade or plied the telephones and the vending machines. It was almost like a country club, except one thing was very wrong. The people were very unattractive: ungroomed, unmannerly, dejected. For a moment, it seemed that the helpers were right: these men were so helpless that it would be cruel to expect them to be somewhere else doing anything useful.

This thought lasted only for a moment. Walking from Loaves and Fishes back to the center of town, I spotted a young blind man going in my direction. He carried a long white cane, which he tapped energetically; the day pack on his back made him look like a graduate student. Whatever he was up to, he had great energy and purpose; he moved along so quickly that I had to trot to keep up with him. When he came to a car parked on the sidewalk, blocking his way, he tapped his way around it. At each intersection, he used the noise of traffic to tell him when the light had turned.

The miasma of Friendship Park helplessness dissolved at once. This young man had more of a handicap than anyone I had seen among the homeless that morning, yet he had obviously not given up on life. Had the help of others been necessary to raise him to his confident, competent state? Of course. But they didn't help him by feeling sorry for him, by making a big deal out of his blindness and urging him to treat it as a crippling disability. They helped by expecting him to achieve, to overcome.

It is right to be sensitive to misfortune. But let us not be so affected by pity that we cease to expect admirable behavior of the needy.

3

Buying Trouble:
The Problems with Sympathetic Giving

Social reformers have often been dismayed by the way problems of poverty seem to grow *after* they begin programs of assistance. It seems profoundly unfair that their efforts should be rewarded not by a solution to neediness but by more of it. The history of the federal government's food stamp program illustrates the pattern.

After operating it as a pilot program in the early 1960s, the Kennedy administration turned food stamps into a permanent program in 1963. The object was to supply the poor with vouchers that they could use to pay their grocery bills. Secretary of Agriculture Orville L. Freeman came to the House Agriculture Committee to explain the administration's expectations about the eventual size and scope of the program. "We estimate," he said in his prepared testimony, "that, with a continuation of current economic conditions, a stamp program could be expanded over a period of years to about 4 million needy people." The eventual yearly cost of the fully established program was expected to be $119 million.[1]

As time passed, the number of food stamp recipients grew and costs escalated, yet the goal of "ending hunger" kept receding.[2] The paradox was highlighted in 1988 when Congress reexamined the program. It was then costing $12 billion, one hundred times what was first estimated, and the number of recipients had grown to 20 million, five times the number of hungry originally thought to exist. Instead of finding that the problem of hunger had been solved by the vast expansion of this and many other food aid programs, Congress discovered a "hunger emergency." So it passed the Emergency Hunger Relief Act, which further expanded food stamp benefits.[3] By 1995 spending for food stamps had increased to $26 billion and the average monthly number of recipients was 28 million, yet food policy specialists declared that "some 13 million children under age 12 in the United States are hungry or at risk of hunger."[4]

What happened to invalidate Secretary Freeman's original estimates? We might understand the numbers if the United States had suffered a series of famines or a military invasion. But the economy was expanding during this period, and welfare experts expected prosperity to reduce the need for assistance. In 1957 the director of the American Public Welfare Association, Loula Dunn, was so confident of the beneficial effect of economic growth that she predicted, "We can expect the volume of public assistance cases to decrease in the future."[5] By rights, the number of people unable to buy food for themselves should have been going down.

The paradox illustrates the aggravation principle of sympathetic giving: giving prompted by misfortune tends to increase the incidence of misfortune. Thus, a program designed to feed people who can't seem to feed themselves results in even more people who can't seem to feed themselves.

The aggravation principle lies at the core of problems with government assistance programs. For some two hundred years, it has loomed over welfare policy—alternately ignored, then painfully recognized, then ignored again. The challenge is not so much to explain the aggravation principle, for it is virtually a truism, but to identify the errors in perception that cause people to disregard it. Only by understanding these errors can we hope to avoid another two hundred years of stop-start anguish on the welfare front.

Poor Law Reform

▼

The aggravation principle has been present throughout history, since it may go into effect whenever gifts are regularly given. However, the increase in production and income during the industrial revolution brought the problem to the fore, notably in the more prosperous European countries.

England was one of the first nations to feel the impact of prosperity. Over the course of the eighteenth century, welfare benefits for the poor—from both governmental and private sources—were considerably expanded. As early as 1766, Benjamin Franklin commented while visiting England that the many different programs to assist the poor "offered a premium for the encouragement of idleness."[6] In 1782 this trend was accentuated with an act for "The Better Relief and Employment of the Poor." This act expanded the system of giving the able-bodied poor cash assistance, funded by local property taxes. Over the ensuing decades, the relief rolls grew, and so did the burden of the taxes. The result was that people who were productive were increasingly taxed to support those who were not productive. Eventually, everyone recognized that the system was economically destructive, as well as socially corrupting, and it was significantly curtailed in the Reform Act of 1834. Benefits were decreased mainly by requiring that most of the needy go into the (unpleasant) poorhouse in order to receive state aid.

It was a widely studied and widely debated episode, and out of it came a new breed of welfare reformers.[7] These "charity theorists" took the failure of the handout system in this period as their point of departure for a more sophisticated approach to helping the needy. In 1836 one of the earliest of these reformers wrote a systematic analysis of alms-giving and its problems, *Essays on the Principles of Charitable Institutions*. This essayist (who chose to write anonymously) laid out the puzzle of the aggravation principle:

> In all ages, the most obvious, and therefore the most usual, method of relieving poverty, has been to give alms. No matter how extensive the distress, or what the cause from which it

arose; nothing could be more simple [it seemed to people] than to give money in proportion to its external signs, and want must inevitably cease. But it began at last to be observed, with surprise, that the more liberally alms were bestowed, the more the indications of poverty were multiplied.[8]

The essayist presented statistics from numerous places—Salisbury, Framlingham, Holbeach, Bristol, Manchester—confirming the rule that the more a town or benevolent institution spent on relieving the poor, the greater the resulting level of poverty.

That this poverty was real was confirmed by a study made by the theologian and charity reformer Thomas Chalmers on the effect of the 1817 depression in the Glasgow area. Some districts—especially Glasgow proper—had long operated a tax-funded cash relief system for the poor, while others, particularly the town of Gorbals, had no such program in place. A committee was set up to distribute ten thousand pounds that had been raised for relief, and it judged every applicant's need for aid. When the successful applicants were tabulated by district, it turned out that inhabitants of Glasgow proper required, on a per-capita basis, twenty-one times as much aid as the residents of Gorbals. In other words, there was more suffering in the district with a long-established welfare system than in the district without one.[9] Apparently, being on the dole had weakened the ability of the Glasgow poor to adapt to hard times.

The essayist then explained the "mystery" of how increasing aid increased misery. The expectation of aid produces a "diminution of the motives to industry and frugality." The result was that the net income of the poor was less than it had been before aid was extended. The essayist insisted that this was not a class or cultural phenomenon: "Nor let the poor be harshly blamed for this. Man is naturally fond of ease, and requires some powerful stimulus to rouse him to exertion."

"Work or Starve"

▼

Between 1850 and 1870, the United States also increased welfare benefits—and then discovered that poverty had not been alleviated, but had increased. According to an account of the period by the charity historian Marvin Olasky, the new largesse was prompted by the emergence of a naive idealism about human nature in certain journalistic and literary circles. Horace Greeley, founder and editor of the *New York Tribune*, was one of the leaders of this native socialist movement. He favored having the state redistribute income by taxing the wealthy and giving their money to the less well-off. He did not worry that the dole might weaken the motivation of the poor because he was convinced that human beings are naturally industrious by nature. "The heart of man is not depraved," said Greeley. "His passions do not prompt to wrong doing, and do not therefore by their action, produce evil."[10]

Greeley and many other journalists, novelists, and academics agitated for, and achieved, a considerable increase in cash assistance by local governments in many cities. The result was that relief rolls climbed. In New York City, for example, the number on "temporary" relief rose from 12,000 in 1840 to 174,000 in 1860. By 1870 one-tenth of the population was receiving doles from the city.[11]

Instead of producing a new breed of enlightened poor, these giveaways seemed only to result in more begging and in abuse and corruption of the welfare system. Public opinion swung against the dole, and government relief programs were curtailed or eliminated in most cities in the 1870s and 1880s.[12] Many of the budding socialists learned a valuable lesson about human motivation. Greeley himself made a dramatic turnabout. By 1869 he was complaining that "the beggars of New York are at once very numerous and remarkably impudent." He judged nine-tenths of them to be "shiftless vagabonds" and concluded that the best way to respond to a beggar was to refuse aid. "Make up a square issue—'Work or starve!'— and he is quite likely to choose work."[13]

These decades taught a generation of American charity workers the perils of sympathetic giving. Even official bodies got the message. The New York State Board of Charities carefully explained why a government cash relief program was unsound: "When persons, naturally idle and improvident, have experienced for a few months the convenience of existing upon the labor of others, they are very likely to resort to this means of living as often and as continuously as possible."[14]

The Economic Effects of Sympathetic Giving

▼

The modern welfare state has repeated the nineteenth century's experience with the aggravation principle. Welfare programs and benefits have been substantially increased over the past half-century, although not necessarily in each program. The overall trend, however, compared with 1950, is higher benefits, more generous eligibility criteria, and many more overlapping programs.

When the benefits of welfare programs are combined, they can add up to an extremely attractive economic package. To document this point, three researchers from the Cato Institute calculated the value of six of the main assistance programs in 1995: AFDC, food stamps, Medicaid, housing assistance, nutrition assistance, and energy assistance. The yearly value of this welfare package, for recipients who took advantage of all six programs, ranged from $27,736 in Hawaii to $13,033 in Mississippi.[15]

To assess how these benefits compared to working a forty-hour week, being taxed, and taking no welfare benefits, the researchers calculated the hourly wage a worker would have to be paid to achieve the welfare level of "take-home pay." In every state, welfare paid much more than the minimum wage of $4.25 per hour. In the state with the median level of benefits, welfare paid $9.18 per hour.[16] In other words, a welfare recipient would have to find a job paying more than $9.18 an hour before his earnings from work exceeded his earnings from welfare.

This study has been criticized because it assumed that recipients benefited from all six welfare programs. However, studies based on actual welfare recipients confirm the general point. Douglas Besharov of the American Enterprise Institute found that in 1992 the average unwed mother on welfare obtained a total of $17,434 a year in benefits, while the same woman working full-time (and also receiving some welfare benefits) ended up with $15,583.[17] The result is a "welfare trap" that makes dependency economically attractive.

The increase in the economic benefits of welfare over the past half-century has attracted a growing number of people to the welfare rolls. At any one time, some 16 percent of U.S. households are drawing assistance from one or more welfare programs.[18] The proportion of the population utilizing welfare is even higher than this, since many recipients follow a pattern of "serial dependency": they leave a welfare program but later return to it—or go on another.

Many studies have documented the point that benefits from welfare programs—unemployment benefits, food stamps, AFDC—reduce work effort.[19] One notable set of findings came out of the studies of guaranteed income in the 1970s. In extremely sophisticated experiments, particularly in Denver and Seattle, poverty-level families were split into two groups: one group received additional income support according to their level of need, and the other group were not given additional support. The families with the income assistance showed significantly lower levels of work effort.[20]

In the typical case, welfare payments promote dysfunctional behavior not so much by making the behavior positively attractive, but by making it *less unattractive* than it would otherwise be. Defenders of the welfare system often miss this point. They cite, for example, the unhappy situation of an indigent teen with an illegitimate child, even with welfare. "Since life as an indigent teen mother is so difficult," they argue, "how can anybody say that welfare payments attract women to this lifestyle?"

But welfare payments have their negative effect, not by making indigent childbearing attractive, but simply by lessening its unattractiveness. Normally, to have a child without being married to a steady wage earner would produce an extremely painful, even tragic, result for the mother. What welfare payments do is lessen the painful penalties associated with indigent unwed childbearing—which is thus increased, as many studies have shown.[21]

The Social Effects of Sympathetic Giving

▼

Economic motives are not the only ones shaping recipients' responses to welfare programs. Human beings are attracted to—and repelled by—activities and roles not only because of material rewards but also because of the social approval and disapproval associated with them. We care what others think about us, and we usually avoid activities that are frowned upon, even if they promise an economic reward.

Social disapproval can play a large role in deterring people from engaging in behavior that leads to neediness. If society frowns on drunkenness, or drug addiction, or unwed childbearing, possible social rejection helps dissuade people from such behavior. Unfortunately, sympathetic giving weakens the social disapproval of harmful behavior by appearing to endorse it.

How should parents react to the pregnancy of one of their unwed teenage daughters? Of course they want to help her, but agreeing to take care of her and her child sends the message that they don't disapprove of unwed teen childbearing. Hence, the other daughters are less likely to expect parental disapproval if they get pregnant—and they are thus more likely to do so. Again, the way out of the dilemma is some arrangement of expectant giving that lets the parents help without seeming to approve of the misbehavior. They can insist that the daughter marry the father of the child, or give the baby up for adoption, or work part-time to help support the baby.

Sympathetic giving, then, communicates social approval of the lifestyle that led to misfortune. This point especially applies to government programs. Government is the source of law and authority in society, and therefore its assistance programs broadly influence social norms. When it gives money to the unemployed, including those who are idle and dependent, it undermines the social disapproval of idle dependency. When it gives benefits to couples who have more children than they can support, it undermines the social stigma of having families larger than one can take care of.

Most school systems today provide prenatal care for pregnant unwed students, as well as day care after their babies arrive. While these benefits have an economic value to the mothers, their main effect is not economic but social. Such programs undermine the stigma of unwed teen pregnancy. Until fairly recently, girls who got "in trouble" were whispered about—and expelled from school. Seeing this social disapproval, other girls made a great effort to avoid pregnancy. Today programs like free day care for student mothers make unwed teen pregnancy seem almost normal—not "trouble" at all, but a viable option intentionally chosen by girls in certain subcultures.[22]

Analyzing government welfare programs only in economic terms is a mistake. By reducing the stigma attached to dysfunctional behavior, their main effect over the years has been social. The arrival of a check every month for a certain type of problem can seem like a natural way to "earn" a living after a while. Even nonrecipients have become habituated. One notices, for example, that workers in most nonprofit charities see federal assistance programs—housing subsidies, SSI, food stamps—as a legitimate long-term means of support for their clients. Government assistance is such a natural part of the landscape that getting people signed up for it seems like a method of self-help!

In Lake Providence, Louisiana, Rosie Watson collects nine welfare checks, which give her and her family a total, tax-free yearly income of $46,716. Beginning her welfare career as an unwed mother on AFDC, Watson turned to the supplemental security income program for disabilities in 1978. She eventually got all of her seven children enrolled for various types of mental disabilities. Her common-law husband was declared disabled on grounds of obesity. In her own case, she was turned down five times because doctors agreed she was not disabled. (One commented, "Patient is determined to become a ward of the government.") Finally, on appeal, an administrative law judge declared her eligible on grounds of "stress."

How do we know all these confidential details? So proud was she of her entrepreneurial tenacity that Rosie eagerly told her story to the *Baltimore Sun* reporters John O'Donnell and Jim Haner. In an earlier day, welfare recipients would have been embarrassed about their dependency. But now, decades of government cash payments for idle people have undermined the stigma associated with being unproductive and dependent. "I've got nothing to hide," Rosie told reporters. "SSI has done a lot for our family. We're not able to work, and it's the best income."[23]

The Static Fallacy

▼

Theory suggests, and history confirms, that sympathetic giving is a self-defeating policy. Through its economic and social effects, it increases the suffering one hopes to relieve. Why is this elementary truth so readily obscured or forgotten? In England, the excesses of the old poor law system convinced practically every thinking person of the folly of state giveaway programs. Yet, by the twentieth century, growing numbers of intellectuals were clamoring for a new welfare state that copied the sympathetic giving of the old system. The United States went through the same process of learning the lesson in the nineteenth century and then ignoring it in the twentieth. What causes this recurrent error?

One answer is the widespread impulse toward shallow compassion. Many people are so moved by immediate want that they cannot discern the ultimate effects of stepping in to relieve it. As nineteenth-century charity theorists kept pointing out, it takes courage and self-discipline *not to give* in situations where giving seems kind in the short run but is harmful in the long run. Programs of sympathetic giving are always probable when people are acting impulsively—which, in politics, is not an uncommon situation.

Another source of the perpetual attraction of sympathetic giving is the "static fallacy." In social analysis, it is easy to forget that people continually adjust their behavior to their environment, moving toward options made more attractive and away from those made less attractive. Instead of grasping this dynamic aspect of behavior, many suppose behavior to be fixed, static even in a changing environment. Suppose there is a narrow highway bridge used by one thousand cars an hour. Engineers assume that this is the traffic level and widen the bridge so that it will accommodate one thousand cars an hour without delays. Within a matter of days, *two thousand* cars are crossing the bridge, because the wider bridge attracts more motorists.

Government policies in many fields are marred by the static fallacy. In taxation, for example, policy makers usually assume that the same amount of a particular good will be produced and purchased even after they increase the tax on it. In practice, the additional tax can discourage consumers, so that sales, and tax revenues, decline.

In welfare policy, the static fallacy leads policy makers into a number of errors. One is to exaggerate the importance of existing programs by assuming that recipients would make no adjustment to a reduction in benefits. This is the error that a baker makes in claiming that he keeps his customers from starving to death. The claim would be true only if his customers had no capacity to find other supplies.

A typical example of this fallacy is the claim of the Social Security Administration and other welfare agencies that their benefit programs keep particular groups "out of poverty."[24] This view sees citizens as helpless and unintelligent. If the Social Security Administration closed its old-age assistance program, officials seem to assume that millions of seniors would keep gathering around social security offices like sheep, waiting for checks to "lift them out of poverty." In reality, there are many ways that seniors would be lifted out of poverty in the absence of a government retirement program. They could work longer, they could sell assets, they could enlist aid from their children, and, especially, they could start saving more money *before* retirement. If the government didn't take away 12.4 percent of their income for the social security program, they would have that much more to save.

When policy makers contemplate new poverty programs, the static fallacy leads to a second kind of error: assuming that the number of needy in a given category will remain unaffected by the new program. This is the error that the baker might make if he decides to give bread away and assumes there will be no increase in the number of customers. Many welfare programs have been based on such specious calculations. Policy makers have determined, for example, that four million Americans need help buying food, but they fail to realize that their program to help these four million will cause changes in calculations, behavior, and lifestyles, eventually resulting in additional millions needing food assistance.

A glaring example of this error was the attempt by the President's Council of Economic Advisers in 1964 to justify the newly announced war on poverty. The advisers claimed that the

> conquest of poverty is well within our power. About $11 billion a year would bring all poor families up to the $3,000 income level we have taken to be the minimum for a decent life. The majority of the Nation could simply tax themselves to provide the necessary income supplements to their less fortunate citizens.[25]

The idea that there would be no additional applicants for handouts after an $11 billion giveaway is as unrealistic as the assumption that a baker who starts to give bread away won't have any additional customers.

Thirty years later, backers of the Great Society programs are still succumbing to the static fallacy. A good illustration is the widely cited Urban Institute critique of the 1996 welfare reform. Its authors concluded that the benefit cuts detailed in the reform legislation would "increase the number of persons in poverty by 2.6 million."[26] The authors conceded that any such calculation was speculative, since it was based on a host of assumptions. The revealing point, however, is not the precise numerical result but the framework used for analysis. The authors examined the effect of the 1996 welfare reform on *current recipients only!* Thus, they missed the dynamic effect that a benefit cut would have on the number of *future recipients*. Lowering benefits to current recipients will reduce their income (if they can't or won't compensate by working), but it will also lower welfare's appeal to the tens of millions of prospective parents considering having children they can't afford to raise. Hence, fewer children will be born in poverty to begin with, and the overall size of the poverty group will decline in the long run.

Static thinking always leads policy makers to ignore how their handout programs draw the poor into poverty. They treat the size of the poverty population as a given, like a mountain that nature has placed on the landscape. In truth, the level of neediness in a society is not fixed but tends to be directly proportional to the size of the giveaway programs intended to treat it. Within a broad range, a nation can have whatever level of misfortune it chooses to purchase.

4

"A More Excellent Way of Charity"

Before the nineteenth century, social assistance had a strongly personal character. In this age of small towns, people tended to stay put. Donors and local charity administrators knew recipients as kinfolk, neighbors, and parishioners. At the same time, economic productivity was low and communities were poor. Even the middle class lived on the edge of a dangerous poverty. The few available funds to aid the poor were dispensed carefully to people who were known to merit assistance. It would have been considered foolish, even wicked, to assist the lazy or the self-indulgent.

Two changes in the nineteenth century revolutionized the face of charity. First, the exponential growth in economic production made possible by the industrial revolution gave rise to a large middle class with much more money to devote to charitable purposes. In addition to direct alms-giving, the newly rich gave through churches and the voluntary benevolent associations that proliferated at this time. In London, for example, there were some 700 charitable societies in 1869; by 1905 there were 1,700.[1]

The second change was the development of transportation and the migration of large numbers of people to cities, a transformation that broke down neighborhood and kinship ties. As a result, the poor were often strangers to those who wished to assist them. While everyone agreed that it was wrong to aid the shiftless, it was no longer easy to know who they were.

The situation was ripe for sympathetic giving. The poor could seek aid from individuals, churches, and charitable associations that knew nothing about their backgrounds and behavior. A needy person could make use of the broad array of assistance opportunities, appealing first to one donor and then, when his purse or patience was exhausted, to another. For many of these supplicants, the result was "pauperization." This word came into use in the nineteenth century to describe how thoughtless benevolence could convert self-reliant poor people into a class that looked to handouts to survive.

Most middle-class givers were unaware of the social blight they were causing. For centuries, the simple religion-based instruction to "give to the poor" seemed to be adequate advice, and the new masses of wealthy benefactors simply carried on this tradition. A few observers—who came to be known as social Darwinists— pointed out that continuously aiding people who could not support themselves would add to misery in the long run. But their recommendation—let the poor shift for themselves—seemed unacceptably harsh.

In this milieu, there emerged a remarkable tribe of reformers who were both practical and analytical. Their theories and writings have been lost from view for several generations, but in recent years they have been rediscovered, especially by the American scholars Marvin Olasky and Gertrude Himmelfarb and the British researchers David Green and Robert Whelan. The nineteenth-century "charity theorists," as they deserve to be called, knew about the poor from extensive personal work among them. They saw how sympathetic giving reinforced the very evils that well-intentioned givers sought to alleviate. However, unlike the social Darwinists, they refused to give up. They insisted on looking for ways of assisting the poor that truly uplifted them. (See the bibliography for a list of the writings of several dozen charity theorists.) Although they did not have much contact with each other, these early workers came to remarkably similar conclusions. Their main findings included these points:

- A personal relationship between the needy person and the helper is the foundation of charity.

- Sympathetic (something-for-nothing) giving is generally harmful to the needy.

- Personal assistance should focus on the individual's future prospects, and therefore on his correctable personal shortcomings.

- Effective helping elicits constructive action from the recipient.

Love, Knowledge, and Sympathy

▼

One of the most notable of the charity theorists was Octavia Hill, an English social worker who lived from 1838 to 1912. She began her work at the age of fourteen, as a volunteer instructor in a London school for poor children, and went on to develop a system for improving the housing, living conditions, and lifestyles of London's poor. Her life exemplifies the approach of these early reformers.

Hill's biographer, E. Moberly Bell, recounts her first day as a volunteer manager of the charity school's toy workshop, where children were supposed to learn good work habits as well as earn a little money with part-time work. The girls, reports Bell,

> were desperately poor and very rough; generally speaking, they came from wretched and degraded homes, some lived in cellars, some were deformed and disfigured by the hardships they had endured. Many of them were older than Octavia, and all were more experienced in wretchedness and vice. They had been accustomed in their work hours to discipline of a repressive kind. On the walls of the room in which they worked hung a list of rules, with the punishment to be inflicted for the breach of each. On her first day in charge Octavia stood before this document, read it through in complete silence, and without a word tore it down from the wall.[2]

Even at age fourteen, Hill had an inner conviction that she could win the children over by establishing personal relationships with them. "I know their tempers," she wrote after she had worked with them for some time, "to whom I may say different things. I have to study how to interest each. I connect all they say, do or look into one whole. I get to know the thing they really care for."[3]

While continuously applying pressure on the students to

improve, she generally avoided punishment or direct correction. When the children refused to scrub their work tables, Hill got her sisters to help and scrubbed them herself under the eyes of the embarrassed rebels, "doing more," as she later wrote, "to convince them of the dignity of labour than any amount of talk on the subject." Constantly, she studied ways to earn the affection and trust of her charges. She taught the children to prepare their own lunches at school, meals both less expensive and more nutritious than the ones they had been bringing with them. Bell reports that "she insisted on a white table cloth and civilized table manners."[4]

On Saturday afternoons, supposedly her time off, Hill took the children on trips to the country. "At first," Bell reports, "the children hesitated; they were actually afraid of walking in the country, believing there might be wolves and bears lurking in the woods, they had no interest in flowers and could not distinguish the very commonest sorts. But Octavia had her way with them." A friend reported seeing Hill and her troop come through a hedge in the north London suburb of Highgate: "She joyfully leapt down from the bank with a staff in her hand, a straw hat on her head, torn by the thicket, followed by a troop of ragged toymakers, happy and flushed, each with an armful of bluebells."[5]

All this love and attention paid off in a respect that transcended the power of rules and regulations. "I have no written or fixed laws," she reported, "simply because in a small business so much has constantly to be altered; but we have a very delightful order, the children all know what they should do, and get into the habit of attending to it."[6]

Throughout her long career, Hill maintained this personal style of helping, always seeking to establish friendly relationships with those she was trying to assist. In a speech given in 1876 to a wealthy London suburban audience, entitled "A More Excellent Way of Charity," she cautioned her listeners not to think that money was the answer to helping the poor:

> Only remember, though you may send your money, and send it to those who use it wisely, the gift is a very poor one compared with that of yourselves. It is you who are wanted there, your love, your knowledge, your sympathy, your resolution—above all, your knowledge.[7]

Volunteer Visitors

▼

Personal relationships are powerful tools in helping the needy because they accomplish so many useful purposes at the same time. First, they are essential to gaining information about the people you are trying to help. All the charity theorists were firm about the importance of detailed, personal knowledge. "You cannot learn to help a man," wrote Hill, "nor even get him to tell you what ails him, 'til you care for him." She chided the do-gooders of the drawing room who wanted to help the poor but who were "thoroughly cowardly about telling them any truth that is unpalatable, and know too little of them to meet them as friends, and learn to be natural and brave with them. We have great relief funds, and little manly friendship."[8]

Another prominent theorist, the Frenchman Baron Joseph Marie de Gerando, made the same point. De Gerando was a wealthy aristocrat, and a prolific writer on social and philosophical subjects, who made it a personal hobby to assist the poor. In *The Visitor of the Poor*, he expressed the conclusions of a lifetime of helping the needy.

> Charity is entirely an individual thing. A largess given in a general way, thrown out to escape importunity, subscribed and published, to nourish pride by the ostentation of false virtue, has nothing to do with charity, with the tie that unites brother to brother. . . . Why do you not go near to the person that implores you; and why do you not seek out those who do not implore you? It is in their dwelling places that you must investigate which is the reality, and which is the phantom; and it is an investigation that requires attentive study. It is not enough that you are open-handed; you must open your eyes too.[9]

Personal contacts are also the key to mentoring: the helper motivates uplift by extending respect and affection in return for improved behavior. As we look more deeply into the theory of mentoring, we discover another point that charity theorists stressed: the relationship should be genuine, not hired or paid for.

Affection and respect extended freely are more effective in motivating change *because they can be withdrawn*. If you disappoint a
friend, the friend is free to criticize you and avoid you for a while. If
you disappoint someone hired to "befriend" you, his job requires
him to continue to meet with you. Therefore, his friendship and
praise means less.

This point is included in De Gerando's fine summary of ideal
charity: "The essence of a good administration of public charity,
then, is the art of creating a voluntary, immediate, and individual
guardianship of the prosperous over the unfortunate."[10]

Today, with the welfare system in the hands of paid social workers, the importance of genuine, voluntary interaction has been
largely forgotten. In the nineteenth century, however, it was a central theme. Charity organizations adopted the practice of using
"volunteer visitors" to carry out their mission. The volunteers
would be responsible for one or two families, regularly visiting
with them in their homes and discovering their real needs. These
volunteers would be linked to the larger organization through coordinators (sometimes called "overseers") who might be paid staff.

Elberfeld, Germany, was one of the first places where this system
was developed, around 1853. Whether through imitation or inven-
tion, it was adopted all over the United States and England in the latter part of the nineteenth century. Writing a comprehensive survey
of American assistance practices in 1884, Josephine Shaw Lowell
emphasized that the importance of volunteer visitors was
"supply[ing] the precious element of human sympathy and tender
personal involvement."[11]

In the matter of volunteering, Octavia Hill set an exceptional
standard. Virtually all the nineteenth-century charity theorists
were volunteers. But most were independently wealthy, so their
volunteering did not affect their standard of living. Hill, the daughter of a bankrupt businessman, lived close to the edge of poverty
and had to support herself teaching and working as an art copyist.
Nevertheless, she always refused to be paid for her social assistance
work. In her system of housing management, for example, she carefully set aside a salary for the manager's job so that she could prove
to investors that her projects were fully self-supporting. But she
never took the salary herself when she was manager. She grasped

that her moral position among the poor as a friend and mentor would be strongest if she in no way made money from them.

Human Ecologists
▼

Another reason for befriending the poor, said the charity theorists, is to find out what your help really means to them. You cannot claim to have helped someone unless you track your gift to the needy person and see what happens. One of the charity theorists' first observations as they made their detailed study of gift-giving was that giving a needy person material assistance to relieve suffering was generally harmful. They saw that every person functioned within a complex setting with subtle combinations of motivations and opportunities. Material relief could profoundly undermine the healthy adaptations that the needy person would otherwise make.

There is a close parallel between the methods of the charity theorists and the methods of modern ecology. People used to believe that to improve on nature, you simply got rid of unfortunate features. To save trees, for example, you put out forest fires. Closer study revealed complex, interrelated systems in which the desirable feature actually depended on the apparently negative one. The heat of forest fires is necessary to open certain seed cones; thus, well-intentioned efforts to prevent forest fires can interrupt the cycle of regeneration.

The charity theorists were "human ecologists." By entering as friends into the lives of their charges, they saw how the undesirable feature—material want—actually played a constructive role in motivating healthy adjustments and improved standards of living. Relieving that want could undermine the process of uplift. In a lecture given in London in 1876, Octavia Hill tried to get her listeners to understand this comprehensive picture.

> You or I go into a wretched room; we see children dirty and without shoes, a forlorn woman tells us a story of extreme poverty, how her husband can find no work. We think it can do no harm to give the children boots to go to school; we give them, and hear

no more. Perhaps we go to Scotland the following week, and flat-
ter ourselves if we remember the children that that gift of boots
at least was useful. Yet just think what harm that may have done.
Perhaps the woman was a drunkard, and pawned the boots at
once and drank the money; or perhaps the man was a drunkard
neglecting his home, and the needs of it, which should have been
the means of recalling him to his duties, he finds partially met by
you and me and others.

She went on to give other illustrations of how the giving of alms
could undermine healthy adjustments, and concluded: "I believe
our irregular alms . . . are tending to keep a whole class on the very
brink of pauperism who might be taught self-control and foresight
if we would let them learn it."[12]

De Gerando made the same point: alms-giving undermines the
disposition to work and harms the poor in the long run. "It is mis-
taken kindness," he wrote, "which turns them away from fulfilling
their vocation on earth, by a useful and honorable life."[13]

Today's social workers see only one side of material deprivation:
it means suffering and therefore should be alleviated as promptly as
possible with a giveaway program. The charity theorists saw the suffering side, of course, but they also saw the positive, motivating
effect of need. Deprivation turned men into breadwinners, trained
housewives to be frugal, and guided children to be helpful to their
parents.

Here is how one of the founders of American social work, Mary
Richmond, diagnosed and prescribed for the "married vagabond":

A man has let himself drift into bad ways: he neglects his work,
spends his money for drink, cares less and less about his family; the
children become more and more neglected and starved. At last
some charitable agency steps in [saying] "The children must not be
allowed to suffer for their father's sins; we will feed and clothe and
educate them, and so give them a chance of doing better than their
parents."

Richmond then took up the perspective of the human ecologist:

All very well, if this were the only family. . . . But next door on
either side are men with the same downward path so easy before

them, and to a large extent restrained from entering upon it by the thought, "What will become of the children?" This restraining influence will break down much more rapidly for the knowledge that Smith's children are better cared for since he gave up the battle, and so the mischief spreads down the street like an epidemic.

Richmond described the therapy for the wayward male recommended by social workers of the day: "It will usually be necessary to let him find out what the charitable community expects of him, and this he will hardly do unless the charitable withhold all aid except in the form of work." In other words, the charity worker must *stop* all outside sources of aid going to this family!

This therapy produced a positive result in many cases, she reported.

Often when a man finds that charitable people are quite in earnest, that they really intend to place upon his shoulders the responsibility of his own family, he will bestir himself and go to work. He is not likely to stay and let his family starve. In fact, I have often found that the withholding of relief from the family of the married vagabond has the immediate effect of improving the material condition of the family—the man has either found work or left home. This method of being charitable requires courage, but if people would only see how wretchedness is perpetuated by the temporizing method, it would require courage to give small doles.[14]

Mary Richmond's analysis dramatizes the gulf between modern practice and the nineteenth-century charity theorists. Today the idea of withholding material assistance to bring about behavioral improvement is unthinkable. Families of wayward males are promptly subsidized by giveaway programs—the very policy that Richmond predicted would lead to an "epidemic" of family breakdown.

The Perils of Relief Funds

▼

Another point on which all the charity theorists agreed was that sympathetic giving is a self-defeating policy. They were fully aware of the aggravation principle: the more you give, the more you have to give. The New York charity leader Edward Devine summarized the consensus of welfare professionals in 1903:

> Relief funds, under the influence of the modern spirit, are no longer to be regarded as sums forever set apart to be expended in meeting an annually recurring number of cases of destitution of particular kinds, merely because those cases fall within the stipulated categories. ... Experience has shown that in almost any community the number of unfortunates of the class for whom it was intended will readily rise to absorb the entire available fund.[15]

In her account of American charity written in 1909, *How To Help*, Mary Conyngton explained that the "charity organization movement" grew up as a reaction against "the dangers of pauperizing and the evils of pauperism."[16] Reformers saw that the needy could make a permanent living by going from house to house and from charity group to charity group, telling tales of woe. To stop this practice, they formed central clearinghouses in each city to which they referred each case of neediness; from there, each case was assigned to a particular church group or friendly visitor. In London, Octavia Hill and other reformers formed the Charity Organization Society in 1869. In Amsterdam, a similar organization was established at about the same time.[17] Buffalo, New York, is generally credited as the home of the first such organization in the United States, in 1877. By 1912 there were charity organization societies in 154 U.S. cities.[18]

While experienced charity leaders knew the importance of limiting relief programs, the general public was not so well informed. Superficial commentators sometimes portrayed charity organization leaders as hard-hearted Scrooges for their opposition to giveaways. One contemporary poet wrote,

> The organized charity scrimped and iced
> In the name of a cautious, statistical Christ.[19]

Today such an accusation of stinginess would arouse a tide of guilt and prompt politicians and social workers to redouble giveaways. The nineteenth-century theorists stood their ground, not only because they knew from their own experience that they were right, but also because their moral credentials as volunteer visitors of the poor were unassailable. Here is how Octavia Hill dealt with the charge of "hard-heartedness":

> My friends, I have lived face to face with the poor for now some years, and I have not learned to think gifts of necessaries, such as a man usually provides for his own family, helpful to them. I have abstained from such, and expect those who love the poor and know them individually will do so more and more in time to come. I have sometimes been asked by rich acquaintances when I have said this whether I do not remember the words, "Never turn your face from any poor man."
>
> Oh, my friends, what strange perversion of words this seems to me. I may deserve reproach; I may have forgotten many a poor man, and done as careless a thing as anyone, but I cannot help thinking that to give *oneself* rather than one's *money* to the poor is not exactly turning one's face from him.[20]

Future-Oriented Charity

▼

In systems of sympathetic giving, the decision to give is based on the apparent suffering of the applicant. The giver asks, in effect, "Is this person sufficiently pitiable to inspire my sympathy?" Thus, a beggar with torn clothes and deformed limbs is a more likely candidate for aid than a healthy, well-dressed beggar. The applicant's past behavior is one factor affecting sympathy: we don't feel as sorry for those who have caused or contributed to their own suffering as we do for the perfectly blameless. We are prompted to give to a beggar who says he is out of work because his factory closed; if we hear he was fired for drunkenness, we ignore him.

The charity system of the eighteenth century and earlier was based on sympathetic giving. It divided the needy into those who were proper objects of sympathy—like the blind and widows—and those who were not—like drunkards and vagabonds. The former would be called the "deserving poor" and the latter "undeserving."

Modern commentators on welfare and social work decry this invidious distinction of the past, but in doing so they miss the welfare revolution of the nineteenth-century charity theorists. One of the remarkable innovations of the last century's charity workers was their orientation toward the *future* of the individual being helped. They overturned the medieval view that poverty was an assigned lot in life, one that the compassionate giver could only ameliorate. They believed in uplift. "The underlying motive of all effort," said Mary Conyngton, summarizing the principles of the American charity organization movement, was "restoring the needy person or family to an independent position in society."[21]

This emphasis on redemption meant that helpers were not so interested in classifying past behavior as worthy or unworthy. If a person is in a ditch, they said, the important thing is to get him out. Whether he jumped or was pushed is secondary. Armed with firm religious principles about the worth and dignity of all human beings, the charity theorists saw it as right to attempt to help everyone. This didn't mean indulgent giving, of course; for many needy, the correct treatment was carefully to deny material assistance and make them stand on their own feet. This view is summarized in the statement of principles drafted by the Buffalo Charity Organization Society in 1910: "In a charity organization society there is never any such thing as an unworthy family, though some cannot be helped wisely with material relief. The word unworthy is uncharitable."[22]

Teaching Values

▼

Since they were dealing with individuals, the charity theorists naturally focused on what individuals could do to improve themselves. They didn't ignore the role of environmental factors in poverty, but they knew it wasn't helpful, in advising individuals, to emphasize those factors. Their position was exactly that of a coach whose players have suffered a defeat in a previous game. Perhaps a bad call by the referee played a role in the loss, but nothing is gained by dwelling on it. To maximize the chance of winning in future games, the coach needs to emphasize what the players can do to improve their performance.

This forward-looking perspective led the theorists to emphasize improving the morale and character of the poor. Helen Bosanquet, one of the most articulate English theorists, put the point carefully and irrefutably:

> Character is one amongst other economic causes, and as such cannot fail to have an economic effect. In other words, I maintain that if you can make a man or woman more honest, sober and efficient than before, he will not only be more likely to find an opportunity of rendering services to the community (i.e., to find work), but will also by his higher range of wants increase the opportunities of other people (i.e., increase the amount of remunerative employment).[23]

An obvious corollary of the character improvement approach is the assumption that the helper is wiser than the helped. There was nothing of today's "value-free" neutrality in the charity theorists' perspective. To use the sports analogy again, the reformers saw themselves as coaches who knew better than their pupils. Of course, they knew they had to use tact and patience to persuade, but they never were in doubt about healthy lifestyles. Their writings are studded with value-laden terms that have utterly disappeared from the modern social work literature: they spoke of dirtiness and cleanliness, of the lazy and the industrious, of the dishonest and faithful.

The judgmental tone of the charity theorists sounds arrogant to modern ears, but it must be remembered that they never intended (as alleged today by writers eager to condemn nineteenth-century charity) to ignore, much less punish, the poor. Their judgments were part of an approach that invested in the poor and aimed to uplift them. This point clearly stands out even in their most untactful pronouncements, such as this one from Josephine Shaw Lowell:

> The main instrument to be depended on to raise the standard of decency, cleanliness, providence and morality among [suffering people] must be personal influence, which means that a constant

and continued intercourse must be kept up between those who have a high standard and those who have it not, and that the educated and happy and good are to give some of their time regularly and as a duty, year in and year out, to the ignorant, the miserable and the vicious.[24]

Octavia Hill agreed with this basic idea but would never have chosen this way of expressing it. For one thing, she never saw helping the poor as a cold duty. She derived immense pleasure from working among the poor and carrying out her tactics of uplift. She also knew that virtue was not a one-way street, and she could point to deprived individuals who had uplifted *her*. For example, she wrote movingly of an old woman who lived in a cramped basement apartment, a person who was spotlessly clean, frugal, self-reliant, and self-disciplined. "It is a life to watch with reverence and admiration," observed Hill.[25]

Modern social workers would see in such a case only an instance of "substandard housing" requiring a giveaway program. Hill, in her role as a "coach of virtue," knew that even an obscure player could set a shining example for everyone.

"To Give Charity upon Conditions"

▼

From their analysis of the defects of sympathetic giving, the charity theorists worked out the right way to give assistance. The basic idea was to look for a *constructive response* from the individual in exchange for the aid—what we have called "expectant giving." De Gerando gave a good statement of the position. While recognizing that simple alms-giving was harmful to the poor, he did not conclude that the poor should be abandoned:

> It would be contrary to humanity to show ourselves so inexorable toward the indigent, who are a prey to intemperance and idleness, as to refuse them all kinds of assistance; and it would indeed defeat the end we ought to propose to ourselves. But it is allowable, it is just, it is useful, to give charity upon conditions; and to proportion it, in a degree, to the merits of those who

receive it; to require that he, to whom we lend support, should also endeavour to assist himself, or at least not destroy the good we wish to do him. Without becoming barbarous, the visitor of the poor may show himself severe. He will become more indulgent in proportion as he sees some attempts at reform; he will encourage and reward efforts.[26]

Daniel C. Gilman, the president of the Charity Organization Society of Baltimore, made a similar statement about expectant giving in 1894. A principle "generally recognized as wise and correct" by all charity workers, he declared, was that "the best of all charities is not that which gives something for nothing; but that which gives something in return for industry, labor, economy, self-sacrifice and self-help."[27]

The most common exchange transaction that charity theorists stressed was work in return for aid. Octavia Hill explained that, in managing apartment houses for London's poor, she put a great deal of thought into lining up repair and cleaning work for the tenants to do:

When a tenant is out of work, instead of reducing his energy by any gifts of money, we simply, whenever the funds at our disposal allow it, employ him in restoring and purifying the houses.

And what a difference five shillings' worth of work in a bad week will make to a family! The father, instead of idling listlessly at the corner of the street, sets busily and happily to work, prepares the whitewash, mends the plaster, distempers the room; the wife bethinks herself of having a turn-out of musty corners or drawers ... and thus a sense of decency, the hope of beginning afresh and doing better, comes like new life into the home.

The same cheering and encouraging sort of influence, though in less degree, is exercised by our plan of having a little band of scrubbers.

We have each passage scrubbed twice a week by one of the elder girls. The sixpence earned is a stimulus, and they often take an extreme interest in the work itself. One little girl was so proud of her first cleaning that she stood two hours watching her passage lest the boys, whom she considered as the natural enemies of order and cleanliness, should spoil it before I came to see it.[28]

Another common type of bargain that charity workers recommended involved a major life change that would permanently lift the family to a better condition. For example, a widow might agree to stop her child from earning money by begging and place him in a trade school in exchange for a pension. Or a family might agree to move to cheaper, more sustainable lodgings in exchange for payment of a debt.

In France and Belgium, reformers organized vegetable-growing by the poor. Charitable associations supplied plots of land and experienced gardeners to supervise. Gardening leaders pointed to more than a dozen benefits of this form of self-help, above and beyond the value of the vegetables grown: energy was increased, self-respect was restored, old people rejected by industrial employers could make themselves useful, a spirit of sociable cooperation was evoked, the saloon was not visited so much, and young children had a place to play in the open air.[29]

Another widely practiced tactic was to develop savings arrangements in which the poor literally financed their own uplift, saving their money to fulfill their dreams and protect themselves from hard times. The reformers contributed the organization and management and, of course, taught the desirability of saving among the poor they befriended.

This, then, was the theory of charity developed by the nineteenth-century charity workers. Effective help, they said, required genuine, voluntary personal relationships between helper and helped, not giveaways of material assistance, for these, they believed, perpetuated or even compounded misfortune. Their aid was future-oriented, directed at improving the character of recipients and their ability to thrive and achieve. And they emphasized arrangements of two-way giving, where some contribution or effort was expected in return for the assistance given.

PART II

The Roots of Failure

5

How Government Gives

In the field of aeronautics, nineteenth-century investigators developed basic principles and carried out the first successful experiments. Building upon this foundation, specialists of the twentieth century made impressive achievements in aircraft design and construction. Nowadays airplanes rarely crash.

In social welfare, as we saw in the preceding chapter, the nineteenth century witnessed a similar progress in developing principles and making first experiments. Yet in this field the hard-won conclusions of the past have been thrown aside. In its charitable practices, the twentieth century has regressed several hundred years to the deficient eighteenth-century attitude that any giving represents kindness. As a result, modern welfare systems are continuously crashing.

What lies behind this repudiation of past wisdom? A number of factors are involved, but the most important is the role of government. The problem is that government has a natural bias toward the handout approach of helping the poor. Hence, when the twentieth century opted for government as the primary vehicle of social assistance, it also chose, unwittingly, the system of sympathetic giving.

The Vast Continent of Welfare

▼

Though almost all Americans have firm opinions about welfare, few grasp the enormous scope of the system they criticize or defend. In the debates about government social assistance programs, most participants are like Pilgrims making statements about North America while pointing at Plymouth Rock.

When most people think of welfare, they have one or perhaps two programs in mind. "The main welfare program in the United States," wrote a researcher for the International Monetary Fund in 1995, "is Aid to Families with Dependent Children (AFDC)." This assumption enabled the author to claim that in budgetary terms, "the welfare program is actually quite small."[1] The tendency to treat AFDC as "welfare" has been a common, but serious, error. AFDC is only one of scores of welfare programs. In 1994 the cost of this program constituted 6 percent of total federal welfare spending.[2]

Those who operate the welfare system have been reluctant to publicize the full size and combined cost of all the welfare programs, perhaps fearing that if taxpayers ever realized how large the system really is, welfare would face even more opposition than it does. In 1993 Robert Rector and William Lauber, researchers from the conservative Heritage Foundation, pored over government budget documents to tabulate the major welfare programs, that is, the "means-tested" programs that give aid to those individuals or communities that can prove they are poor. Rector and Lauber came up with eighty major federal and state government programs, which, since 1965— the beginning of the war on poverty—have cost the country *$5.4 trillion.* Just in 1993, by their computation, the total cost of welfare programs was $324 billion.[3]

In terms of size of spending, the largest welfare program is Medicaid, which pays medical and rehabilitation costs for low-income recipients. The next largest category of spending is disability, which gives cash to those deemed unable to work. Other programs include housing subsidies; job training programs; numerous feeding and nutrition arrangements, including food stamps, WIC (Special Supplemental Nutrition Program for Women, Infants, and

Children), and school lunches and breakfasts; assistance with heating bills; education programs for low-income children, including Head Start; assistance programs for Indians, migrant workers, and refugees; block grants to low-income communities; day care for low-income parents; a wage subsidy for low-income workers (EIC); and foster care assistance. Oh yes, and AFDC—which has lately been renamed TANF (Temporary Assistance for Needy Families).

This listing doesn't even begin to portray the vastness of the welfare system. Consider just one area, job training. The Heritage Foundation researchers counted nine employment and job training programs costing $5.3 billion. However, the government's own General Accounting Office, making a more thorough tabulation a year later, found "about" 163 job training programs (even the GAO wasn't sure it had counted all of them), costing $20 billion.[4] Government welfare programs are rather like petroleum deposits: the harder you look, the more you find.

The profusion of welfare programs needs to be appreciated in order to draw conclusions about the operation of the entire system. When considering the positive or negative effects of reductions in a particular program, many commentators assume that the program is the only one supporting recipients. In practice, most recipients receive benefits from numerous programs. For example, in 1995, 97 percent of AFDC recipients were on Medicaid, 87 percent were on food stamps, 63 percent benefited from school lunches and breakfasts, 31 percent received housing benefits, and 25 percent received additional food assistance from the WIC program.[5] Recipients are also "serially dependent": after exhausting benefits in one program, they go on to others.

The multiplicity of programs makes it just about impossible to reform the welfare system in any prompt way. The 1996 welfare reform legislation illustrates the problem. The popular view was that this was a "sweeping overhaul of welfare," as the *Wall Street Journal* put it.[6] But the legislation attempted major changes in only two programs—AFDC and food stamps. A few other programs, including disability (SSI), wage subsidies (EIC), foster care, child nutrition, and Medicaid, were slightly adjusted to exclude certain beneficiaries and to alter benefits, but their basic features were not addressed. And the many dozens of other welfare programs, from job training to housing subsidies, were totally unaffected. At best, then, the 1996 legislation tried to "overhaul" only about one-eighth of the U.S. welfare system.

The tendency to underestimate the number of welfare programs is reinforced by a tendency to underestimate their costs. Almost invariably, welfare programs cost more than they are thought to cost. To some extent, this distortion is fostered by administrators and lobbyists who conceal the true costs of programs to avoid criticism. It is also aided by the complexity of the budget. Most welfare programs are funded from a variety of government accounts, and it can be quite difficult to track them all down. For example, working with readily available budget figures, the Heritage Foundation researchers reported that the Job Corps program cost $926 million in 1992.[7] This tabulation left out, among other things, the administrative costs. A comprehensive audit of this program by the accounting firm of R. Navarro & Associates, performed under contract for the Department of Labor's inspector general, included these and other costs. It found that for the same year—1992—the total cost of the Job Corps was $1.561 billion, a figure 69 percent higher than the Heritage Foundation number.[8]

One expense always left out of the welfare picture is the fund-raising cost. The government dollars spent on welfare programs do not float effortlessly into the Treasury. They are extracted from the public through the tax system, a system of raising money with enormous overhead costs. These burdens include the disincentives to productive economic activity, compliance costs (record-keeping, studying tax law, filling out forms, making deposits), the costs of penalty disputes, tax litigation, tax avoidance, and so on. A compilation of these costs for 1985 found that they amounted to sixty-five cents for each tax dollar collected.[9] In other words, every welfare program costs society 65 percent more than the tax dollars actually spent on it.

It is important to keep tax system overhead costs in mind when considering the relative merits of private and governmental funding of welfare programs. Many private charities find that they have rather substantial fund-raising costs, and their leaders often look to government and its tax system as a way to avoid these costs. However, the idea that government money can be raised cheaply is an illusion. The overhead costs of taxation are much higher than the fund-raising costs of any legitimate private charity.

In Search of Welfare "Cuts"

▼

In addition to underestimating the size and costs of the American welfare system, the public is also unaware of its steady growth. This misperception can be traced to the biased way the media report on welfare debates. Few in Washington want to truly cut welfare spending, to actually reduce the amount of money spent on "the poor." For more than thirty years, the debates in the capital have been over how fast welfare spending should rise. Those campaigning for rapid increases accuse those who favor slower growth of "cutting" welfare, and the media repeat the charge as if it were a fact.

Decades of this misreporting have given rise to a widespread belief that under Republican administrations—Nixon, Ford, Reagan, Bush—welfare was cut. The truth is that under every recent administration, overall welfare spending has always grown. The few programs that have been terminated have been replaced by more—and more costly—programs. Sometimes some recipients have lost benefits, but other recipients have been added. Since 1968, just before Richard Nixon took office, welfare spending, in inflation-adjusted dollars, has more than quintupled; on a per capita basis, spending has more than tripled.[10]

The 1996 welfare reform provided another round of this misleading statistical sparring. Official projections made by the Congressional Budget Office in 1996 showed that federal welfare spending in the reformed programs was projected to rise by 50 percent over the period 1996–2002—much more, even, than the projected increase in inflation. Food stamp spending was projected to rise from $26 billion to $31 billion in 2002, disability spending (SSI) from $24 billion to $35 billion, Medicaid from $96 billion to $165 billion, and child nutrition from $8 billion to $11 billion. It is true that some recipients in some programs would lose benefits, but this would be more than counterbalanced by the expected addition of new recipients and by increases in services and benefits. Total spending in the affected welfare programs was projected to rise $98 billion over the six-year period.[11] Unfortunately, most journalists failed to examine the actual numbers. Instead, they succumbed to the spin put out by the welfare lobby and reported that "cuts" were being made in welfare programs.[12] The numbers represent "cuts" only in the sense that if the programs had been left untouched, spending would have gone up slightly more, by 55 percent instead of 50 percent.

Despite their criticisms of welfare, conservative policy makers join liberals in endorsing comprehensive government welfare programs. Over the decades, this bipartisan consensus that government should render aid to the poor has resulted in a vast array of programs and continually increasing welfare spending.

An Engine of Sympathetic Giving

▼

While the specifics of government welfare programs differ, they have one thing in common: until recently, they have been handouts. In fact, most of them still are handouts. Program after program gives goods and services without seeking a meaningful reciprocal act from the beneficiaries. The Medicaid program gives individual recipients medical care worth thousands of dollars, yet the beneficiaries are not expected to do anything in return after they recover from their illnesses. They don't have to sweep the hospital floor or repay even a few cents on the dollar. In return for free school lunches and breakfasts, neither parents nor children are expected to do anything. They aren't expected to volunteer in classrooms, or supervise the playground, or help in the cafeteria. In the Job Corps—a $2 billion job training program with 111 residential centers around the country—students get free instruction, free room and board, free transportation, free recreational facilities. They aren't expected to pay anything for this training, or take out loans, or work nights, or mow the lawns at the work centers. Instead of being asked for a meaningful contribution in return, students are given an additional sixty dollars a month in spending money to encourage them to remain in the program.

In the Head Start program, the giveaway approach is so ingrained that it undermines the effectiveness of the program. The original idea behind Head Start was to give poverty-level preschoolers social and educational enrichment that would help them succeed in school. Since the children are in class only a few hours a week, it is vital that anything learned be reinforced at home by parents. Consequently, as an authoritative review of the Head Start program put it, "parent participation is recognized as crucial to the success of early intervention."[13] Logically, parental involvement should be required as a condition of the program. Unfortunately, the idea of a requirement goes against the giveaway principle on which Head Start is based. "Can you get kicked out of Head Start?" I asked an official in a Head Start program in Spokane, Washington. "No, not really," she laughed. "You can't kick them out. We try to figure out what their needs are and meet their needs."

As a result of this indulgent approach, most parents have no significant involvement with the Head Start program, and for them and their children it is little more than a baby-sitting service and welfare agency. (A main job of Head Start social workers is to see that parents and children are signed up for all applicable welfare benefits.) In the Head Start office in Sandpoint, Idaho, I asked a teacher how often parents volunteered to be in the classroom with their children. "We'd *like* them to come in once a month." The emphasis she put on *like* indicated her understanding that even this marginal level of parental involvement was an unrealistic hope. I happened to see the class roll and time sheet for one class: it showed that not one of the parents of the eighteen children had volunteered in the entire month.

The giveaway feature of government programs has led to mounting public dissatisfaction, and both practitioners and observers are coming to understand that the ineffectiveness and harm of welfare is rooted in this characteristic. In his 1986 book *Beyond Entitlement*, the political scientist Lawrence Mead set out to explain "why federal programs since 1960 have coped so poorly with the various social problems that have come to afflict American society." His answer is that they "have given benefits to their recipients but have set few requirements for how they ought to function in return."[14]

This argument has become increasingly persuasive to state and federal policy makers. By 1995, twenty-four states had added some type of work requirement to a few of their welfare programs. Federal welfare reforms have paid lip service to work requirements since 1967. The federal welfare reform of 1996 put rather strong requirements in two programs, AFDC and food stamps. At least some recipients in these programs would henceforth be expected to work part-time in order to obtain benefits. Other types of requirements cropping up in welfare reform measures include expecting recipients to make a job search, to finish high school, or to make their children go to school.

These recent reforms raise the question: can we get rid of the objectionable handout feature of government welfare programs? Can they all be turned into healthy programs of expectant giving that put strong demands on the needy and uplift them? Most welfare reformers, including many conservatives, seem to believe they can. They propose that government aid policies be continued, or even expanded, but with the inclusion of exchange features.

I believe this hope is unrealistic. We did not end up with eighty giveaway programs because policy makers, in a moment of absent-mindedness, simply forgot to add an important ingredient. Instead, the institutional forces at work within government continually push assistance programs toward the handout mode.

This is not to criticize the idea of requirements in welfare programs. As part of a transitional effort to cut welfare caseloads, requirements are a useful way to help screen out recipients who can thrive on their own. For example, in 1994 New York City put 122,700 of its most employable welfare recipients into a workfare program in which they were expected to work part-time for city agencies in return for their benefits. Two years later, 89,000 had simply dropped out, having found other more attractive ways of coping than the city's work program.

We also don't want to say that a government assistance program can never achieve a degree of expectant giving, uplifting recipients by making demands on them. The past decade of work-oriented welfare reforms has produced useful programs in places like Riverside County, California, and Grant County, Wisconsin. In these settings, well-motivated caseworkers energetically prod welfare recipients to enter the labor market. They are backed by committed administrators who, in turn, are politically supported at the highest level.

But we should not take such success stories as representative of the whole. Work requirements have been attempted in thousands of counties, and the overall results have been disappointing. Furthermore, these programs are probably achieving their best results now, when they are new and fresh, their promoters are most committed, they are tackling the easiest welfare cases, and they are least encumbered with political compromises and judicial restrictions. "You have to have a lot of stamina," says Wisconsin Governor Tommy Thompson, explaining the difficulties in keeping that state's work-oriented program on track.[15] The question that must be asked is: why should the next governor, and the next, and the next, bother to fight these battles?

We should remember that the programs of the past forty years, rightly criticized by Mead for their something-for-nothing form, were not intended to end up that way. The prime architect of the 1960s war on poverty, which gave us handouts like food stamps and the Job Corps, was Sargent Shriver, who headed the Johnson administration's task force on poverty and later its Office of Economic Opportunity. He declared to the press in 1964, "I'm not at all interested in running a handout program, or a leaf-raking program, or a 'something for nothing' program."[16]

It would be unwise to see in today's government workfare programs, even those exhibiting a degree of success, a model for a permanent governmental approach to social assistance. Officials who make this error will find, decades later, that they originated yet another dismaying system of handouts.

The Quality-Quantity Dilemma

▼

In explaining how government programs become giveaways, we need to begin with the observation that politics deals with most public policies in a superficial, distant way. This is a natural consequence of the highly overloaded state of government decision-making systems. Voters and legislators lack the time to inquire closely into the thousands of policy matters that government tries to manage. Therefore, as many commentators have ruefully observed, they react on the basis of first impulses, bumper sticker slogans, and sound bites.

This superficiality has marked consequences for welfare policy. An underlying cause of sympathetic giving is inattention. The giver doesn't have the time to look deeply into the supplicant's situation and to see the ineffectiveness or harm of a handout. He gives because, at first glance, it seems kind to provide what is lacking. Politics amplifies this bias toward superficial good intentions. While voters and politicians want programs to be "a hand up and not a handout," they can seldom tell which is actually occurring. Most of the time, all they can judge is the number of people served in the programs and their overall cost.

This perspective creates a bias, because sympathetic giving is generally cheaper than expectant giving. To throw a dollar to a beggar costs only a dollar. To pay him in exchange for, say, learning to read requires the donor to invest in a system of motivating, teaching, and testing him. This cost difference leads to a quantity-quality trade-off in giving. You can treat more people through a simple giveaway program than with an arrangement incorporating exchange and self-help. In practice, the "help" of the giveaway program may be superficial or even unhealthy, but distant spectators, such as voters and legislators, are unlikely to grasp this point. They want to see more people served rather than fewer. Hence, broad political pressures encourage officials to boost the caseload numbers of the needy being "helped" and to shortchange the more costly phase of uplift.

Expectant giving is especially costly in government programs because of government's high costs and inefficiency. In small-scale, personal, and voluntary assistance arrangements, helpers may perform many roles at no cost. For example, a volunteer might counsel a jobless worker at no charge, or a neighbor might drive an invalid to a rehabilitation session on the way to work. In a large, formal institution like a government agency, the requirement that all functions be carried out by high-priced personnel—often unionized and often licensed—makes programs of expectant giving extremely expensive. A job counseling session in a government program—including all the administrative and facility overhead— is likely to cost taxpayers hundreds of dollars.

The expense of expectant giving has been recognized at least since the New Deal's Works Progress Administration (WPA). Though everyone agreed that it was healthier for the unemployed to work in WPA projects for their assistance than to be given a dole, the WPA cost more to get the same amount of money in beneficiaries' pockets. This was one of the reasons it was discontinued.[17]

Today's programs that attempt to implement work requirements face the same problem. The typical program continues to give welfare recipients all their previous benefits (including cash, housing, food stamps, and Medicaid), while at the same time incurring additional expenses for the supervision and leadership. These typically run more than $3,000 per year per participant. Most of these programs also pay carfare expenses for getting to work (around $1,000 per year) and day care expenses (between $3,000 and $4,000).[18]

The same kind of fiscal crunch affects welfare-for-education programs. In 1995 reformers in Ohio proposed that AFDC recipients be required to work toward a high school general equivalency diploma. This was an excellent idea in principle. Instead of just handing out money, why not expect welfare recipients (about half of whom lack a high school diploma) to complete their high school education? However, a look at the cost of such a program showed how unrealistic this would be. Estimates indicated that the cost of supplying the necessary education and supervision would be $8,892 per recipient per year. This cost would be on top of all the welfare benefits they were already getting. Hence, a program that would serve the fifty thousand eligible welfare recipients would cost more than $400 million yearly. As it happened, the reform was stillborn because even the $13 million appropriated to implement the idea on a small scale was left out of the budget.[19]

The overall result, then, is that welfare programs with work requirements cost much more than giveaway programs. In the early years of such a program, this increased cost may be disguised by falling caseloads. But once caseloads stabilize, budgetary pressures lead politicians and welfare administrators toward relaxing requirements and shortchanging the costly phases of uplift in order to serve more needy people with cheaper handout programs.

Equal Treatment and Red Tape

▼

Expectant giving involves crafting requirements that fit the individual case. Each recipient must be given a significant load, but not one too heavy for him to bear. Expectant giving therefore requires that subjective judgments be made about what the individual is capable of under the circumstances. In small, personal systems, subjective distinctions are made all the time. In a family, for example, each child is given duties according to his abilities.

This kind of subjective, unequal treatment tends to be unacceptable in a government agency. Because officials are spending tax money, taxpayers of all possible persuasions have the right to object to any unequal treatment. To prevent favoritism or prejudice, the public insists on controlling administrators through rules and regulations that dictate how they must treat all clients.

In the welfare system, half a century of political agitation and judicial decree has resulted in a body of law and regulation that tends to prohibit the introduction of positive requirements in welfare administration. I asked an administrator of an Idaho food bank why his organization didn't demand something in return for the food boxes it gives away. The group is a private, nonprofit organization, but it gets substantial government funding:

Q.   Have you ever thought of something like a work test, like you have to pick up litter for an hour to get a food box?

A.   We can't do that! We can't do that! You violate their rights [said sarcastically]. These young people coming through. They're living off the land. That's all they're doing. They go south in the wintertime, come back north because it's so pretty, camp on the bank of the lake out here, fish, come up to the food bank, get whatever.

Q.   Why don't you have them wash your windows?

A.   You can't do that! We're told [by the state funding agency] that you cannot make people repay for the food.

In order for work, job search, and schooling requirements to succeed, the long-established norm of bureaucratic neutrality must be overturned. To a certain extent, this is starting to happen in connection with recent welfare reforms. Administrators of successful workfare programs agree that staff must be given the freedom to treat individual cases differently. In Riverside, California—which has the state's most successful welfare-to-work program—flexibility has been the watchword. John Rodgers, the assistant to the director, told me that managers and caseworkers in the work-focused program are "given a lot of latitude. Management and administrative staff gave them the resources, gave them the message, gave them the training they needed, and then got out of the way. And gave them an opportunity to figure out what the best way was for them to help people go to work." In the Wisconsin program, county welfare officials are free to contract with any agency, including private, profit-making firms, to carry out the welfare-to-work program.

A recent Urban Institute survey of eight welfare-to-work programs observed that "program flexibility is critical" in dealing with dysfunctional families. "Because these families' circumstances are so diverse," the report concluded, "a broad range of services and approaches to strengthening families is needed to help them achieve self-sufficiency."[20]

More freedom is needed in a successful program of expectant giving than simply the flexibility to adjust formal punishments and rewards. In successful programs, staff members become friends and mentors to their clients. They create emotional ties with them, both to give them emotional support and to instruct and criticize. The Urban Institute study emphasized the importance of developing these "trusting relationships." It observed that "program administrators repeatedly stressed the importance of hiring staff who were genuinely committed to helping families bring about change in their lives."[21]

Unfortunately, personnel policies in government agencies work against this ideal. Consider hiring policies. To select employees who are "genuinely committed" to clients and capable of building a "trusting relationship" with them, managers would have to make rather subjective decisions about prospective staff. Once given the power to make subjective decisions, managers might use it irresponsibly, hiring their friends and family members, for example. To prevent this kind of misuse of taxpayer funds, government personnel systems use mechanical criteria in hiring personnel, such as formal tests, academic training, and years on the job. But these criteria are irrelevant to—and often opposed to—the task of finding caring, committed caseworkers.

The issue of terminating employees raises the same problem. Many, perhaps most, caseworkers "burn out" after years of working with needy families. They are likely to become cynical and pessimistic and to view their jobs merely as a nine-to-five source of income. To maintain the idealism and effectiveness of a system of uplift, these employees should be discharged. But to achieve this flexibility, job security in government welfare agencies would have to be abolished. Also, managers would have to be given the power to fire employees who have lost their sensitivity and enthusiasm. But the freedom to make these kinds of subjective decisions would also give managers the autonomy to fire employees who are personal or political enemies.

There is a dilemma here with no easy resolution. In practice, the century-old tendency of government agencies has been to evolve personnel policies that protect employees from unfair termination and give them virtually lifetime job security, even if their enthusiasm falters. Unless this orientation changes, in the long run caseworkers in government welfare agencies will tend to lack empathy and enthusiasm in dealing with welfare clients.

When they first begin, welfare-to-work programs may be relatively unhampered by red tape. But each day of legislation and litigation is bound to bring more regulations that restrict the ability of caseworkers to discriminate between clients and make demands on them. New York's program, only three years old, has already seen a number of challenges. In August 1996, welfare rights lawyers prevented the city from including residents of a South Bronx homeless shelter in its workfare program; they obtained an injunction from a state supreme court judge who felt that interviewing these welfare recipients in connection with the work program would be "traumatic" for them.[22] The 22,000 New York City welfare recipients who attend college objected to workfare requirements, since the part-time work assignments might interfere with their college careers. A *New York Times* editorial supported them, and two state legislators introduced a bill to require workfare officials to assign "convenient" on-campus jobs to these recipients.[23]

In an effort to be more flexible, many programs have contracted with private firms to prepare and motivate welfare recipients for work. But in the long run, these firms will also be subject to restrictions as litigation and regulation follow the flow of tax dollars. There are bound to be scandals and shortcomings, cases in which money is wasted or stolen or in which recipients seem to be shockingly indulged, or shockingly harmed. Officials will try to fix problems the only way they know how: with new regulations that apply to all such programs.

Unfortunately, we do not yet realize that there is no solution to the problem of rigidity within the doctrine of taxation with representation. We are not about to set welfare bureaucrats loose, telling them to do whatever they think is best. We—taxpayers, voters, pressure groups, newspapers, lawyers, churches, university professors, social workers, beneficiaries—all have a much-cherished right to intervene, to stop what we think are abuses, unkindness, and scandals. So we try to control what welfare officials do through laws, regulations, and court decisions, thus producing the inflexible, deadening red tape that undermines meaningful programs of expectant giving.

6

Paying for Failure

In cataloging the pressures that push government aid systems into the handout mode, we need to note a factor common to all institutionalized giving: the separation of donors from recipients. When we directly give our own resources to those in need, we don't want our aid to create an open-ended dependency because that would drain us financially. So we look for ways to help that will make the recipient independent and let us end our aid. Hence, personal systems of assistance have a bias toward expectant giving, toward helping the needy stand on their own feet.

In an institutional system of assistance, with workers being paid to help the needy, the incentives run in the opposite direction. Welfare officials are not dispensing their personal funds; they are giving away other people's money. They do not suffer financially from open-ended giving. For them, the financial pinch comes when the money *stops* being given away, when the program is shrunk or closed down and their jobs disappear. Thus, the self-interest of workers and managers in institutional systems creates pressures to keep caseloads up, even if the program is ineffective, and even if it causes harmful dependency.

A social security official in a Midwest field office candidly described for me the institutional pressures in the disability program (SSI). A healthy disability program, of course, would urge people to transcend their disabilities and continue working, not declare themselves disabled and useless. In the SSI program, he found, the incentives were just the opposite. Social security staff were urged "to do anything—just get these people on the rolls."

> In the field—I was a supervisor out there for years and years—your staffing, your budget for supplies, and your awards money for the employees was based on work units. Now, work units were assigned based on the number of claims you took. So we would sit around and figure out how we could get more people on the SSI rolls, because it would benefit us. The more applications we took, the more work units, the bigger the staff: we could build up an empire.

The pressure to build and maintain caseloads works against having programs that make real demands on clients, because doing so would involve turning potential clients away. As a result, institutional systems tend to slide into something-for-nothing giving.

"We'd Lose Just About Everyone"
▼

Relaxing standards to maintain caseloads takes place even in programs whose only justification is to raise standards. Job training programs illustrate the problem. Their aim is to give poverty-level individuals preparation—special courses, trade school, community college—for the job market. As conceived by Congress, the programs are supposed to embody expectant giving. In return for financial assistance and training, the students are supposed to pursue diligently their course of study, increase their abilities, and get better jobs.

In practice, it seldom happens this way: job training doesn't produce significant increases in skill or capacity, and graduates end up about where they were before—perhaps, in some ways, further impaired—because the programs are not demanding enough.[1] They do not insist that participants show a high level of commitment and motivation. The presence of unmotivated recipients drags down standards and impairs the morale of staff; typically they, and the program, end up merely going through the motions.

Why don't these programs insist on a high level of effort from participants? The answer is that a demanding program would screen out large numbers of participants. That would reduce the caseload, then the appropriations, causing lost jobs and career opportunities for the staff.

The Job Training Partnership Act (JTPA) gives financial aid to low-income individuals seeking vocational training in trade schools and colleges. I asked an administrator in a North Carolina JTPA program about the policy toward unmotivated students:

Q.   If people are not going to class and you hear about this, how many times do you call them until you say, "You're off the program?"

A.   I immediately start calling or sending letters or going to try to find this person and say, "Where are the time sheets?" And they'd either moved or whatever, but say you ran into a person who just says, "I don't want to go." The first thing you try to do is find out if there's something underneath all that. The last thing that we try to do is take them off the program. That is not a viable threat. It's a problem. There are people that know we are not going to say, "You're off JTPA." They know the next thing we're going to say is, "Can we help you get back into other classes?"

Q.   Why wouldn't it be a threat?

A.   Because the way JTPA is driven. It's driven that you have to have so many people positively terminated to continue to get money, so . . .

Q.   And recipients know that?

A.   It gets found out very quickly.

Hence, in the JTPA program fiscal pressures keep administrators from imposing rigorous requirements. As a result, for recipients not already motivated to succeed, the program drifts into the giveaway mold and cultivates irresponsibility: recipients learn that if you slack off, the world will keep rewarding you anyway.

This pattern of laxness is not confined to government agencies. Private groups spending tax dollars can drift into it as well. They want to make their programs look good to legislators and administrators, so they too are tempted to keep their head counts up by relaxing standards. In the early 1980s, the Manpower Development

Research Corporation (MDRC) ran a number of "supported work" programs financed by the federal government. The aim, as an MDRC vice president told a Senate subcommittee, was to instill "positive work habits and attitudes."[2] To implement this goal, moderately firm attendance standards were adopted: no more than three unexcused absences or five unexcused latenesses in the first ten weeks of training class. The reporter Ken Auletta attended one of these courses in New York City and discovered that the rules were not being applied. The trainer in charge explained that if the rules were applied, "we'd lose just about everyone in the class." Students were allowed to come and go as they wished, even to sleep or read the newspaper in class. As a result, a program that was supposed "to induce trainees to accept the responsibility for their own fate" actually reinforced irresponsibility.[3] When they didn't keep their commitments, clients were shielded from the consequences.

The trainer did not intend this outcome, of course. It was simply a consequence of the normal desire to create some appearance of success. Imagine what his superiors would think if he reported that he simply had no students left after applying attendance standards!

"A Story We Are Proud to Tell"

▼

If welfare bureaucracies pursue their self-interest at the expense of clients, why don't welfare workers themselves expose the hypocrisy? They are people of goodwill and integrity. If billions of taxpayer dollars are being wasted in programs that don't help, and even positively harm, recipients, why don't they come forth to tell the world about it?

The answer is that a number of defense mechanisms keep employees from noticing what's wrong—and from telling anyone when they do notice. Perhaps the most basic is "task commitment," our tendency to believe that whatever we are doing is worth doing. If we are paid to do a fairly pointless or even harmful job, we protect our self-esteem by finding ways to see the job as worthwhile. It would be psychologically stressful for an employee to say to himself (and to others), "What I do is wasteful and harmful."

Higher-level administrators are especially vulnerable to task commitment because they have the job of defending the agency to the outside world. "The history of Social Security is a story that we are proud to tell," said Shirley S. Chater, social security commissioner in 1996, in an agency pamphlet entitled *A Brief History of Social Security*. "From its modest beginnings, Social Security has grown to become an essential facet of modern life." The pamphlet boasts that "the SSI program has nearly doubled in size over the years from its inception in 1974."[4] To a thoughtful outsider, the doubling of the SSI rolls probably represents a tragedy: twice as many people have been coaxed into idleness. But the social security officials responsible for the program could hardly entertain this view. They are paid to "sell" the agency to Congress and the public; to maintain a positive self-image, they must sell themselves on the program first.

Another psychological mechanism leading to the suppression of criticism within welfare bureaucracies is the "not for me to reason why" syndrome. The workers—even top administrators—see themselves as cogs in a much larger system created by higher powers: Congress, the Supreme Court, and the American electorate. If they do notice a harmful aspect of their program, they say there's nothing they can—or should—do about it because their "boss" apparently wants it that way. "Don't blame me, blame Congress" is frequently heard in the corridors of bureaucracy.

This mentality is enshrined in rules that require employees to support and defend programs regardless of their own views. The regulations for standards of conduct for employees of the Department of Health and Human Services illustrate the basic approach:

> When a Department program is based on law, Executive Order or regulation, every employee has a positive obligation to make it function as efficiently and economically as possible *and to support it as long as it is a part of recognized public policy*.[5]

Thus, if an agency employee came to the conclusion that a welfare program, like SSI, was a tragically misguided policy, destroying millions of lives, and wrote a letter to a newspaper detailing his views, he would be violating HHS regulations.

Another factor limiting criticism within bureaucracies is outright muzzling. All organizations develop ways to present an attractive image and to keep employees from revealing flaws to the public. Ironically, in most government units, including welfare agencies, the task of keeping outsiders from finding out anything negative is often carried out by "public information" officials.

Here's an example of how the system works. I called the Harrisburg, Pennsylvania, office of the Social Security Administration and asked the local manager whether I could interview him about the SSI program. He thought this would be fine, but said he had to check with the regional public information officer. The next morning I found a message on my answering machine from the public information officer denying my request for an interview.

When I called him, he explained that he turned me down because I was seeking "opinions on SSI, about how it works." This, he said, was "absolutely forbidden." "Social security folks cannot give opinions."

"So if," I asked, "an employee saw an abuse, or thought a program unsound . . . ?"

"They have proper channels to go through within the government," he replied. "It is not their responsibility to go to the press, or to go outside of the organization to alert individuals that there is an impropriety going on."

The New York City welfare department has muzzling honed to a fine art. In preparation for my trip there, I called several local welfare offices to try to set up interviews. All the managers said the same thing: we can't talk without permission from the press office. "What would happen to you if you talked to someone?" I asked the manager of an uptown Manhattan food stamp office.

"I really don't know, because I'm not going to take that chance," she replied.

"But who would ever find out?" I persisted.

She lowered her voice. I could feel her looking around the room for informers. "I don't trust nobody. We're talking about feeding my kids, you know."

Blocked at every turn, I finally gave in and asked the media relations officer to set up some interviews with local caseworkers and branch managers. My request was ignored. Further pestering finally yielded one interview—with a public relations specialist in the workfare program whose sanitized account of the city's workfare program neatly skirted all its problems. When I asked him about the muzzling of welfare workers, he denied that any such policy existed. "People are free," he said. "No one is abridging First Amendment rights."

Fortunately, the efforts of bureaucracies to muzzle their workers are imperfect. With persistence, a reporter or scholar can usually find someone willing to talk. Generally speaking, liberal reporters have a much easier time of it, because welfare workers see them as allies in the campaign to preserve and expand programs. The workers feed them studies, data, and case histories that seem to document a need for the program. Conservatives who want to report on program weaknesses have no natural allies at any level of a welfare organization. The result is a serious bias in welfare reporting: the public gets vast amounts of coverage in support of programs, but very little information that reveals their real costs and harm. In chapter 13, I suggest a method for counteracting this imbalance.

Who Cares About Fraud?

▼

In exploring why government officials don't apply standards and don't demand performance of recipients, it is useful to look at the problem of fraud. Comprehensive data on fraud and error in government programs are not readily available. Nevertheless, the partial data we do have indicate that it is a serious problem. The food stamp program has probably received more official attention than any other. Systems for detecting certain kinds of errors have been in place for more than twenty years, and they reveal a stubbornly high rate of error and abuse. In the mechanical process of giving out benefits, for example, there is a 10 percent error rate—a flaw that runs, as might be expected, in the direction of overpaying benefits. In 1995 these overpayments resulted in nearly $2 billion in excess payments.[6] Another kind of abuse is trafficking—illegally selling food stamps for drugs, alcohol, cigarettes, and so on, instead of using them to purchase food. The GAO estimates that 10 percent of benefits are trafficked.[7]

The welfare program with the highest officially documented level of abuse is the earned income credit, the wage subsidy program that provides $20 billion in benefits. A careful audit by the IRS in 1988 found that 42 percent of recipients were overpaid and that erroneous benefit payments amounted to 34 percent of the total amount disbursed.[8] A less comprehensive measure of the fraud in the program in 1994 found that $4.4 billion was falsely claimed and paid out.[9]

All governmental attempts to determine the level of fraud in welfare programs have a double weakness: (1) officials are inclined to understate fraud because they are reluctant to let it be thought that their programs are seriously marred (the task commitment phenomenon), and (2) officials are unable to earn the confidence of welfare recipients to learn about all the misrepresentations they employ. For this reason, all official studies of welfare fraud greatly understate the true level of corruption.[10] A valid study of welfare fraud would need to gain confidential information about the financial condition of the welfare recipients.

Perhaps the most searching study of this kind was conducted by Kathryn Edin in 1988 in a midwestern city. She gained the confidence of twenty-five women receiving AFDC payments, who were introduced to her through friends, and found that all twenty-five had unreported income. Therefore, they all were defrauding the AFDC program. Most had unreported full- or part-time jobs; others were getting income from boyfriends and family members.[11] This study suggests that the level of fraud in programs like AFDC and food stamps may be close to 100 percent, with virtually all recipients at least shading the truth about their financial circumstances and their ability to obtain outside income.

Welfare officials are often aware that high levels of fraud are occurring, but they seldom take strenuous steps to prevent it. Edin's research illustrates the point. She interviewed several dozen welfare case workers and pointed out that the reported budgets of many clients didn't add up, and that this had to mean they received unreported income. Though all the caseworkers agreed that this strongly indicated fraud, none of them wanted to act: "The case workers Edin interviewed all turned a blind eye to such indirect evidence of cheating because investigating a recipient's unreported income would have required extra work and would not have earned them any credit with their superiors."[12]

Welfare agencies and welfare workers are rewarded for higher caseloads and for dispensing more benefits. Since fraud control takes resources and only results in a reduced caseload, it is slighted. In a comprehensive book on fraud in the AFDC and Medicaid programs, John Gardiner and Theodore Lyman concluded that fraud control efforts are limited because "agencies' [fraud] control goals often conflict both operationally and politically with their service goals."[13]

A good example of this pattern is the Social Security Administration's management of the federal disability system. Fraud in this system has attracted considerable media and congressional attention. In California, the complaints and tips about SSI fraud became so numerous that the state Medi-Cal office conducted an investigation in 1993 using undercover agents posing as SSI claimants. Investigators uncovered systems of middlemen who coached clients in faking disabilities and medical practitioners who submitted phony reports. One clinic specialized in providing hundreds of diagnoses of "mildly mentally retarded" without even examining the claimants. That one clinic had fed 1,981 successful applicants into the SSI system, at a cost in benefits of $39 million.[14]

Yet, the Social Security Administration has refused to make a significant effort to control the fraud in its program. Indeed, it doesn't even want to hear about it. A House subcommittee found that workers in the disability field offices were dismayed by the stonewalling:

> Many SSA field offices and State DDS [Disability Determination Service] offices informed the Subcommittee of their frustration with SSA headquarters and the HHS OIG [Office of Inspector General of the Department of Health and Human Services]. Employees frequently recognized the pattern of fraud schemes by middlemen, only to have their referrals and complaints "fall on deaf ears." Eventually, some offices just quit making referrals.

The subcommittee noted that even after California investigators had exposed fraud schemes, the Social Security Administration dragged its feet doing anything about the documented abuses: "At the time of the hearing, SSA had not reopened any of the thousands of suspected SSI cases."[15]

Administrators say that fraud cannot be more energetically pursued because there are no funds for it. It's certainly true that anti-fraud efforts are expensive. To reopen, say, 1,981 suspected SSI claims—giving every case a complete hearing—would mean diverting many people from other administrative activities.

But what are those "other administrative activities?" Mainly, they are the work involved in getting people *on* the disability rolls. Nothing in the social security law requires the agency to give first priority to this function. The social security commissioner *could* recommend that the agency suspend taking new applications for as long as it takes to deal with the fraud backlog. But that, of course, would interfere with the doubling and redoubling of SSI rolls, the "story" that Commissioner Chater was so "proud to tell."

The inability of government welfare programs to root out fraud in their programs is a warning sign. Before we can pronounce a government agency capable of expectant giving, capable of demanding an intricate quid pro quo from its beneficiaries, it first needs to prove that it has the will to prevent the massive cheating that has been going on for generations.

Implications of Tax Funding

▼

Any degree of separation between donors and recipients in an assistance system creates a bias toward sympathetic giving. It creates a class of workers and administrators who have a vested interest in the continuation of the giving. That is why the best welfare system would be staffed by volunteers who have no financial interest in prolonging programs or in making the poor dependent on them.

Paying welfare workers does not automatically create a fatal bias toward self-interest. A paid worker who has previously served as a volunteer is likely to retain a noninstitutional perspective, at least for a time. Temporary workers, part-time workers, and workers with outside sources of income are also more likely to be independent of career biases. Another factor affecting careerism is the size of the organization. A small group is likely to have closer contact between paid staff and donors. In a local group, like a small church, donors are likely to keep rather close watch on how a charity administrator spends their hard-earned money, and they are likely to impart their perspectives to him. In larger organizations, to which donors give rather blindly, with little knowledge of how their money will be spent, the danger of programs lapsing into the handout mode is greater.

However, in any kind of organization based on voluntary donations, no matter how large, there is one ultimate check. If programs become too unattractive—if they are clearly seen to create dependency or to assist recipients who are not trying to help themselves—donors are free to stop contributing. In the end, notoriously bad programs will be cut back or terminated.

Programs based on the tax system—whether operated by government agencies or nonprofits using tax money—lack this safeguard. If donors are forced to give through the tax system, they cannot decline to support programs, no matter how much they disapprove of them. In theory, democracy should provide a way for the public to terminate failing programs, but in practice, it is almost never possible. Decisions on renewing and expanding welfare programs are handled mainly through a closed, unnoticed process dominated by special interest groups and self-serving administrators. They are rarely the subject of a full, informed national debate that examines their pros and cons.

The Job Corps, an employment training program for disadvantaged youths established in 1964, illustrates the pattern. It is a markedly weak program that, despite its high cost ($21,333 per student per year), does little to move its clients into mainstream employment. In 1992 the accounting firm of R. Navarro & Associates performed an audit of the Job Corps under contract for the Labor Department's inspector general. The firm found that only 12 percent of people leaving Job Corps programs found work in the field for which they had been trained, and only 44 percent found jobs of any kind. Of those who did find jobs, the average wage was $5.09 per hour, or about the same pay they would have received skipping the Job Corps and just getting a job at the nearest fast-food outlet.[16]

In spite of the massive evidence that the Job Corps is a wasteful failure, there is little chance that this war-on-poverty dinosaur will be slain. The 111 Job Corps centers are like little military bases scattered around the country, each with hundreds of employees, each run by contractors who make a healthy income from the business, and each with a congressman ready to defend the local pork barrel. Hence, appropriations for this $2 billion program are ensured by a quiet process of logrolling and lobbying among insiders. It is worth noting, in this regard, that the Job Corps was one of the welfare programs specifically slated for spending *increases* in the 1997 balanced-budget agreement approved by President Clinton *and* Republican congressional leaders.[17]

If welfare programs were supported on a voluntary basis, not one citizen in ten thousand would donate his money to the Job Corps—and the program would quickly disappear. Continuously funded by the coercion of the tax system, and quietly shielded from direct public control by the complexity of the governmental process, it goes on and on, no matter what its actual results in helping the poor. In conclusion, one reason we end up with welfare programs nobody wants is that nobody is free to stop paying for them.

What the Charity Theorists Knew

▼

The preceding pages explain what many sense about government welfare programs: they tend to be harmful giveaway programs. Most nineteenth-century charity theorists noticed the connection and condemned government welfare programs. We could have learned from them had we but listened.

Writing in 1899, Mary Richmond explained some of the objections to government welfare programs:

Public relief comes from what is regarded as a practically inexhaustible source, and people who once receive it are likely to regard it as a right, as a permanent pension, implying no obligation on their part. Even where it is well and honestly administered, as in Boston, the most experienced charity workers regard

it as a source of demoralization both to the poor and the charitable. No public agency can supply the devoted, friendly, and
intensely personal relation so necessary in charity. It can supply
the gift, but it cannot supply the giver, for the giver is a compulsory tax rate.[18]

Because of their tendency toward sympathetic giving, government programs of assistance to the needy are inherently unsound.
They ought to be avoided in the first place, phased out where they
exist, or trimmed back where they cannot be phased out. Introducing requirements in welfare programs is a useful way to begin the
retrenchment process. But in the long run, meaningful work and
performance requirements are not likely to be sustained in a governmental program of assistance.

7

Can the Poor Survive Income Redistribution?

For millennia, social philosophers have dreamed of a society in which wealth is evenly distributed. In 400 B.C., Plato pointed to this goal in his great treatise *The Republic*, describing an ideal state where the ruling philosopher-kings prevented extremes of wealth and poverty from arising. Sir Thomas More, in his classic work *Utopia*, written in 1515, criticized the inequality of his day:

> What kind of justice is it when a nobleman or a goldsmith or a moneylender, or someone else who makes his living by doing either nothing at all or something completely useless to the public, gets to live a life of luxury and grandeur? In the meantime, a laborer, a carter, a carpenter, or a farmer works so hard and so constantly that even a beast of burden would perish under the load; and this work of theirs is so necessary that no common wealth could survive a year without it. Yet they earn so meager a living and lead such miserable lives that a beast of burden would really be better off.[1]

It's not difficult to see why equality has been such an appealing social goal. In addition to seeming unfair, income differences are socially corrosive. The rich tend to separate themselves from the poor and look down on them, while the poor are inclined to envy the rich. The resulting class tension undermines the possibilities for friendly intercourse and social cooperation. To achieve a society in which human beings live in harmony with each other, the ideal is a community of equals. This was the vision of Henry Wadsworth Longfellow when he described the idyllic life of the French Arcadian farmers in the poem *Evangeline*:

> Neither locks had they to their doors, nor bars to their windows;
> But their dwellings were open as day and the hearts of the owners;
> There the richest was poor, and the poorest lived in abundance.

Since the nineteenth century, the concern with equality has gone beyond utopian thinking and poetic imagery to become a major principle of economic policy. In many lands, revolutionaries have confiscated the properties of the wealthy—and sometimes murdered the owners to boot—in the name of equality. In modern Western states, the preoccupation with equality has subsided somewhat in recent decades, but the principle remains embedded in policy. Public opinion still supports the idea of using the power of government to take away from the rich through progressive taxation and death duties and to redirect this wealth to the poor. To a considerable extent, then, modern welfare policy is an outgrowth of this focus on redistributing wealth.

Traditionally, the debate over income redistribution has assumed that the poor always gain from a program of redistribution, and the argument has focused on whether it is fair to take away the wealth of the rich and middle classes. Opponents of redistribution have claimed that it is wrong to penalize the better-off, since they have worked hard and made sacrifices to gain their wealth. Defenders of redistribution have said that the rich have been lucky, or that they have inherited wealth created through no effort of their own. Both sides have tacitly assumed that the poor would always be better off with the rich man's dollars in their pockets.

This assumption needs to be questioned. A close analysis of the problem reveals that whether or not the rich deserve their wealth, attempting to transfer it forcibly to the poor *hurts the poor*.

Government Is No Fairy

▼

Philosophers live in a frictionless world, a geometric plane where going from point A to point B can be accomplished in an instant of thought. Real people in the real world cannot go from A to B so easily. We have to trudge through rainstorms, detour around muddy ditches, and crawl under bramble hedges. So it is with income redistribution. Abstractly, it is easy to visualize as a mathematical goal, but how do we carry it out in practice?

It might be that society could be improved by shifting wealth from the rich to the poor—if this could be done in some delicate, unnoticeable way. The scheme might work if fairies could slip into rich people's houses at night and, undetected, extract banknotes from their wallets, and then flit into the homes of the poor and deposit them so subtly that the poor did not perceive the transfer. But, alas, the state is not a frictionless machine. It is more like a rhinoceros than a fairy, and its intrusions into people's lives are neither delicate nor unnoticed.

Let's look at the taxation side first. Perhaps the most remarkable fact about the history of the welfare state is that, until quite recently, no one was concerned with the overhead cost of taxation. The lack of interest in the harm caused by taxation goes against logic. The first thing a welfare state does is take money away from people against their will—an obviously harmful, destructive activity. Only after it has inflicted this *certain* harm is it in a position to do some *possible* good by giving it away.

When reformers began taking an interest in the welfare state idea a century ago, scholars should naturally have studied the harm caused by taxation first. But they didn't. In their optimism, they tended to assume that government could do no harm when it meant well. As a result, the destructive side of government's revenue-raising activities went unnoticed. The welfare state was considered a beautiful, frictionless machine that transferred wealth back and forth without wasting any resources in the process.

Eventually, however, scholars get around to studying everything, and the injury of taxation has finally made it to the research agenda. One of the first burdens of taxation to be studied was the "disincentive cost," that is, the way a tax system discourages production by denying workers and investors some of the fruits of their efforts. The first empirical studies of tax disincentives appeared in the 1970s.[2] This subject has now become a major interest of economists, and the literature on it is massive. Everyone understands that taxation lowers production, destroys jobs, and leaves a country poorer than it would otherwise be. A representative finding from this field is the calculation made by Charles Ballard, John Shoven, and John Whalley published in the *American Economic Review* in 1985. Their study, which calculated the combined effect of all existing taxes, found that raising one dollar through the tax system causes a waste of 33.2 cents in lost production.[3]

Indiana, Iowa, and Maine in Bondage

▼

Another major waste of the tax system is the compliance cost—the time and energy spent in keeping records, making calculations, and filling out tax forms. The first effort to assess this burden was made in 1966 by a Montana economics professor who sent his students home with a questionnaire for their parents to fill out.[4] Since that time, a number of compliance cost studies have been carried out, the most sophisticated being an IRS-commissioned survey by the Arthur D. Little Company. This study found that in 1985 the country was wasting a total of 5.4 billion man-hours on tax compliance labor. Since 1985 the tax code has become more complex and affects more taxpaying units, and compliance burdens have grown—to 10.2 billion man-hours in 1995. This is equivalent to 5.5 million workers—the entire labor force of Indiana, Iowa, and Maine put together—working all year long on just this activity.[5]

There are additional costs and wastes, including those associated with tax litigation (hundreds of thousands of people contest IRS actions each year), tax avoidance activities, and tax enforcement and forced collection procedures. When all the burdens are added up, the total came to $593 billion in 1993. To make the point a different way, each dollar of taxes collected costs society sixty-five cents in overhead costs.[6]

These are sobering numbers for devotees of income redistribution. Money cannot be made to slide effortlessly out of the pockets of the rich. It has to be wrenched away through a costly and destructive tussling. And the costs of this tussle are borne not only, nor even mainly, by the rich. They are spread throughout society and may well have a greater impact on the poor than on anyone else. We were given a graphic illustration of this point when Congress imposed a tax on powerboats in 1990. Legislators assumed that this was a "luxury tax" that would be borne by the wealthy. They never stopped to trace the full economic consequences of their action. The tax caused sales of the boats to decline, and the firms that made them laid off workers—who were then thrown into poverty. The injury was so blatant that Congress reversed itself and repealed the tax three years later.

The cost of tax compliance for businesses—the red tape involved in signing up workers and forwarding data and documents to the IRS—is a huge deterrent to the hiring of low-income, temporary workers. A GAO study found that a typical Cleveland small business has to make fifty-six different employment tax deposits a year to keep up with all state and federal requirements.[7] Imagine how these requirements would discourage a potential entrepreneur who is thinking of giving work to a few poverty-level individuals.

The High Cost of Giving Money Away

▼

Just as the tax system is not a frictionless system for extracting wealth, so government programs are not frictionless machines for passing it out. To begin with, there are administrative costs: the government must pay people to disburse the benefits, as well as give them office space, telephones, computers, pensions, and so on.

Furthermore, procedures have to be implemented to make sure that the money goes to those who need it—by whatever definition we want to apply. If we have no such procedures, then the nonpoor will also get money, leaving less for the needy. To keep the nonpoor out of the program, extensive systems of control—questionnaires, background checks—are needed, and these raise administrative and compliance costs even further. For example, in the food stamps program, administrative costs amount to 12 percent of the total spent on the program.[8] This figure does not include the administrative costs borne by recipients: the time and effort they expend in obtaining documents, filling out fourteen-page forms, waiting in offices, and litigating for benefits.

Administrative overhead isn't the only cost. Income redistribution programs can have serious disincentive effects, undercutting the willingness to work. Take a simple redistribution scheme that plans to guarantee everyone a minimum income of $10,000. This means it is pointless to work if your earnings are below this figure. Thus, the guaranteed income becomes a "welfare trap," and anyone earning less than $10,000 is strongly encouraged to quit. But if he does quit, he loses work experience and the chance to gain the skills and contacts that would eventually let him earn more than the $10,000 threshold.

Everyone agrees that there must be some incentive to work, but the only way to include this factor in an income support plan is to weaken the redistribution. We must either give middle-income workers some of the subsidy or reduce the subsidy for the lowest-paid workers. The mathematical implications of redistribution were explained by the economist Edgar Browning in a comprehensive study, *Redistribution and the Welfare System*, which appeared in 1975—the heyday of the debate over a guaranteed annual income. He pointed out to the activists that their hope for a sizable income guarantee was illusory. The elementary arithmetic showed that "it is much more difficult to finance a redistribution of income than is generally understood." He demonstrated that pumping more money into existing welfare programs would not help the poorest of the poor very much. Assuming that we intended to avoid a serious welfare trap, "the United States was approaching the limit of its ability to redistribute income in 1973."[9]

Wasted Years

▼

Politicians have paid little attention to analyses that demonstrate natural limits to the redistribution idea. As long as they could see rich and poor, it seemed to them that more redistribution was possible. The result, in virtually all the Western democracies, has been a serious welfare trap of the kind Browning warned against. As we pointed out in chapter 3, a proliferating array of support programs has made it increasingly uneconomical to work, and the result is the creation of a large economically dependent class.

In the English town of Exmouth, where I lived in 1993, I encountered one of socialism's unexpected casualties—a middle-aged man who frequently passed his time leaning on the railing of a bridge over a disused railway line. One day I stopped to talk with him. It turned out that he had been a fireman on this branch railway line, which was closed in the early 1970s. He had begun work when he was eighteen and had been laid off at age twenty-six when the line shut down. "I gave the best years of my life to that railway," he said bitterly. The statement rather shocked me, since I was about his age and assumed that the best years of my life lay ahead.

He was unemployed and had been unemployed for the past two decades. I don't know what combination of assistance programs he relied on—whether he got a severance package from the (state-owned) railway or relied on other British welfare programs. Whatever it was, it enabled him to get by without working.

"I gave the best years of my life to that railway." He kept repeating this phrase, obviously the focus of his thinking. He was voicing a point often made by socialist leaders. The poor, they say, give the best years of their lives to employers and the economy. When misfortune strikes through no fault of their own, society should take care of them. A century of implementing this idea has left Britain with a multitude of welfare programs that cushion the unemployed from hardship.

Even if we concede that such programs are fair, that still doesn't make them healthy. Though cushioned, this man was far from happy. He didn't die at age twenty-six, or lose his legs, or lose his mind. Twenty years later, he was still a normal, healthy human being. Why didn't he get another job? The welfare benefits—however well-intentioned, however well-deserved—had helped draw him into a state of permanent idleness, wasting his life sullenly gazing down an empty railway line.

The phrase "welfare trap" can seem technical and abstract until you meet the people caught in it. Most human beings—perhaps nearly all of us—require the pressure of economic need to make healthy adjustments, to seek new ways of serving others. Remove that pressure and the stage is set for dependency and wasted lives.

The Welfare Rights Movement
▼

The 1960s gave rise to some unusual lifestyles and strange social crusades in the United States. One of the most remarkable of these was the welfare rights movement, a campaign that made war on the welfare system in the name of income redistribution. It was a bizarre episode, and though mercifully short, it added some lasting scars to the U.S. welfare system.

To some extent, the movement grew out of the dissatisfaction of welfare recipients, especially women receiving AFDC payments. For most recipients, welfare is no bargain: the benefits never seem high enough to cover their needs, and they have to jump through many bureaucratic hoops to get them. Down through the years, recipients have complained about low benefits; in the late 1950s and early 1960s, the pace of this protest activity increased substantially.

A small number of academic ideologues saw in this protest an opportunity to create a revolutionary movement that would shake the foundations of society. The idea was elaborated by two left-wing professors, Richard Cloward and Frances Fox Piven, in an article entitled "A Strategy to End Poverty," published in *The Nation* in 1966. Their aim was to use welfare protest to provoke "a political crisis" that would lead to a government program "to eliminate poverty by the outright redistribution of income."[10]

Unfortunately for the radicals, by 1966 the age of revolutionary idealism had long passed away. Few people were disposed to risk personal convenience to implement socialist ideals—and recipients of public assistance seemed the least idealistic of all. So Cloward and Piven hit upon a loony way to overcome apathy: the poor would be mobilized by urging them to pursue their economic self-interest and clamor for welfare payments! The poor were to be told they had a "right" to welfare. "The strategy we propose," said Cloward and Piven, "is a massive drive to recruit the poor *onto* the welfare rolls."[11] This would overload the welfare system, producing "the collapse of current financing arrangements." Out of this crisis, it was supposed, would somehow come the radicals' dream of dreams: a guaranteed annual income.

The scheme was put in motion. Welfare recipients were prodded to mount angry demonstrations at local welfare offices around the country. Lawyers from the federally funded Legal Services Corporation took up the cause, litigating to overturn welfare regulations and procedures that stood in the way of higher benefits and more beneficiaries. To coordinate the campaign, the National Welfare Rights Organization (NWRO) was founded in 1967, headed by a Syracuse University professor; it even managed to receive some federal funds.

The welfare rights movement was short-lived. By 1975 the NWRO had been disbanded and agitation against the welfare system subsided. Commentators from within the movement have pointed to "internal and external conflicts" to explain its demise,[12] but the real explanation was much simpler: the welfare rights movement was plagued by too many fallacies. Although the movement's leaders were articulate about the plight of the poor, they were painfully unaware of the pitfalls of income redistribution.

For one thing, they completely ignored the tax system and its overhead costs and failed to see how destructive it would be to attempt to raise the funds needed for their desired redistribution. Browning showed, for example, that funding the guaranteed $5,500 income the NWRO proposed in 1970 would have required a marginal tax rate of at least 83 percent on all families—including the poorest of the working poor. "That level of taxation would obviously produce economic ruin," he noted.[13]

The welfare rights activists also ignored the administrative problems of giving money away. They wanted to do away with the intrusive welfare bureaucracy but never realized that the "poor" still had to be identified before they could be given any money. Bureaucrats were needed to question applicants about their income and investigate them to prevent cheating. Cloward and Piven even insisted that assets should have no bearing on entitlement: "Income should be distributed without requiring that recipients first divest themselves of their assets, as public welfare now does, thereby pauperizing families as a condition of sustenance."[14] They failed to notice the embarrassing result of this postulate: owners of new Cadillacs could still get welfare benefits.

They also ignored the aggravation principle of sympathetic giving. Succumbing to the "static fallacy" we discussed in chapter 3, they assumed that the number of "poor" was fixed, so that reallocating wealth to this group would bring "an end to poverty."[15] But the strata called "poor" is constantly changing. Vast numbers of persons enter it all the time, owing to personal problems (family breakup, bad habits, bad choices) as well as economic dislocations like layoffs. *And if incentives encourage economic striving*, the number of people leaving the low-income category will be just as large or larger. They will enter into new family arrangements, overcome vices and bad habits, relocate, retrain for different jobs, and so forth. One study of tax returns filed between 1979 and 1988 found that after ten years, 86 percent of those who had been in the lowest fifth of income had moved to higher income groups.[16]

In this fluid situation, offering a substantial economic reward for being "poor" in the form of a guaranteed income will undermine the incentives propelling people out of poverty. The result will be that the size of the "poor" group requiring the subsidy keeps expanding.

The lawyers and academics who organized the welfare rights movement believed that by breaking open a cornucopia of welfare benefits they were benefactors of the poor. In fact, they were modern lady bountifuls thoughtlessly showering alms—and aggravating the very culture of poverty they deplored.

Formula for Sympathetic Giving

▼

While the agitation for income redistribution has subsided, it has left a significant intellectual and administrative legacy, one that seriously hampers government welfare policies. The premise of the policy of income redistribution is that the poor have a right to the funds of the rich. When you have a right to something, the implication is that you don't have to do anything to get it. For example, you have a right to the money in your bank account. Therefore, the bank teller cannot demand that you work toward a high school equivalency diploma, or clean the bank's windows, before allowing a withdrawal. It's your money, no strings attached.

Applied to welfare, the conception of assistance as a right requires programs to follow the sympathetic giving model; they cannot have requirements or expectations. Cloward and Piven were quite explicit on this point: "The right to income must be guaranteed, or the oppression of the welfare poor will not be eliminated." They condemned even the feeble efforts of government welfare agencies to include some kind of quid pro quo. "People have been coerced into attending literacy classes or participating in medical or vocational rehabilitation regimes, on pain of having their benefits terminated."[17] Much of the opposition to recent welfare reforms stems from this sentiment. For those who see welfare payments as a way to implement "economic justice," as a way to boost the income of the poor simply because they are poor, requiring recipients to do anything in return seems inequitable.

The problem, of course, is that a policy of promoting "economic justice" directly conflicts with the idea of uplifting the poor. The redistribution idea leads to giveaways that don't demand any kind of performance or improvement in return. Whatever the vice of the recipient—indolence, crime, drugs, alcohol—the money must still be given out, and no change in behavior can be required. The result is that vice and social dysfunctions are prolonged and multiplied.

The "rights" approach to welfare has also led to self-defeating attitudes: it has encouraged the poor to believe that the world owes them a living, and that therefore no self-discipline and sacrifice are required on their part. Eloise Anderson, a social services administrator who became head of California's welfare department, made this point in a 1996 interview. Anderson, who is black, recounted for me the disagreements she had with white welfare rights activists in Wisconsin:

> Some social workers I worked with [in the 1960s] in my agency were going to graduate school at the University of Wisconsin in Milwaukee. They were going to be community organizers in the [Saul] Alinsky model—three white social workers—and I said, "You're going to go out and lead the charge, and when you get tired of playing Mr. Poor and Mr. Radical, you're going to go back into your communities and these people are going to be here with nothing."
>
> "Oh, no, that's not the way it is," they said.
>
> I said, "You haven't taught them how to do anything within the economic system. All you've taught them to do is hate, and think somebody owes them something. I'm sorry, this is not the way the world is. Don't nobody owe you anything! Why are you setting up these kinds of expectations in this community?"

Similarly, the sociologist William Julius Wilson finds that the perverse "you-owe-me" attitude is today a major reason why employers are reluctant to hire the poor, especially inner-city blacks.[18]

Making welfare a right has yet another harmful effect: workers and donors in assistance systems tend to be abused. When social workers are obligated to take care of you, you can be ungracious, dishonest, or even disruptive and your payment is still secure. If you throw litter on the floor of a welfare office, you don't jeopardize your payments. You're still entitled to them. Having to put up with inconsiderate and irresponsible behavior naturally demoralizes welfare workers and greatly contributes to their burnout.

Sensing these drawbacks of treating social assistance as a right, organizers and volunteers in most private programs firmly oppose the entitlement perspective. Their programs incorporate requirements, rules aimed at uplift, and rules that protect the needs of donors and workers. For example, the Saint Paul's Lutheran Church in affluent northwest Washington, D.C., has a long-term shelter with a capacity for five homeless men. It has been a delicate undertaking because many in the church and in the community feared the blighting effect that a shelter might have in this upscale neighborhood. The fear is understandable, since homeless men tend to have objectionable behavioral problems, such as drug and alcohol addiction, bad grooming, aggressiveness, and thieving. Church leaders were especially sensitive to this issue since the church also runs a Montessori day school for small children.

Therefore, shelter managers established conditions designed to protect donors and neighbors, and clients must agree to them to enter the program. "In order to be courteous to others," reads part of the contract, "shelter guests agree to: not engage in loud, boisterous behavior; shower daily between 9:00 and 10:30 P.M.; perform scheduled chores to ensure that shelter area is clean and neat." The men are required to be in the shelter by 7:00 P.M. and have to stay until 7:00 A.M., when they must leave the shelter grounds. The men are also required to save 50 percent of their earnings, attend group meetings, and refrain from alcohol and drug use.

This spirit of firm expectation is opposed to the idea of assistance as a right, and the shelter contract explicitly says so:

> Admission to Saint Paul's shelter pursuant to these house rules does not create any property rights or entitlements for sheltered guests, and Saint Paul's shelter reserves the unconditional right to expel any guests from the shelter for any reason.

A Community Ensnared

▼

In reviewing the flaws of government redistribution of wealth, we need to mention one more point: the coercive foundation of these arrangements. Supporters of the welfare state seldom give this aspect much attention. In describing welfare programs, they speak of a "community" taking care of the needy through the "generosity" of its members. It is this image of a caring society that the distinguished Swedish economist Assar Lindbeck has in mind when he says, "I have often described the modern welfare state as 'a triumph of western civilization.'"[19]

It may be that the impulse to take care of the needy has a generous origin, but unfortunately, government welfare programs do not function on the basis of generosity or community spirit. They rest on the coercion of taxation. Anyone who declines to give—whether because he lacks sympathy for the poor or because he lacks confidence in the programs of assistance—is still forced to contribute. Supporters of the welfare state defend the use of coercion on the grounds that taxation raises more money than could be raised by voluntary giving.

Perhaps, but the fact remains that tax-funded assistance programs are not imbued with noble motives. Acting under the threat of coercion, donors can take no satisfaction from their contributions. Instead, they experience feelings of resentment at having their privacy invaded and their funds extracted from them. To counter growing resistance, government has an ever-expanding system of surveillance and punishment to force citizens to comply. Today employers, bankers, and many others are required to report every significant transaction to the IRS, which each year collects more than one billion pieces of personal financial information on every man, woman, and child in the country. The IRS assesses more than thirty million penalties each year against taxpayers who have failed to live up to its demands. To uphold the fear on which the tax system depends, the IRS promises cash rewards to anyone who snitches on friends, neighbors, or family members. The entire system is based on thousands of pages of burdensome, confusing regulations that spawn millions of Kafkaesque taxpayer disputes every year.

These sinister and frustrating features might be excused if the welfare-giving side of the redistribution process were gracious and uplifting. Unfortunately, it is frustrating and degrading. Welfare recipients do not view their benefits as a reflection of the generosity of others; they see them as an entitlement. They are not grateful to the "community" that has sacrificed to help them out; instead, they are peeved that this community doesn't provide more help. This grasping attitude underlies the fraud and dishonesty that pervade welfare programs. Just like taxpayers, welfare recipients are out to cheat the system.

The result is that the welfare office is the mirror image of the tax office. On the welfare agent's desk is a thick compendium of regulations that have grown in number and complexity beyond the capacity of human beings to understand. Applicants for benefits must fill out lengthy forms documenting their claim to neediness and supply personal information to enable bureaucrats to check up on them. Because most clients are seeking to take advantage of the system, a massive machinery of surveillance has been established that attempts to enforce honesty. Welfare department computers are linked up to state and federal databases that provide tax information and details about automobile ownership, employment, and so on. Like the tax system, the welfare system tries to intimidate clients into telling the truth. In many places, welfare recipients are fingerprinted in an effort to control fraud. California is developing a "secret witness program" to reward people who turn in friends and neighbors for welfare violations. At a food stamps office in Sandpoint, Idaho, a poster on the wall says, "It's all plugged in," and lists some of the databases that the welfare department uses to check statements made on applications. In large type, it menacingly announces, "If you don't tell us, somebody else will."

The problem with redistribution of wealth lies not in the basic concept. Equality is a noble social goal that, when pursued through voluntary means, enhances the spirit of community and strengthens the bonds between individuals. Constructive, voluntary redistribution takes place in dozens of ways. Wealthier parents assist poorer children; wealthier children assist poorer parents. Richer friends pick up the tab for poorer friends. Better-off professionals shade their bills for clients who are less well off. Philanthropists endow public facilities that the poor may use at below cost, or no cost. Wealthier individuals sustain voluntary groups, like churches and Boy Scouts, that the less fortunate may use at little or no cost. These are all positive, commendable acts of voluntary income redistribution.

When force is used to implement equality, however, the ideal turns sour. Relying on the coercion of the state to promote equality mocks generosity and poisons the wellsprings of genuine community. In the end, the welfare state produces donors who resent recipients, and resentful recipients who clamor for their "rights." And both wind up ensnared in a Big Brother apparatus of surveillance and control operated on the assumption that everyone is trying to cheat everyone else. Surely, we may be forgiven for doubting that this arrangement represents "a triumph of Western civilization."

What Social Workers Believe

The modern welfare system is the product of a structure and an ideology. The structure is government, which imparts a bias toward something-for-nothing giving, and the ideology is state redistribution of wealth, a philosophy that justifies blind giving to the poor. Yet these two factors alone might not have been sufficient to force welfare into the handout mold if the leaders in the field of social assistance had resisted. The welfare professionals could have made a stand at the gates. They could have publicized the danger and destructiveness of sympathetic giving, challenged the politicians who wanted to build welfare empires, and debated the socialists who urged income redistribution. Relying on their expertise and authority, they could have warned the country against putting something-for-nothing giving arrangements in place.

Instead of resistance, however, there has been enthusiasm among welfare professionals for the modern welfare system. The social workers who staff and direct American welfare programs embrace government as the proper agency for helping the poor and strongly endorse income redistribution. They have become a main pillar of the existing system of something-for-nothing giving. Down through the years, they have played an important role in shaping welfare programs, and their opposition to changing its assumptions has been a major obstacle to genuine reform.

There are roughly 700,000 social service workers in the United States, filling a wide variety of roles, from eligibility clerks in government benefit programs to career counselors in high schools. At the center of this profession are the 420 schools of social work whose faculty prepare students for work in social service agencies. Each year, they award 11,000 baccalaureate degrees and 13,000 master's degrees in social work.

The policy-oriented core of the social work profession includes a number of influential lobbying organizations. The main groups are the American Public Welfare Association (APWA), among whose members are numbered more than 800 state and local welfare agencies, including all the state departments of human services; and the National Association of Social Workers (NASW), with 155,000 social worker members. As a measure of their political activism, one poll of NASW members found that 64 percent contributed money to political campaigns in 1984, and 33 percent reported lobbying for legislation.[1]

Members of this occupational sector strongly lean to the left. The NASW regularly backs Democratic candidates; in 1996 its leadership endorsed the Clinton-Gore ticket, voting 168 for Clinton against 6 for Republican Bob Dole.[2] Even more distinctive than this political bias, however, is the professional bias. Today's social workers hold views about the treatment of poverty that are practically the opposite of those held by the nineteenth-century charity theorists who founded the profession.

Give, Give, Give

▼

The nineteenth-century charity theorists advocated a highly personalized approach to working with the needy. Emphasizing the capacity of the poor to respond to life's demands, they believed in pushing them to achieve independence and a better life. The social worker was first and foremost a mentor and adviser, one who guided individuals to improve themselves and make better choices. They all agreed that programs of sympathetic giving—giveaways of cash, food, housing, clothing—were generally harmful to the poor.

Of course, they knew that the poor needed these things, but they also knew that it was vitally important to let them fill these needs for themselves. Well-meaning reformers who stepped in with doles undermined the self-esteem of the poor and impaired their capacity to thrive independently.

Modern social work has completely abandoned the idea that neediness can play a positive, motivating role. For the modern social worker, any kind of suffering or being in need is wrong. "Human suffering is undesirable and should be prevented, or at least alleviated, whenever possible," declares Herbert Bisno in *The Philosophy of Social Work*.[3] This declaration ignores the complexity of human motivation. Extreme forms of suffering are indeed incapacitating, and therefore harmful. But intermediate levels of deprivation—or the anticipation of such—motivate all sorts of constructive choices, from getting up in the morning to go to work, to controlling bad habits like gambling, alcohol abuse, and overeating.

Armed with the idea that neediness is always wrong, modern social work has developed the notion that filling someone else's needs is always right. The giving of material assistance is now seen as the primary mission of social work. The NASW's "Definition of Social Work" makes "helping people obtain tangible services" the first aim of social work practice.[4]

One introductory text announces the giveaway mission in its title: *Social Welfare: A Response to Human Need*. Like so many of the social work textbooks, it downplays the idea that the poor should be expected to work for a living; indeed, "work" is never mentioned as a solution to poverty. The "belief that each person should be responsible for meeting his or her own needs" is labeled "rugged individualism" and dismissed: "This situation is neither possible in contemporary society nor desirable in terms of optimal human growth and development."[5]

Another text, *The Practice of Social Work*, incorporates the philosophy of sympathetic giving in a broad collectivism. "Social work believes that society has a responsibility to all of its members to provide security, acceptance, and satisfaction of basic cultural, social, and biological needs."[6] Nothing is said about the responsibility of the individual to do anything in return, whether this be to work, to raise children properly, or even to be courteous.

The "code of ethics" of the National Association of Social Workers defines the social worker as a giveaway agent in sweeping terms: "The social worker should act to ensure that all persons have access to the resources, services, and opportunities which they require."[7] Instead of urging people to obtain what they require through their own energy and perseverance, social workers are instructed to give it to them.

The ideology of "meeting needs," of forestalling any type of suffering, permeates welfare practices. In New York City, someone who rents an apartment he cannot afford can have it funded by the Human Resources Administration by applying for a grant to stave off eviction. Instead of questioning the client's decision to rent the too-expensive lodging, the HRA steps in and pays the rent. "The overriding policy in the Human Resources Administration is to prevent the loss of accommodations at all costs," says an HRA spokesman.[8]

What about the effect of giveaways on undermining the motivation of the poor? Today the social work discipline is silent on this subject. In contrast to the nineteenth-century writings, which are full of strictures against giving handouts, *modern social work texts never point to a situation when the social worker should not give material aid to a needy person.* In the indexes to these volumes, there are no entries under "dependency" or "incentives" or "motivation." The massive economic literature on the negative behavioral effects of welfare programs is ignored.

A Washington University professor of social work calls it a "myth" that "recipients use welfare year after year, generation after generation," even while reporting his own finding that 25 percent of current welfare recipients grew up in families that also received welfare.[9] The *Encyclopedia of Social Work*, published by the NASW, considers the idea that "income maintenance assistance robs recipients of their incentive to work" to be an unfounded "suspicion."[10]

Privately, social workers mention cases where welfare encourages idleness and other dysfunctional behavior, such as having babies one cannot support. But in official pronouncements, social work leaders avoid or dismiss the point that benefit programs might be drawing vulnerable individuals into dependency and even ruin.

No Judge of Lifestyles

▼

The nineteenth-century charity workers expressed strong convictions about the behavior that would help people rise from poverty. They had clear opinions on the obvious vices, such as drunkenness, gambling, unmarried sex, and idleness, as well as on many ordinary choices. For example, Octavia Hill believed it was unhealthy for families to live in one room, as most of them wished to do to save the cost of renting a second room. As a volunteer housing manager, she used her powers of gentle persuasion to get tenants to pay extra and take two rooms. (After the move was made, she reported, tenants themselves would admit it was a wise use of their money.)

This emphasis on values has all but disappeared from modern social work. Today's orientation is on *not* swaying welfare recipients in their choices. The NASW *Encyclopedia of Social Work* acknowledges the change. At the turn of the century, it reports, "an important part of the caseworker's mission was assumed by many to be the inspiration of clients to learn to lead morally upright, prudent lives." As the twentieth century progressed, "concern about clients' personal morality waned."[11] Today social workers prize the doctrine of "self-determination": clients should be free to do whatever they want, and social workers must not influence their choices.

One value of social work, says John Brown's *Handbook of Social Work Practice*, is a "nonjudgmental attitude": "social workers should not judge clients' behaviors by imposing a moral value on it."[12] One introductory text, *The Practice of Social Work*, criticizes "the layperson's views that a social worker seeks to 'remold' clients into a pattern chosen by the worker." The professional view is that clients "should be permitted to determine their own lifestyles as far as possible."[13] Social workers apply this indulgent approach to children, even when the children are making a self-destructive lifestyle choice. Consider the NASW's official policy position on unwed pregnancies among indigent teens. The child is to be neither criticized nor urged to give up the baby. Instead, her decision to have a baby she cannot raise or support is to be reinforced with a vast range of handouts: "Adolescents who choose to parent need a range of services to help them complete the developmental tasks of adolescence while assuming the adult responsibilities required to care for themselves and their children."[14]

The notion that social workers must be neutral paralyzes them as advisers or mentors. Of course, in any advising situation a dogmatic style is generally counterproductive, and no one piece of advice fits everyone. The nineteenth-century workers, with their individualized approach, knew this well. They stressed the importance of tact and patience in projecting their healthy values. But they were in no doubt about the need to project these values. Today's social workers have genuinely internalized a value-free approach. Instead of guiding clients away from foolish choices, they set up systems to reinforce them.

Never Their Fault

▼

Who's to blame for poverty? The nineteenth-century charity theorists knew that both environmental and individual factors played a role. They were fully aware of the unhealthy living conditions of the poor and the dreadful lack of opportunities they faced. To remedy such environmental problems, they worked on public policies that addressed them, such as making sanitary improvements and developing parks and gardens. But they also knew that the poor were held back by their own shortcomings: vices, family breakup, unhealthy habits, and shortsighted choices. In their policies of individual social assistance, therefore, they endeavored to improve character.

Octavia Hill emphasized this point. In 1875, after a decade of serving as a befriending manager of low-income housing units, she emphasized the importance of personal behavior.

> The people's homes are bad, partly because they are badly built and arranged; they are tenfold worse because the tenants' habits and lives are what they are. Transplant them to-morrow to healthy and commodious homes, and they would pollute and destroy them. There needs, and will need for some time, a reformatory work which will demand that loving zeal of individuals which cannot be had for money, and cannot be legislated for by Parliament.[15]

Most modern social workers have abandoned this balanced, logical view. Textbooks smugly criticize nineteenth-century charity workers for their "judgmental attitudes toward the poor." They find it lamentable that social workers in those benighted days "held to the notion that individual failure was the reason for poverty."[16] The modern view is that the needy cannot be held responsible for their problems. Indeed, anyone who suggests otherwise is engaging in the cardinal no-no of "blaming the victim." Neediness, says social work, is caused by external social and economic factors.

In expounding this position, social work professionals often exhibit a rather weak grasp of economics. In *Social Welfare: A Response to Human Needs*, we find this tautological explanation: "The distribution of income, the way that income is distributed, is what causes poverty."[17] One social work professor likens the economy to a game of musical chairs with a fixed number of opportunities: "This musical chairs analogy can be applied to what has been taking place in this country economically and socially. Some people will lose in the game, given that there is unemployment and a lack of jobs."[18] This static, zero-sum conception of economic life ignores the fact that people continually create new jobs for themselves and for others—if we don't undermine their motivation to do so.

The social workers' bias toward the environmental explanation of poverty underlies their policy recommendations. Whatever the problem, it's not up to the needy person to reform or strive; "society" has to give more. A 1990 editorial on homelessness in the NASW magazine *Social Work* criticized programs to treat drug addiction and alcoholism because

> they define homelessness in terms of private troubles. . . . Homelessness is a result of the steady disappearance and unavailability of low-cost housing. We must be clear that homelessness cannot be reduced appreciably by treating individual troubles. The problem of homelessness is a public issue and can be resolved only through public action and major changes in public policy. Poverty must be reduced and low-cost housing must be made available.[19]

Some social workers have been trying to break away from the approach of blaming society. They include therapists in private practice who try to help individuals with problems like drug abuse, anger, and stress, and whose therapies emphasize individual responsibility. This departure from orthodoxy aroused the ire of mainstream social work leaders like the late Harry Specht, the former dean of the School of Social Work at the University of California at Berkeley (and winner of the 1993 NASW Presidential Award for Excellence in Social Work Education). With junior author Mark Courtney, Specht wrote an entire book in 1994, *Unfaithful Angels*, denouncing the renegades.

Psychotherapy is unsound, say Specht and Courtney, because instead of accepting the axiom that society is to blame, it advances the "dark" doctrine "that most suffering is a matter of personal responsibility." Those social workers who stress individual responsibility are "unfaithful angels"—unfaithful because they depart from the mission of expanding tax-funded giveaways to the poor. "The major objective of social work practice," they say, "is to develop and strengthen communally supported services and to enable participants to make use of social resources available to them."[20]

Millions of Checks, Millions of Deserving Poor

▼

How did social work abandon the theme of personal responsibility? One explanation is that both social work and government social policy fell under the sway of a superficially attractive, but deeply flawed, belief: the needy simply lack money, and the way to fix their problems is to give them money and the things that money can buy. Today we are becoming wary of this idea, but generations ago it dominated the social policy field. Arthur Altmeyer, the first commissioner for social security and a leading mover and shaker of New Deal social policy, expressed this mentality in a comprehensive outline for poverty policy in 1946. "The individual without private resources," he wrote, "requires, first of all, of course, cash assistance so that he may purchase the minimum necessities of physical existence."[21] And it wasn't just cash that government was supposed to provide. "Needs that cannot be met merely by the assurance of cash incomes," he went on to say, "call for the expansion and development of community resources and social services." This is the philosophy of the "supplier state." The poor are seen as passive consumers, almost like domestic animals, and it is the job of social workers to see that their needs are filled.

The idea that neediness is a purely external condition, unrelated to character or motivation, was reinforced by historical accident. Modern social work came of age during the 1930s when, more than at any other time before or since, environmental factors accounted for neediness. Masses of ordinary workers had been thrown out of their jobs by the Depression. The social work profession imprinted on the Depression, and it made "blame the economy" into a permanent diagnosis of social ills for all time.

But there's more to the story. The nineteenth century also saw a number of depressions, some of them quite severe. While these crises certainly alerted charity workers to the environmental factors bearing on poverty, they did not cause them to ignore the role of character. The early charity workers were in the business of improving the individual's future prospects, and they knew that character always plays a role in personal success. Even if a person was unemployed through no fault of his own, they didn't want to give aid in a way that would weaken his healthy motivation and make him *unemployable* when trade picked up.

This focus on character and motivation grew out of the personal nature of nineteenth-century charity, which was based on small, private organizations. When government became the major welfare provider and legislators decreed that millions of people in this or that category were to get money, government social workers were left with the job of handing it out. They were no longer expected to chide or discriminate; indeed, they could get into trouble for doing so. They had to find a way to be comfortable with wholesale giveaways, including giveaways to many individuals who were vice-ridden, irresponsible, dishonest, or lazy. The solution was to stop trying to judge recipients, to see them all as "deserving poor," victims of "society" or "the economy."

Social work's reluctance to see that personal failings play a role in poverty is worse than unrealistic: it positively hurts the poor. Modern social workers have taken the position that environmental factors—the economy, racism, sexism, and so on—account for neediness, and sadly, many have preached this doctrine to their clients. By telling them that someone else is to blame for their fate, they encourage scapegoating and whining, and undermine the motivation to succeed.

In the game of life, just as in sports, it is not useful to dwell on the past and to blame others. What would we think of a coach who tells his team that the reason they lost was the rainy weather and the bad calls of the referee. *Even if this were mainly the truth, it would be unhealthy to dwell on it*. A coach who follows this approach will find that his team loses even when the weather is fine and the referees are fair.

Welfare Reform: Bigger Is Better

▼

Paradoxical as it may seem, social workers are not happy with the welfare system they have shaped. "I hate welfare," declared former HEW Assistant Secretary Peter Edelman, looking back on thirty years of his involvement with the welfare system.[22] Most social workers agree with him, and their criticism would seem, from a distance, to afford a healthy basis for reform. A closer look reveals, however, that social workers are not dissatisfied with giveaways. The defect of the welfare system, to their way of thinking, is that the giveaways are not large enough, and that it shouldn't be putting strings on the aid it does give.

The county director of welfare of Sacramento, California, spelled out this view at a 1995 conference of social workers: "For us, real welfare reform has to involve the stakeholders, including the people you serve. You have to find out what they need. You have to find out what they want. And you have to find out what you can do to help them get what they need and want."[23] In its 1997 policy recommendations, the National Association of Social Workers declared that welfare reform must never involve cutting benefits: "States should be allowed to diverge from the national base only if they scale benefits upward from it." The organization sets its face against experiments that demand something from recipients: "NASW opposes the imposition of any compulsory work requirement for AFDC recipients."[24]

In contrast with the NASW, the American Public Welfare Association has accepted the idea that some kind of work obligation is appropriate for certain welfare recipients. But this principle is undermined by the profession's more deeply held conviction that welfare recipients must be shielded from any possible suffering. Even if a client flatly refuses to participate in an employment plan without good cause, the APWA recommends cutting benefits by only 25 percent. Furthermore, although the APWA agrees that welfare recipients should be expected to work, it does not expect them to go to work *tomorrow*. The APWA approves of a work requirement *only if* government programs first supply a vast array of additional services to help recipients find and hold a job.[25]

A spokeswoman for Delaware's First Step Program gives an idea of the support that welfare administrators feel is necessary to implement the welfare-to-work concept. This program offers a broad smorgasbord of additional benefits to cajole recipients into taking care of themselves: "basic academic and life skills development," career counseling, child care, transportation, eye exams, eyeglasses, and even clothing. "If we don't have these supportive services," says the Delaware official, "then the participant cannot succeed."[26] "Cannot" is a strong word when you consider that tens of millions of working poor get and hold jobs without any of these services.

Can Social Workers Overcome Their Training?

▼

Officials in the welfare industry resist the charge that welfare workers are dragging their feet on real welfare reform. When I interviewed the executive director of the American Public Welfare Association, Sid Johnson, in 1996, he stated his belief that social workers have recently adopted "a surprisingly different approach," which he traces to the 1988 adoption of the Family Assistance Act. "The dramatic change in 1988 was that a system that for fifty years had been, by public policy, aimed at providing income maintenance made a major shift toward the promotion of self-sufficiency."

But can fifty years of training and ideology be overcome so readily? In most parts of the country, social workers are still wedded to a policy of nonjudgmental giveaways. In Michigan, social workers have largely undermined the state's policy of requiring unwed teen mothers to live with responsible adults simply by exempting the teens in question. In Ingham County, 74 of the 85 indigent mothers under age eighteen were allowed to keep their welfare checks and their independent lifestyle because social workers decided that adult supervision would jeopardize their "emotional and physical well-being."[27] In New York City, a workfare trainer who is supposed to motivate welfare recipients to take responsibility for their lives encourages her students to blame others: "The welfare system is using you," she tells her class. Instead of preaching self-help, she encourages clients to turn to politics and overturn the Republican mayor's workfare program. "I hope you vote in November," she tells the students, the implicit assumption being that they should vote for Democrats opposed to workfare.[28]

In those few places where welfare reform has had some success, traditional social workers are noticeably absent. In California, all fifty-eight counties are supposed to be pushing welfare recipients into work under the GAIN program, which began in 1988, but only one, Riverside, has a well-documented record of success. I asked John Rodgers, the assistant to the director, what proportion of Riverside's caseworkers are professional social workers. "That's basically a nonexistent classification in GAIN," he replied.

> There are some counties in California that did that, took social workers in their existing organization and moved them over into GAIN. We did not do that at all. We had an open recruitment, and in fact strongly encouraged people from the community who had never worked in a social services agency to apply for the jobs. We were looking for people that had a variety of skills, but specifically people that had experience in the employment sector, of helping people go to work.

California's director of social services, Eloise Anderson, believes that social workers are badly instructed in schools of social work. When I asked her what they should be taught, she replied:

> They ought to learn something about capital formation, something about work, something about free markets, something

about economics. They need to learn something about what does it take to make it out here. They don't know any of that stuff! And they're running out here and talking to people and going [mimics a saccharine, pitying tone], "Oh, dear. Something's wrong with you? Oh, let me help you." It's just wrong. The question is, "What do you need to get on your feet?" They don't know anything about that. They're the wrong group of people.

Another sign that social workers aren't behind meaningful welfare reform is the lobbying of the National Association of Social Workers. The organization strenuously opposes the welfare reform passed by Congress and signed by President Clinton in August 1996. The NASW has vowed to undertake a "state-by-state monitoring of the welfare reform bill's impact on poor women and children."[29] This is another way of saying that social workers are preparing to provide the media with a diet of hardship cases attributable to the reform.

Social work's indulgent orientation seriously cripples the profession. In other disciplines, the professionals play the role of telling hard truths to an unsophisticated public. When a child has to have a vaccination, the child may cry and the mother may wring her hands; it is the professional, the nurse, who says, "This is going to hurt, but it's best in the long run." A century ago, this was the role played by social work leaders, by the Octavia Hills and Mary Richmonds. They took up the task of instructing bleeding-heart clergymen and hand-wringing matrons that, painful as it seemed, *not* giving material aid is often the best policy.

Today the roles have been entirely reversed. The official stance of social work is that the poor should always be given what they need, and that no suffering or deprivation must ever be permitted. So it has fallen to outsiders to point out that this position is naive and destructive. To a considerable extent, the current debate over welfare reform is precisely about this issue. In contradicting the doctrine of give, give, give, the lay reformers are trying to bring social work back to its roots, and back to its senses.

PART III

Varieties of Expectant Giving

9

The Health of Commerce

Since ancient times, teachers and philosophers have realized that alms-giving and other simple giveaways are an inadequate response to neediness, since they tend to prolong the misery of recipients and undermine their motivation and morale. For this reason, they have favored expectant giving: arrangements that make the recipient a partner in the process of uplift.

Of all the forms of expectant giving, providing a job—exchanging money for useful labor—is the most obvious and probably the most effective. The medieval Jewish philosopher Maimonides made this the highest of his "Eight Degrees of Benevolence": putting the needy person "where he can dispense with other people's aid" by "accepting him into a business partnership or by helping him find employment." Many other maxims and teachings repeat the idea that giving the poor employment is by far the best way to help them. The British charity theorist Thomas Mackay made this point elegantly in his 1898 book *The State and Charity*:

Trade and commerce, and the practice of the professions, justly and successfully carried on, are centres from which the contentment and happiness of many homes will be found to radiate. The truest philanthropist is he who . . . can extend the contentment of this honourable interdependence.[1]

Despite the obvious value of commerce, most journalists, politicians, and voters are quite ambivalent about it. Businesspeople are not viewed as saviors of the poor, but as threats to them. The underlying reason for the suspicion is the frank recognition that commercial exchanges are based on self-interest. Employers hire workers not to do good, but to do themselves good. Since their intentions are not benevolent—this reasoning goes—employers will probably exploit their workers, and they must be tightly regulated by the state to prevent them from doing so.

To explore this view and the misconceptions behind it, let's take a close look at one employment situation, the hiring of underclass workers by temporary labor firms.

A Seventeen-Cent Profit

▼

Dave is a black ex-convict in Dallas. He's hooked on cigarettes and alcohol and I'm not sure what else. He has little education, little money, poor manners, and no credible job experience. He also happens to be a likable person once you get to know him, but the typical employer or landlord is not going to find this out. In the normal course of events, Dave could be jobless and homeless.

But today Dave is lucky, for an unusual organization has taken him under its wing. It has given him a bed in a warm, safe place to sleep, a hot shower, and doughnuts and coffee for breakfast. It has found him a job, given him the equipment he needs for the job, provided transportation to and from the work site, supplied a sandwich for lunch, and advanced him five dollars on his pay in case he needs to buy something more during the day.

The organization helping Dave onto his feet is not a federal job training program, not a church shelter, not a city youth corps. It's a private, profit-making company that receives no government aid of any kind. In fact, it pays $1.4 million in federal, state, and local taxes.

The Dallas branch of Industrial Labor Service Corporation is the largest employer of temporary manual laborers in the city. On a typical day, it sends out 650 workers, transporting them to and from job sites in its fleet of vans. It also operates a shelter, the Bunkhaus, which accommodates up to 180 men per night. It pays its workers an average of $4.70 per hour and collects $7.50 per hour from the employers who use them. From the $2.80 left over, it pays dispatchers, van drivers, salesmen, the computer operators who issue some 195,000 individual pay vouchers per year, 24-hour security guards, license fees, van rentals, rent, utilities, and, of course, taxes. After all these expenses, ILS still makes a profit—about seventeen cents per hour of labor contracted.

This achievement is remarkable given the competitiveness of the industry: some fifteen firms in Dallas supply temporary manual workers. Furthermore, ILS's clients are also its competitors. They always have the option of hiring workers directly, skimming away ILS's best workers by offering them permanent jobs at a higher wage.

Yet ILS's success in the marketplace is not its greatest achievement. It is, almost without knowing or caring about it, a highly effective social welfare program.

This observation is bound to come as a surprise. We've all heard about Adam Smith's theory of the invisible hand, how profit-seeking can unintentionally serve the public good in the realm of production and distribution. But it's difficult to imagine that the same idea applies to helping the needy. The down and out are supposed to require handouts and compassion, not capitalists trying to make money from them. Yet a close look at ILS operations reveals that the theory of the invisible hand applies even to welfare.

This is not to say that this company is a welfare panacea. It aids only a particular kind of worker. Physically handicapped workers, for example, cannot be helped at ILS, nor can those whose financial needs are beyond minimum-wage employment. ILS occupies a specific niche in the welfare services industry. But within its scope, the results are impressive. In seeking their own self-interest, the owners and staff of Industrial Labor Service have evolved a system that aids the down and out more effectively than the programs that well-intentioned politicians have put together.

Giving Lodgers What They Want

▼

To learn about the ILS operation, I entered the system for a few days, sleeping in the Bunkhaus and taking jobs through the hiring hall. It was uncanny to see how, on point after point, the pressure to make money produces a socially constructive result.

The Bunkhaus charges five dollars a night. This puts it in an exchange relationship with the men who lodge there, so naturally the company has to give something in return. Its biggest service, I felt, was security. As I gradually learned, most of the men staying in the Bunkhaus have done time in prison. Yet somehow, just one manager and one security guard keep good order among this rough humanity. The staff knows how to screen out the worst trouble-makers, exclude drugs, and defuse altercations before violence breaks out.

Part of their successful strategy is allowing the workers considerable freedom and finding ways to accommodate their needs. Smoking is permitted (there are many chain smokers in this group), as is beer, although it cannot be brought in after 10:00 P.M. These concessions respect the worker's dignity (after all, you can drink and smoke in a hotel room) and seem to result in a more relaxed atmosphere. Whatever the ingredients, ILS has contrived a small miracle of harmony with this socially difficult clientele. The workers are racially mixed, and predominantly black, yet there is little sign of racial hostility. As I, a white man, walked around the Bunkhaus one evening during a televised Dallas Cowboys football game, half a dozen black men cordially offered me a beer.

In addition to television, the Bunkhaus has laundry facilities, vending machines, microwave, free coffee, free baggage check, and free blankets. It also sells used work shirts and jeans for one dollar. Some aspects would offend middle-class sensibilities. The toilet bowls have no seats; the beds have bottom sheets but no top sheets. The night noises in the one-room dormitory keep the newcomer awake at first. But one adjusts. On balance, the profit-seeking entrepreneurs of ILS have developed an excellent lodging value, in my opinion a better deal than the thirty-dollar-a-night seedy motel beside the nearby freeway. A number of workers who have progressed beyond ILS's temporary jobs stay on at the Bunkhaus to keep their expenses down.

Real Jobs for Real Self-Esteem
▼

The steadying, motivating influence on this little community is work. The fact that there are real jobs to be had and money to be earned underlies the order and the camaraderie of the shelter. The discipline of work sends the men to bed early, with lights out at 10:00 P.M., and propels them to rise when the lights pop back on at 4:00 A.M.

The hiring hall is located just around the corner from the Bunkhaus. For a newcomer, the system is simply to wait until a dispatcher at one of the windows announces a work opportunity.

When jobs are few, the workers crowd around the windows to be the first in line. This seemed at first to be somewhat unfair and arbitrary, for it tends to reward aggressiveness and might penalize a worker who had waited patiently and politely for hours. Later I began to see the problem with trying to use a queue system. Many of those who come to the hiring hall are unmotivated; sometimes they are sleeping off the effects of drugs or alcohol. If the firm sent such workers out on a job, employers would quickly be disappointed. Selecting candidates from those who crowd around the dispatchers' windows is a cheap, informal way of screening workers according to their motivation.

The jobs provided at the hiring hall give the men a sense of accomplishment. In the literature of social reform, much is made of self-esteem. Unfortunately, too many theorists treat self-esteem mechanically, as if it were a substance that could be given out in doses like a pill. Self-esteem cannot be raised with posters that say, "You're the greatest," or with encounter groups in which participants are instructed to stroke each other. Everyone knows the praise is hollow. To raise self-esteem, the individual has to *know* he has done something worthwhile.

Many government agencies will give you money under the guise that you are "working" for it, but the clients know this is a sham. In a dozen ways, they sense the pointlessness of the projects. They see the time wasted standing around, long breaks, endless "instructional videos," and silly "orientation sessions." They notice that tasks are left unfinished, that foremen disappear from the work site for long periods. These are clues to the fact that *no one really cares whether this work is done.*

In a real job, an employer is selfishly demanding productive labor in exchange for money; the worker can hardly escape gaining a sense of accomplishment. This applies even to manual labor—in some ways, *especially* to manual labor. When you've dug a ditch or unloaded a sixty-foot trailer truck, you get a feeling that you've accomplished something that sets you apart from—and somewhat above—the cultured and coddled sectors of society.

Meaningful jobs don't grow on trees, however, and they cannot be dreamed up by administrators twiddling pencils at their desks. They come from the real world of commerce and production. This means that the most important staff members in a work opportunity program are not trainers or counselors, but salespersons who find the real work opportunities. While in a charitably focused agency this aspect could easily be overlooked, in a private firm the sales function is critical for survival. ILS has a sales force of five employees who continually visit workplaces, pointing out the advantages of using ILS's temporary workers. Their efforts guarantee that every ILS worker admitted to the "program" has a meaningful, dignity-enhancing job.

Labor Discipline

▼

Workers at the bottom of the social scale often lack good work habits, such as arriving on time, doing what they are told, and not talking back. Government job training programs and make-work programs have difficulty inculcating good work habits because they are funded according to the number of people the program serves. This encourages administrators to be lenient with unmotivated participants. The result is that, too often, a government jobs program tends to condone—indeed *teach*—bad work habits.

In the profit-making commercial world, the incentives are reversed. Employers are supported by the output of their firms, and that depends, in turn, on workers with good work habits. Therefore, private employers systematically discourage bad work habits. On my first day with ILS, I saw how this works. Six of us were dispatched to a construction project in the Dallas suburb of Plano. After fifteen minutes on the job, only four of us were still working. The other two workers were at the bus stop, waiting for a ride back to Dallas. The foreman fired them because, among other things, they failed to stand up when he began to give instructions, and because they failed to put on their hard hats after he told them to.

I felt the lash of labor discipline myself on the following day. Like most ILS workers, I had become a repeat, asked back to the same job by a satisfied employer. This puts the worker a step up, since he doesn't have to wait for a job; the dispatcher calls him by name at the beginning of the day. I had collected my job ticket and equipment to return to the construction site and was waiting under an awning during a heavy cloudburst when my van was called on the loudspeaker. I figured I could wait a few minutes until the shower passed, but I figured wrong. By the time I got to the van, I had been replaced. This meant I dropped back into the newcomers' labor pool and didn't get another job for the rest of the day. Henceforth, I paid obedient attention to what the loudspeaker said.

Treating Workers with Dignity

▼

Beyond wages and hours, every job involves many less tangible working conditions. In the world of marginal manual laborers, one of the most important of these side issues is social treatment. Because of the low status, shabby dress, and poor grooming of temporary manual workers, those in higher positions may be tempted to be rude and inconsiderate toward them. I was surprised to discover that at ILS the staff treated the workers with a professional courtesy. On the loudspeaker at the Bunkhaus, we were addressed as "gentlemen." At the dispatch windows and equipment counters,

I saw no instance of a worker being treated discourteously; in fact, most of the clerks were remarkably patient.

One explanation for this politeness is the background of the staff: many had started as temporary workers and sympathized with their plight. "Some guys think I'm too hard on 'em," says the Bunkhaus manager, Brien Colvin,

> but with the majority of the tenants here, I feel pretty much well-liked. At least they know everything that I do, I'm doing for their benefit. I've been on the other side of the fence, I know how it is. 'Bout seven years ago when I first came to Texas, I was homeless. So they can't tell me anything.

There's also an economic pressure to be courteous. No matter how grubby and unimpressive they may appear, these workers are necessary for the success of the business. They are customers, and the company needs to keep them coming back, for an empty labor hall spells trouble. When the employment market was especially tight in the summer of 1994, ILS offered a five-dollar sign-up bonus to attract laborers. Courtesy is just another employment incentive.

The pressure to treat workers well comes from the highest level. "That was one thing Charles really came down on us about on his last visit," reported the assistant manager, Eric Veblen. "In the day-to-day rush, you know, you get careless about how you treat the workers, and it's good for someone to call you out about it." Veblen was referring to the principal owner of ILS, Charles Joekel, who drops by the Dallas branch office from time to time. Again, one is struck by the contrast with government. One could hardly imagine a senator or mayor visiting a tax-funded job center and reminding staff to be courteous.

In Trouble with the Media

▼

The firms that supply temporary manual labor make up a substantial economic sector. ILS has twenty branches in different cities. Nationwide, temporary service agencies employ more than six hundred thousand manual workers. However socially useful these firms are, it is extremely difficult to get journalists to see them as beneficial. Public opinion is shaped by what is seen at first glance, and when journalists encounter a company that makes a profit by hiring members of the underclass, their first impulse is to assume that workers are losing out. As a result of this bias, media coverage of firms that hire temporary manual workers is almost uniformly negative.

An example is a piece that appeared in the *Dallas Observer* in 1993 about a crew of ILS workers who erected temporary stands at a Dallas Cowboys practice field. Entitled "A Dirty Job," the piece set out to show that it is "a fairy tale" that temporary manual laborers are treated fairly and with dignity.[2] Yet in his minute-by-minute account, the reporter could not find any actual abuse or mistreatment. The negative picture had to be built up entirely with adjectives and innuendo.

For example, he devoted four paragraphs to insinuating that laborers were overworked because they were asked to carry certain beams across a field, one beam to a man. How heavy were these beams? The reporter didn't say, but he tried to leave the impression that they were unbearable. When a worker carried one, he declared, its weight "squashed the carrier's feet into the moist soil." While we are almost ready to shed tears for the overloaded laborers, the reporter inadvertently destroys the effect by shifting attention to a "40ish white guy" with "something to prove" who "put one beam on each of his shoulders, and carried two at a time."[3] So one beam per man was, if anything, a rather light load.

This hostile, straining-at-gnats coverage of the private employment scene compares strikingly with the way reporters cover government units in the same field. Just a few months before the story trashing the ILS appeared, the *Dallas Observer* ran a piece on the Dallas Youth Services Corps. Like Industrial Labor Service, the DYSC takes unemployed, uneducated workers and gives them a minimum-wage job. Yet the coverage of the DYSC was upbeat and enthusiastic, starting with its headline, "Building up Hopes." From beginning to end, the reporter gushed uncritically about this "program to give uneducated, jobless kids a chance."[4] The officials operating the program were invited to sing its praises, and their claims were never questioned or investigated. Whereas the workers in the

ILS operation were portrayed as "dogs," lacking any constructive plans for their lives, the same kind of workers in the DYSC operation were portrayed as nobly striving to better themselves.

What's the difference between the two operations? It is certainly not a difference in the number of workers assisted. ILS helps 650 workers a day and keeps going strong, while the DYSC, faltering because of budget cuts and compassion fatigue, was serving only 18 clients. The difference between the two organizations is in the public face of their motives. ILS is a moneymaking company based on the principle of self-interest. The DYSC—a money-losing operation that costs taxpayers and private donors $500,000 a year— claims to be based on compassion. This claim of good intentions sways reporters and the public.

Rethinking "Exploitation"

▼

Afflicted by a negative image and a bad press, the temporary worker firms are particularly vulnerable to government attack. Every new tax or regulation—however well-intentioned—adds to their costs and brings them closer to shutdown. For example, in 1993 ILS was compelled to close its hiring hall in Phoenix because Arizona workmen's compensation taxes became prohibitively expensive. Even in Texas, these charges are almost crippling: ILS has to pay the state workmen's compensation system fifty-one cents per man-hour worked, a figure three times its profit margin.

One way local governments make life difficult for labor halls is through zoning and licensing regulations. In Dallas, the entire industry was nearly destroyed in 1991 by the city council, which tried to adopt deliberately stringent licensing and location standards for hiring halls. The ostensible reason for attempting to close these firms was their supposed blighting effect on local neighborhoods. It was claimed that they were attracting crime and drugs; real estate developers asserted that the hiring halls made it difficult to upgrade the run-down parts of town where they were located.

But the prejudice against capitalism was also at work. The leader in the crusade to stamp out the labor halls was the council's foremost liberal Democrat, Lori Palmer. When day laborers came to a council meeting demonstrating in support of the companies like ILS that gave them jobs, Palmer never got the point. "They make a lot of money at your expense," she told the workers.[5] She missed the idea that A can make money from B's labor while B also benefits by getting a job, money—and self-respect.

Why Aren't There Enough Jobs?

▼

The 1996 federal welfare reform makes finding a job and going to work a requirement for receiving benefits, at least for some recipients in some programs. Thus, even official government policy has now recognized that gainful commercial employment is a solution to poverty.

But are there enough jobs? Will they pay enough? These are questions that many critics of the reform are raising. As the experience in the temporary labor industry illustrates, government policy has much to do with the answers. Through its policies of taxation and regulation, government often undercuts commercial activity, preventing employers from providing jobs, and preventing workers from earning enough income from them. The result is painfully paradoxical. With one hand, the government adopts policies to press the poor to get jobs, while with the other it takes jobs away or makes them financially unattractive.

Look at pay levels. One of the principal reasons the poor who work at entry-level jobs have difficulty making ends meet is that government drains their wages away. Many suppose that because the poor pay little federal income tax, they are not significantly affected by taxation. In fact, they face a crushing tax burden. The point has been documented by Martin Buchanan of the Cascade Policy Institute in a study of Oregon's working poor. He found that the working poor in Portland were affected by more than two dozen direct and indirect federal, state, and local taxes: social security tax, Medicare tax, federal and state unemployment taxes, workman's compensation taxes, telephone taxes, gas taxes, property taxes, business taxes, even a water runoff tax. A worker earning $3.85 per hour ended up with a net income of $5,881 yearly. Without these taxes, the worker would have had an effective income of $9,786—a wage 66 percent higher![6] Clearly, the first solution to the problem of low wages is to reduce the burden of taxation.

To create jobs for the poor, many reformers have tried to develop business opportunities for the poor. But they discover that government throws up roadblocks at every turn. Red tape is an enormous deterrent to starting up a small business, especially for lower-income individuals who might lack the assertiveness and skills needed to counter bureaucracy. On River Road in Bethesda, Maryland, is the Hunan Kitchen, a small Chinese take-out shop. The owner has mounted on the wall the government licenses and certificates he needed to open. There are seven, including three from the county, three from the state, and a certificate of registration from the Maryland Department of Agriculture for "Maryland Egg Law Packers and Distributors." In addition, the business is subject to health and fire department inspections and regulations, as well as demands from the alphabet soup of federal regulatory agencies and from the IRS. Imagine what a barrier this regulation represents for someone struggling to leave the underclass by starting a business!

Reformers working to teach entrepreneurship and establish businesses have noticed that government regulations impede the ability of the poor to raise themselves. Michael Bernick, who founded the Renaissance Entrepreneur Center in San Francisco, thought government was a benign force when he began his programs to create inner-city jobs. But "participation in running the six Renaissance businesses," he said, "taught me how serious a drag on new business growth the taxes and regulation can be."[7] For example, the convenience store Renaissance was trying to start was shut down by the local health inspector for selling coffee without the proper permit.

The harm of government regulation is not spread evenly. It particularly hurts firms with low-income owners, workers, and consumers. For one thing, regulation is often used by powerful, politically connected businesspeople to hamper their competition. Many trades and professions—taxis, barbershops, beauty parlors, day care, foster care facilities, hospitals, schools—are strangled by restrictions that established providers lobbied for as a way of keeping lower-cost firms and workers out.

Another reason regulation especially hurts the poor is that the regulators have been especially trying to help them! At first glance, it seems that if some good or service consumed by the poor is substandard, then the solution is to legislate higher standards. If nursing home care is inadequate, for example, the solution seems to be to mandate better care. The mistake of this approach is that it prices the poor out of the market. Instead of getting low-quality goods they can buy, the poor are left with high-quality products they can't afford.

Lawmakers have run wild with this approach in the housing market, where a vast array of regulations attempts to protect tenants and homeowners from any conceivable unfairness or harm. The problem is that all these higher standards mean higher costs. For example, in 1996 more than twenty states adopted building codes that increased the required size of stairs from nine to ten inches deep, although there is little evidence that the larger step is safer. This change alone could add several thousand dollars to the cost of a home.[8] This new regulation may not matter to a wealthy person who wants to buy a top-of-the-line house, but it hurts those of modest means.

The campaign against the single-room occupancy rooming house illustrates how regulation hurts the poor. Over the years, reformers have urged numerous regulations to discourage this "substandard" type of accommodation and force owners to raise its quality. The result is that in city after city this vital first step in self-sufficient housing has been all but destroyed. In an article in the *New York Times Magazine* in 1996, the reporter John Tierney detailed the plight of one of New York's last "flophouses," the White House Hotel, which rents simple cubicles to extremely low-income tenants.[9] The city has highly complex "tenant rights" regulations that make it difficult and costly for a landlord to evict nonpaying tenants. In the fall of 1995, federally funded antipoverty lawyers convinced a judge to extend these regulations to flophouses. The practical effect is to make it impossible for the White House Hotel to collect rent from those who don't want to pay.

"I've given up," says the manager-owner, Mike Ghelardi, about the twenty-seven men who had stopped paying for their cubicles. "I can't afford to file the paperwork and pay a lawyer to go after them—I'm having a hard enough time paying the heating bills and the taxes. And if you can't evict guys, you can't run a place like this on the Bowery." He expected to close within a year.[10]

Tierney contrasts the lodging service provided for tenants at the White House Hotel with that at city homeless shelters. The White House charges ten dollars a night, including tax, and gives tenants not only a sense of dignity, by enabling them to pay their own way, but a valued degree of privacy and security. The city-run homeless shelters cost taxpayers fifty dollars per person a night; a demeaning giveaway, these shelters are so lacking in privacy and security that many homeless people refuse to stay in them. "If he winds up on the streets," concludes Tierney, "New York's crusading lawyers and other reformers will feel terribly sorry for him, but they won't rent him a warm cubicle on a winter night." In another article on housing, Tierney focused on a bitter paradox: New York reformers have "passed more laws, built more homes and spent far more money on housing than any other city," yet their legacy is "a housing shortage and a system that discriminates against the young, the poor, the nonwhite and above all against the new."[11]

Clearly, the idea of using government agencies, laws, and court decisions to harass landlords has reached a dead end. In San Diego, reformers discovered that the poor could be helped by working in the opposite direction: encouraging businesspeople. To foster construction of new single-room occupancy hotels for the poor, they convinced city and state governments to relax a wide array of code and zoning regulations and also to cut taxes bearing on this type of low-income housing. As a result, 2,770 new and renovated SRO units have been added to the housing stock. Constructed by profit-making commercial builders, without government subsidy, they provide a poor person a private, safe room for rents as low as fifty dollars a week.[12] That, the reader will notice, is one-seventh what it costs New York City taxpayers to house one homeless person in unpleasant government shelters.

Helping the poor in the twenty-first century will require a profound rethinking of our theories about the role of commerce. For the past century, reformers have regarded business as the natural enemy of the poor, and government as their natural savior. We are now beginning to discern that both impulses were tragically misguided. Business is not the foe of the poor, but the provider of the jobs, goods, and services they need to make their way up in the world. And government, with its blind doles and cynical regulations, turns out to be an inept, destructive patron of the poor.

The thrust of the next century of reform will turn the old models upside down as reformers find ways to help business help the poor and work to get government out of the way.

IO

Charitable Capitalism

Bangladesh is a land plagued by hurricanes, floods, and abject poverty. When Muhammad Yunus returned there in 1972 after obtaining his Ph.D. in economics from Vanderbilt University in Nashville, Tennessee, he naturally wondered what he might do to combat the suffering in his native land.

Being of an analytical turn of mind, he did not simply engage in alms-giving—the typical response of the well-to-do, both native and foreign. He and his students investigated villagers' economic activities in an attempt to discover blocks to productivity. They found that many tiny family operations were crippled by the lack of credit. They couldn't buy enough raw materials to do their manufacturing efficiently, and when they did borrow, they were charged exorbitant interest rates by moneylenders. The banks refused to deal with them because such tiny loans, without collateral, would be hard to collect.

So Yunus and his graduate students began a special kind of bank that lent to poor, landless villagers, especially women. Since it began in 1974, the Grameen ("village") Bank has grown to more than one thousand branches. An economic anchor for several million small traders and manufacturers, it has improved their productivity and life prospects.[1]

The Grameen Bank confounds the usual stereotypes about charity and capitalism. Charity, in the old-fashioned image, is suppose to involve straight generosity, giving things away to people. But the Grameen Bank doesn't give anything away. In fact, it is strikingly hard-nosed with its clients. It charges interest rates four points above the commercial rate; repayments must be made weekly; and it never forgives loans, even in the event of a natural disaster. Even when it distributes essential items such as water purification tablets and iodized salt, it charges its customers. While it has obtained some financing from private foundations and government agencies, it is now turning down grants and raising capital through commercial channels.

In spite of its capitalist face, however, the bank does not have a capitalist soul. It was not founded to enrich its creators, and its purpose is not to make money. It was set up by do-gooders to improve the lives of others.

Beyond Profit

▼

To many, this amalgam of charity and capitalism seems confusing, if not downright sinister. The preceding chapter on the role of profit-making firms in uplifting the poor helps us see that there is no real contradiction. A commercial firm that does business with the poor is often an excellent institution for helping them. It establishes the exchanges that supply their needs, and these exchanges help develop self-confidence as well as healthy habits of industry and responsibility.

Reformers who grasp these points realize that one of the main problems faced by the poor is that there aren't enough companies to give them jobs, to lend them money, to develop housing for them. The reasons for this lack of commercial activity vary. Sometimes— as with the Grameen Bank—the needy consumers have to be organized and motivated in a special way to make the enterprise successful. In other cases, government regulation—taxation, licensing, zoning, threats of confiscation, litigation, and so forth—make commercial activity unattractive to ordinary entrepreneurs.

So reformers try to overcome these barriers and organize the commercial activity for the community in need. Although the resulting firm has many capitalistic features, it is charitable in two senses. First, its main mission is not to make money, but to assist the needy by involving them in its system of exchange. Second, it relies—at least in the start-up phase—on donations. That is, it cannot cover all its costs on a strictly moneymaking basis. For example, the Grameen Bank began with donated capital (from the Ford Foundation and the United Nations) and took advantage of the unpaid services of organizers and advisers like Yunus.

In the long run, a charitable-capitalist enterprise may evolve toward complete economic self-sufficiency and become a commercial firm. Savings banks are a good example. These began as philanthropic institutions to promote thrift among the poor. In England, the first two savings banks were founded in the early 1800s by Anglican ministers, John Muckersey and Henry Duncan. In 1816 in Boston, James Savage led fellow philanthropists to form the first American savings bank, the Provident Institution for Savings. The founders agreed that "it is not by the alms of the wealthy that the good of the lower class can be generally promoted. By such donations, encouragement is far oftener given to idleness and hypocrisy. . . . He is the most effective benefactor to the poor who encourages them in habits of industry, sobriety, and frugality."[2] In the savings bank organized in Philadelphia, the founders donated between $10 and $250 to get the bank going and volunteered their time to serve as managers and clerical workers.[3]

By 1860 there were more than 1,500 savings banks in the United States. But they gradually lost their charitable character. They ceased to rely on idealism, donations, and volunteer labor and evolved into pure commercial establishments. The positive side of this evolution was that society gained healthy, constructive economic institutions. The drawback was that they were no longer serving those at the bottom of the social ladder.

Ironically, to fill the low-end gaps in credit markets today, some American reformers have turned to Bangladesh for inspiration. Organizations like the Good Faith Fund of Pine Bluff, Arkansas, and the Lakota Fund on the Pine Ridge Reservation in South Dakota have consciously copied the Grameen system, especially the idea of grouping small borrowers into peer support circles—a fascinating case of technology transfer from one of the poorest countries to one of the richest.[4] A recent study by the Aspen Institute counted more than one hundred microenterprise lending programs in the United States serving low-income clients.[5]

In addition to incorporating the healthy principle of exchange, capitalism has another advantage in a social assistance program: financial strength. An organization that only gives things away faces an uncertain future, since its entire income must come from private donors or governmental sources. Changes in public sympathies or political alignments can result in a crippling financial cutback, even outright collapse. An enterprise based on supplying things people pay for can sustain itself over the long haul.

Charitable capitalism as defined here is an arrangement that involves needy clients in productive economic exchange. It is important not to confuse this technique with what might be termed "fund-raising capitalism." Some nonprofit leaders have argued that charities should develop a commercial, moneymaking arm. The idea is that the charity should make and sell something of value, rather than depend on philanthropic contributions.

The charity advocate Bill Shore makes the case for this approach in his book *Revolution of the Heart*.

> There's nothing wrong with appealing to people's generosity and charitable instincts. But why stop there? Why not appeal to their self-interest as well? . . . To meet the challenge of the future, nonprofits must be thoroughly reinvented to create new wealth—that is, nonprofits for profit.[6]

He cites his group, Share Our Strength, which raises money by organizing food and wine events that customers are willing to pay for. He also notes the example of the actor Paul Newman's food company (Newman's Own), which donates all its profits to charitable causes.

These are interesting fund-raising techniques: ways of obtaining a pot of money to do something with. However, they are not social assistance systems; they do not involve the needy in the capitalistic exchange. The money raised by one of Shore's "Community Wealth Enterprises" could be turned over to any group following any kind of social assistance strategy, including straight handouts.

Another possible point of confusion concerns the terms "profit" and "nonprofit." Many organizations practicing charitable capitalism are legally recognized as "nonprofit" organizations. But this legal designation is not part of our definition. Many nonprofits—universities, labor unions, symphonies, fishing clubs—are not involved in social assistance. Some nonprofits that do work with the poor simply give handouts; they are therefore not practicing charitable capitalism, which involves the poor in an economic exchange.

Not Warehousing the Disabled

▼

Pride Industries of Roseville, California, illustrates how a business-oriented approach can improve the quality of social assistance. Pride, which was founded in 1966, helps disabled individuals to find work. It was started as a sheltered workshop in the basement of a church by parents of disabled youths who wanted something better for their children than leaving them in front of the TV. In its early years, it was funded almost entirely by grants from the federal government, the state of California, and United Way, and it followed the service delivery model. Managers vaguely hoped that the disabled clients would do some work, get some satisfaction from work, and move into the world of employment, but the emphasis was on taking care of them. As a result, the organization didn't have much work, and fifteen years after it was founded, clients "were still watching television," as a Pride official put it. A former board member who joined the organization in the late 1970s described the group's nonmarket approach:

> They had no salesmen! I don't think anything happens anywhere, ever, without somebody selling something. They didn't have one! They had a bunch of do-gooders doing good, but nobody was making any money. It was a lousy way to run a business. The president was of a social-service bent, so he really didn't know a salesperson when it hit him in the eye.

In the early 1980s, several key board members decided that dependency wasn't good enough. They were fed up with "warehousing" the disabled and irritated by having to knuckle under to the meddling of government and United Way grant supervisors. The board adopted a resolution to become self-sufficient, to earn enough money from the labor of handicapped workers to support the operation.

The transition provoked a major dispute. The social service–oriented leaders were alarmed at the idea of expecting the disabled to work and produce. One Pride officer describes the tension between these "advocates," who wanted to give things to people, and the business-oriented manager who thought in terms of exchanges:

> Advocates are wonderful people, you need them in the field, but they don't care about "where is the money coming from?" What they care about is, "I want to deliver this service, and gosh darn it, it's the right thing to do, and gosh darn it, somebody better give me the money to do it."

These "social service types," he reported, "couldn't see the idea [of adopting a business orientation]. They thought that we were just going to work these people like slaves." In practice, the handicapped individuals were the greatest beneficiaries of the change. Once the organization decided it had to make money, managers saw that they could not just play at rehabilitation; the workers *had* to be rehabilitated so they could do real work and earn real money. There would be no more warehousing, no more watching TV. The result was that the handicapped got full-time, well-paying jobs out of the deal.

The emphasis on commercial success enabled Pride to expand enormously. In 1983, the year before the transformation began, Pride served 50 disabled individuals with a staff of 15 nondisabled workers. About 90 percent of its funding came from federal, state, and United Way donations. In 1996 it had 1,200 disabled workers on its payroll, and its grant income had shrunk to a token United Way contribution (less than 1 percent of its income). More than 80 percent of its revenues are generated by its manufacturing and service subdivisions: electronic assembly, packaging, snowshoe manufacture, landscape service, property maintenance, wood products manufacture, and so on. Another main source of income, about 15 percent of the total, comes from fees paid by the state of California for rehabilitating handicapped individuals.

I asked the president of Pride, Michael Ziegler, if the disabled are better off as a result of the organization's switch to commercial principles.

> Most of them will tell you it's the best thing that ever happened to them. It gives me goosebumps to work here. I walk through this company and marvel at what this company accomplishes. The people with developmental disabilities, they'll tell you, they're working, they're happy, they get a paycheck, like you and I, they smile just like you and I do on payday.
>
> Gentleman over here named Freddy, probably close to sixty, can't hear, can't speak, but he's high skill level. Every payday, Freddy would come and find me. The first time he ever did this I was in the men's room, standing at the urinal, and Freddy's tapping me on the shoulder. He makes a ritual of this. He opens his wallet, unfolds the check, and points to it. He had the biggest smile on his face you could ever see.

Does a commercial thrust lead to worker mistreatment or a lack of worker safety? A past president and board member, Bob Selvester, answered this way:

> It's very difficult for social service people to understand the concept of free enterprise. They still equate business with some nasty thing that takes away the freedom of the worker. That's absolutely dead wrong. The people who work for us in our contracts are the highest-paid people around. They love their work.
>
> Very early on, we invited OSHA [Occupational Health and Safety Administration] to come in at any time. We have an open-door policy with them. We want them in there. If they can find a way for us to keep our workers safe, we want that. We're not out to kill people, we're out to find jobs for them. If we can keep them healthy, we'll make more money. Our workmen's comp insurance premiums alone are much lower. It's like any other corporation: you want to keep your employees healthy and happy. That keeps them coming back and doing the best they can do.

Although Pride makes a "profit," its aim is not to make a profit, but, according to its mission statement, "to create opportunities for people with disabilities." Its commercial success has enabled it to generate money to fund first-class programs to assist more seriously disabled individuals and train disabled workers to work for other employers. Selvester explains:

> When you're struggling financially, you really can't offer much. It's a bare-bones deal. Whoever's giving you funding, that's like a minimum wage. It's really not enough to do a whole lot of good. No program's going to flourish on what the state's willing to give you.
>
> When we want a program, we can afford to hire the best people. It takes a lot of skilled people to take folks from zero to where they can actually go work for somebody else, and live by themselves, and get off social security. Our business is the part that makes the money.

I asked Selvester whether Pride, as a commercially oriented enterprise, is now serving handicapped people better than it used to?

"In all ways," he said.

Building Self-Esteem

▼

One advantage of charitable capitalism as a method of assistance is that it builds the self-esteem of its clients. When needy people provide for themselves through their own efforts, instead of being the object of giveaways, they feel better about themselves. Octavia Hill often made this point about the housing projects she undertook in nineteenth-century London. A classic example of charitable capitalism, these were set up as paying propositions for investors who, in what became known as "five-percent philanthropy," were offered near-market rates of return on their money. But Hill's purpose in organizing the purchases and managing the properties was, from the first, to improve the lives and character of the poor living in them. Nevertheless, the principle of economic exchange was firmly applied. She advocated "extreme punctuality and diligence in collecting rents, and a strict determination that they shall be paid regularly." It was not capitalist greed that prompted this policy:

I have tried to remember, when it seemed hardest, that the fulfillment of their duties was the best education for the tenants in every way. It has given them a dignity and glad feeling of honourable behaviour which has much more than compensated for the apparent harshness of the rule.[7]

The idea of preserving dignity by economic exchange is one of the principles cultivated by the Christian Community Development Association, a network of urban social assistance organizations inspired by the charity philosopher John Perkins. At one of its member organizations, Building Together Ministries in Raleigh, North Carolina, I asked the director, Fred Johnson, whether the group has programs that give away food, clothing, or other things.

"We give nothing," he replied emphatically. "We don't charge a lot. But we firmly believe that every time you give to somebody, you are stripping them of their self-esteem and their dignity." He explained the operation of the center's store:

We're not in it for the money. We're in it to redistribute necessities into the neighborhood at affordable prices. So we may have a three-hundred-dollar men's suit there with a five-dollar price tag on it. But there will be some sacrifice by whoever buys it. And if that person can't afford five dollars, they can contribute to the store by volunteering in it. One hour's volunteering equals five dollars' purchasing power.

The ministry has an inspired way of dealing with Christmas gifts. Many charitable organizations around the country run Christmas drives, collecting toys, or money to buy toys, to give to needy children during the holiday season. It's an appealing cause, and fund-raising for it is generally quite successful. In my own village of Sandpoint, Idaho, the Lions Club regularly raises more than $20,000 in its Toys for Tots campaign. But like all programs of sympathetic giving, the giveaway has harmful side effects. The children's realization that their parents are not supplying the toys can undermine parental confidence and authority. To avoid this problem, Building Together uses the idea of a commercial exchange. In its Christmas toy program, Pride for Parents, it raises money for toys, which are then *sold* to parents at less than market value.

Healthy Training

▼

Expecting people to make sacrifices in exchange for things is not only ego-building; it's also good training for the real world. If the ultimate object of helping the needy is to make them non-needy, capable of supplying their own wants, a commercial setting is the ideal format for training people out of poverty. It's like a game that resembles the real world.

Fred Johnson explains this theory as it applies to the program Building Together has for junior high boys in its after-school program. Participation in the "leadership academy" is set up as a job. The boys are treated as employees: they check in on a time clock and are paid for the nine hours a week they participate. "And we're hard on 'em," says Johnson.

> We consider ourselves their employer, and we consider that a very responsible position. We're trying to teach them what to expect when they go out and get a job elsewhere. If we let them get away with something they can't get away with in private industry, then we've done 'em a disservice and they're going to be shocked when somebody says, "You can't be late to work," or, "You can't dress like that," or, "You can't treat your fellow employees the way you're treating him." So we're trying to set a very high standard.

Has the ministry fired any of these workers? "Yes, we have."

Another example of a training program that implements the idea of monetary exchange is Enterprise Mentors, a foreign aid program of the privately funded International Enterprise Development Foundation, based in St. Louis. This program, first operated in the Philippines, aims to encourage small entrepreneurs and helps train them in accounting, marketing, and production. The program has a strong emphasis on self-sufficiency, on sticking to the principle of giving "a hand up, not a handout." In keeping with this aim, says the founder, Menlo Smith, "nothing is given away. Some price, however modest, is always charged for materials or services."[8]

Cultivating Idealism

▼

As we noted earlier, charitable capitalism requires an ingredient of generosity, of idealism. People connected with such ventures have to be willing to make sacrifices that they would not normally make if they were involved in a strictly commercial enterprise. The point always applies to donors, and often to managers and customers as well. Only a spirit of cooperation and generosity will keep the enterprise going.

The Grameen Bank illustrates the point. Commercial banks in Bangladesh could not successfully lend to tiny entrepreneurs because the loans would have been too hard to collect. It would have cost too much to track borrowers down and motivate them to live up to their responsibilities. The Grameen Bank's founders saw that they would have to create a system to motivate borrowers to behave more generously, more cooperatively, than they normally would. They have done this by setting up local loan committees that establish mutual accountability. Each prospective borrower joins a five-member loan group, which meets weekly; the group approves the candidate and takes responsibility for her repayment of the loan. This committee structure creates ties of friendship and commitment that make possible the bank's remarkable 97 percent repayment rate.

Another example of charitable capitalism that stresses personal ties of obligation and trust is Habitat for Humanity. Founded in 1976 in Koinonia, Georgia, Habitat provides housing for people in need by stressing the participation of the needy family itself. The system, which has spread around the world, is based on local, volunteer-run chapters—more than one thousand in the United States—that select the families who are to receive homes. The recipients are required to contribute five hundred hours of labor ("sweat equity") building their own homes and to make payments on a no-interest mortgage.

In addition to formal financial connections, the Habitat system involves recipients in a number of ongoing personal relationships with the Habitat volunteers. Habitat's president and founder, Millard Fuller, explained the value of these contacts when I asked him how Habitat maintains a default rate of less than 1 percent.

> First of all, we have a family selection committee that chooses the families, and then a family nurturing committee that works with the families after they move into the houses. People don't like to disappoint somebody they know who loves them. We try to develop that relationship with the families: a close, loving, caring relationship.

Fuller went on to identify another advantage of involving people economically in their own assistance programs.

> The families help build their own houses with the sweat equity. A person does not like to lose that which he or she built with their own hands. They have an emotional, psychological investment in it. Finally, a no-profit, no-interest house is the best deal in town. If you lose that, you've just lost the best deal in town.

He paused a moment, then continued.

> I say there's no better deal in town. There are some deals which might appear to be better, where the government gives away houses. But really and truly, the people who get those kinds of deals don't feel connected to them. People don't feel connected to government housing units where they rent, and they pay in accordance with their income. Because they had nothing to do with building it. They didn't even design anything about the houses, even to select the paint colors. Everything is decided for them by someone else. I think you feel cheapened.

A Remedy for Burnout

▼

The focus of most discussions of social assistance is on the recipients, the needy individuals being helped. We tend to forget about the helpers, the people who contribute their time and energy to provide services. They should not be taken for granted. After all, these helpers make the difference between success and failure. If they are enthusiastic and energetic, the program is likely to work

well; if they are discouraged or burned out, then the assistance program, whatever it is, is likely to be ineffective.

While many factors affect the morale of workers in a social assistance organization, one of the most important is the role of recipients. When clients are the object of sympathetic giving, simply taking and taking, workers tend to be unenthusiastic and even
resentful. When clients try hard to give something back, it inspires
staff, donors, and volunteers. They feel that clients are showing their
gratitude and have become part of the team. When you ask managers
of assistance organizations to recall a particularly happy moment,
they often report that it was when someone they'd helped returned
to volunteer in the organization, who "gave something back."

In a rehabilitation organization like Pride, the managers and
therapists are motivated to work harder by seeing how their clients
contribute to the success of the operation. As the president says, "It
gives me goosebumps to work here." In contrast, the staff of welfare programs based on sympathetic giving are often bored, if not
annoyed, by the unhelpful attitude of clients.

One who noticed the motivational importance of the exchange
principle was the great humanitarian Albert Schweitzer. Schweitzer
left a promising career as an organist and musicologist in Europe to
become a doctor and establish, in 1913, a clinic in the French African
colony of Gaboon. In his autobiography, Schweitzer explained how
he incorporated the idea of charitable capitalism in operating his
jungle hospital:

> So far as the rule could be carried out, I used to extract from my
> native patients some tangible evidence of their gratitude for the
> help they had received. . . . I gradually got it established as a cus-
> tom that in return for the medicines given, I received gifts of
> money, bananas, poultry, or eggs.

He pointed out that this had practical value for the recipients in
that it made the resources of the hospital go further, and it also gave
patients a stake in the hospital. He also saw that receiving something in return from the patients was important for the morale and
motivation of donors and charity workers: "Again and again I used
to remind them that they enjoyed the blessing of the hospital
because so many people in Europe had made sacrifices to provide it;

it was, therefore, now on their part a duty to give all the help they could to keep it going."[9]

The proponents of giveaway systems have got it wrong. Unrequited giving does not represent the highest kindness; it is a truncated, defective charity. To give back, to give in return for gifts given, is how we express our gratitude, our pride, and our humanity.

11

Contracting for Uplift

In 1991 volunteers in the town of Sandpoint, Idaho, got serious about helping the homeless. They obtained a donated lot and an old house that could be moved to it. For more than a year, they struggled to raise the seemingly impossible sum of $47,000, the cost of the move. Scores of local individuals, businesses, and groups contributed, including the association of realtors, the Lions Club, the Chamber of Commerce, the Mall Trade Association, and churches. Fund-raisers included a fun run, a dance, a movie showing, a wine auction, and a raffle of a Pontiac Sunbird convertible.

At last they succeeded, and the great day for the house moving came. News photographers came from as far away as Spokane, Washington, to record the massive building—to be called Blue Haven—making its ten-hour trip through town to its new location half a mile away.

Once the house was in place, there was more work to be done: foundations, plumbing, wiring, stairways, partitions, sidewalks, driveway, roofing. One after the other, local contractors volunteered their services to take care of each need. Others stepped forward to finish the individual units. For example, the First Lutheran Church took responsibility for one apartment, and its high school youth group put up Sheetrock and painted the walls in one of its bedrooms.

After three years and thousands of volunteer hours, Blue Haven was a reality, a facility capable of housing twenty-five homeless people in different apartment and group living units. The question then arose: how should this facility be managed? Under what terms should homeless families be allowed to stay in it?

Having made such an investment of time and energy—and with the entire community looking over their shoulders—the volunteers of Blue Haven were not about to treat their shelter as a giveaway, thrown open to any needy person, no questions asked. "This is not just a shelter," said one of the volunteer organizers. "We are here to help people get back on their feet, to help them with job interviews, budgeting, and to help them become independent."

To ensure that their effort was effective, organizers hit on the idea of striking a bargain with recipients: housing in exchange for self-improvement. Prospective clients have to sign an agreement to abide by certain rules and regulations and take steps of self-help. The contract is five pages long, single-spaced. It lists many obvious rules—no alcohol, no drugs, no pets, no smoking—along with other requirements: agreeing to take mandatory baths, keep units clean, open units for inspections, abide by a 10:00 P.M. curfew, refrain from cohabiting (for unmarried couples), and—in a clause that rings with the sane discipline of nineteenth-century charity—use no "boisterous or obscene" language.

To accomplish self-help, residents agree to meet with a case manager and develop a personal plan. Although each plan is individually tailored, all residents are obliged to work or seek work (unless excused for education or essential child care), to participate in budget counseling, and to put at least 10 percent of their disposable income in a savings account.

This system of "contracting for uplift" has become an increasingly popular approach to social assistance. It is especially prevalent in the housing and shelter fields; thousands of local organizations around the country have, more or less independently, arrived at the same principle. Instead of simply giving shelter, they draw up a quid-pro-quo agreement with the people they are trying to help.

It is important to notice how the pressure toward expectant giving comes from private donors and volunteers. These programs of supervised contracts are not initiated by nine-to-five bureaucrats spending public funds. Government employees want to do good, of course, but for them it is no tragedy if a program is marginally effective. They keep their jobs whether a program uplifts or not, and the money wasted does not come from anyone they know.

A closely watched, private, volunteer-based program is unlikely to be so complacent. It has taken too much personal sacrifice to be treated as a giveaway that only "might" do some good. The volunteers want to make *sure* that both their efforts and the generosity of their friends and neighbors are not abused, that they bear fruit. Instinctively, they reject sympathetic giving and devise arrangements of expectant giving. The result is a program that requires recipients to live up to standards of behavior and make an effort to improve.

"You've Got to Trust Us"

▼

In contracting for uplift, attention naturally goes to the contract, to the rules and requirements that have been put down in black and white. These are important in defining the program, of course, but the real strength of the program does not lie in these legal documents. Their effectiveness comes from the personal relationships involved, from the encouragement and advice of the volunteers. This point applies to all types of assistance programs. Anne Burke, director of Urban Ministries of Raleigh, North Carolina, puts it this way: "The greater the opportunity to build a relationship built on trust, the better the chances of success." When a strong personal relationship can be established between helper and helped, she says, "people will respond beyond expectations."

Contracting programs vary considerably in the extent to which they provide for personal relationships. One that gives an outstanding example of human support is the Step-Up Ministry in Raleigh, North Carolina. The program began in 1988 as an outreach project of the White Memorial Presbyterian Church; it now receives additional support from other churches and civic groups.

The Step-Up Ministry provides a rent-free apartment for four months to families in need. Each family is assigned to a team of four volunteers, called co-partners, who meet each Tuesday night with the family to discuss goal-setting, budgets, and employment opportunities. Other volunteers, called co-hosts, visit the family at their apartment and help them cope with home management and school problems. Still other volunteers prepare supper for the Tuesday night meetings and baby-sit while the parents meet with their co-partners. Altogether, the program supplies ten volunteers for each family.

The volunteers, especially the co-partners, become intimately involved with the personal lives of the people they are trying to help. Ginger Webb, the program's director (and its only paid employee), explains the complexity of this mentoring task:

> We tell people, "We're really going to get in your business. You'd better be willing. You've got to trust us. We're here to help you, and if you don't want that, then don't enter the program." It's an in-your-face kind of thing. The hard thing about being a volunteer is, you know exactly what that family ought to do. You can figure it out if you've got common sense. Trying to teach the family to set their own realistic goals is the tricky part, and not imposing values that aren't theirs. We can hope to influence their values, like on honesty, but you can't just say, "You must be an honest person the rest of your life. . . . "
>
> I have to be real careful putting a team together. We had a retired executive and an attorney we mistakenly put on a team together once, and they could hardly work. One would talk, and the other would interrupt, and the poor family was just done in, so we never did that again. You have to balance the personalities. You need a very quiet, caring person, and you need somebody who is upbeat. We have a lot of young people who are young singles, some young, really enthusiastic volunteers.

Webb describes the spiritual commitment of volunteers:

> Q. Do you in any sense communicate a spiritual aspect? You don't require it, obviously.
> A. No, we don't require it. All the volunteers we have are Christians. They're different denominations, but basically they're coming and volunteering because they have that spirituality themselves and they'd like to share it. We have what we call

"circle time" at the beginning of the meetings [each Tuesday] when the families come. Sometimes we have a guest minister who comes, and sometimes we have one of our volunteers to lead, and we gather in a circle, children included—last night we probably had twenty-six to twenty-eight people. First we introduce ourselves, and then we share any general concerns. If somebody has an aunt who is sick, or somebody says, "I'm afraid my husband is going to lose his job," we share those concerns. We may sing a song, "Amazing Grace" or something, and then we have a prayer. If we know . . . for instance, we had a Muslim family one time several years ago, and we just said, "If this is in any way offensive to you, you can come five minutes later, but this is what we're going to do."

Q. Did they come five minutes later?

A. No, actually they decided they were converted [laughs]. They said, "We like to do this, and actually we used to be Christians." What did we know? It's a witness. You're witnessing to your faith by having the program, but we decided a long time ago that people will share their faith if they have a faith.

Through the personal give-and-take, many volunteers and clients establish a bond that continues long after the basic program has been completed. And because of all the personal attention and support, almost all the families complete the program. Webb reports that of the eighty-two families that have entered the program (which manages seven apartments), only three have had to be dropped. The ministry further supports some successful Step-Up graduates with the Second Step Program, through which families pay some of their rent and utilities and meet only monthly with their advisers.

While the Step-Up Ministry relies almost entirely on volunteers, the program of the Delta Housing Agency in Harrisburg, Pennsylvania, relies on one paid staff member working with two volunteers for each supervised family. But the same principle of establishing a close human contact applies. Director Ed Trask explains the philosophy:

We're in the people business. We think we need to know the technologies of helping people move from point A to point B. But there's something more basic than that, and that is the connection with people. There is some kind of human transference that has to take place. We probably violate every canon in social work because we get personally involved with people, because we think that's where it's at. We can't treat them clinically. You can't just give them the technology.

We want staff to know the participants as real human beings. I say to them, "Go to the park and talk. Take one of our women, don't deal with her just as a client, don't just say 'Okay, today we've got to work on your budget,' or, 'Did you read to your kids three times?' and, 'Did you go to class?' No, no, no. Go talk to her about her sex life, or her dreams, or whatever she wants to talk about, or whatever you want to talk about. Just connect."

We have clients here who say, "Nobody ever treated me like a person before." And they mean *nobody:* mother, father, brother, sister, teacher, and everything. That's how human beings are reclaimed: give them a chance to be a human being. We call it love, the feeling of "I'm going to keep coming at you, I'm going to keep caring about you and try to find some way to connect with you nevertheless."

The Problems of Professionalism

▼

The success of a contracting-type program depends on two crucial pillars: (1) the personal encouragement given to clients and (2) the firmness with which the requirements are applied. In the ideal arrangement, supporting friends boost the client's morale, give advice in difficult times, and observe instances of backsliding and push for correction.

In the early stages of most organizations, this mentoring and supervision role is carried out by volunteers, just as it still is at the Step-Up Ministry. In many organizations, however, there is a tendency for professionalism to set in as the organization matures. The actual work of screening candidates, meeting with them, and advising and mentoring them is given to paid staff. Volunteers still serve on the organization's board and make final decisions, but they increasingly defer to the paid staff, who are assumed to know how to run the program.

From a distance, this professional model of assistance often seems ideal. The caring function is put in the hands of trained experts who presumably do a better job than amateurs. A closer look suggests that the move to paid staff generally sets the stage for the deterioration of the program. The basic problem is that paid staff are less likely to supply the powerful redemptive friendships that volunteers can form with clients. This is not always the case, of course. In some organizations, paid staff have grown up with the organization and are idealistically committed to it. They work long hours at low pay and are willing to take on many responsibilities beyond their job description; they are, in effect, "supervolunteers" who inspire everyone else in the organization. This is the case at Delta Housing. This eight-year-old organization began with volunteers who later became paid staff members. As Director Trask puts it, "We're still in our formative, idealistic stage."

As an organization matures, the original idealistic workers are likely to drop out, and paid staff members are more likely to be workers with no particular tie to the organization, and no special commitment to its ideals. Trask believes that this mentality characterizes the older nonprofits—and especially government agencies:

> A lot of them have become bureaucratic: you know, you have an opening, you plug the space, put a body in it. Their line people don't have the same commitment. They're thinking, "Nine o'clock, I'll start working. It's five o'clock, I'm done. And I'm going to make sure I get my hour for lunch." The worst example is the department of welfare, the public assistance office in this county. We have dehumanized the whole system, and then to think it's going to help people to change their whole lifestyle— the absurdity of that is beyond me.

In the long run, a staff-centered organization lacks the personnel needed to form deep, sympathetic friendships with needy clients. But, as we just noted, such friendships, more than any material benefits, uplift clients and motivate them to rise above self-defeating impulses. The result is that in older, staff-based organizations, clients more frequently backslide. They revert to drugs, alcohol, or violence, or quit their jobs, and have to be dropped from the program. Instead of having a successful completion rate of 85 percent, as the volunteer-intensive Step-Up Ministry does, the success rate in staff-centered programs falls to 50, 40, even 30 percent. Instead of uplifting, the program mainly becomes a further step along the path of an unhappy, drifting life.

As volunteers disappear from an operational role, the program can also lose its idealistic energy. The generous example of volunteers prompts clients to be generous as well. Being motivated to rise above selfish, cynical perspectives is important both for their own rehabilitation and for the efficiency and morale of the organization. Clients can plant flowers, tutor other clients, baby-sit for each other, and so on. Volunteers who give the first shining example of generosity help establish this ethic of mutual assistance. One sign of a successful assistance program is that it encourages clients to volunteer in it once they get on their feet. Organizations run by paid staff find it more difficult to inspire altruism. Paid employees are, necessarily, less effective in projecting the idea that "I am here only because I care about you"—because, of course, it isn't true.

Another disadvantage of relying heavily on paid staff is that staff can come to have a vested interest in the program. If a program is failing, volunteers close to it are more likely to insist on major changes—or even to scrap it. They are likely to say, "If it's not working, what am I doing here?" Paid workers, on the other hand, earn their income from the program, and this dependency biases their perceptions and their reports to the board and to the public. They are likely to feel that their program, which independent observers would rate a failure, is working as well as it can under the circumstances. Among other things, they are likely to turn a blind eye to violations of self-help requirements so that the "head count" can be maintained. In large assistance organizations whose boards have little knowledge of what is really happening to clients, this problem of self-justification and distortion is particularly serious.

How to Motivate Volunteers

▼

To stay healthy, then, an assistance organization needs to maintain a strong volunteer base and limit its dependence on paid staff. Some paid employees are usually necessary, and they can be wise and inspiring leaders. But a robust organization should not depend on paid staff for its main activities. It is one thing to state this as a principle, but quite another to apply it in practice. In many groups, paid staff members seem to be needed because not enough dedicated volunteers can be found to do the job. How, program managers ask, does one attract an adequate contingent of volunteers?

A first answer is that one needs an exhilarating, effective program. This returns us to the issue of morale raised in the preceding chapter. A giveaway program that expects little of clients is generally not inspiring to the people working in it. It has a plodding, mechanical quality. A program that makes high demands on clients, on the other hand, is exciting. Workers come to empathize with—and admire—those they help; they see their efforts bear fruit in uplift. An organization like the Step-Up Ministry, with a demanding program of expectant giving, is able to attract and retain a large number of volunteers. It is also able to appeal to private donors to meet its financial needs and therefore doesn't require, and doesn't seek, government funds.

A lack of volunteers and donors should be taken as a warning sign. Instead of filling the deficit with a government grant and paid workers, leaders should reexamine their approach. They will often find that their problem stems from having a bureaucratic program of sympathetic giving that provides volunteers and donors with little to admire or to be enthusiastic about. The cure for a lack of volunteers, then, would be a radical redesign of the program so that it strongly challenges clients.

Even within effective programs, however, volunteers need to be attracted and nurtured. The Raleigh Step-Up Ministry, with its rich complement of volunteers, offers some useful ideas on their proper "care and feeding." First, the organization offers a compact, short-term commitment to prospective volunteers: just four months as a co-partner for one family. Contrast this to a request "to work in a homeless program." The prospective volunteer doesn't know how long she is expected to participate and can't visualize a point at which the job is "done." A short-term commitment does not create a high turnover of volunteers. After getting their feet wet in the initial term, most volunteers find the work attractive and rewarding and reenlist for additional terms.

Second, the Step-Up Ministry puts inexperienced volunteers alongside experienced ones on its co-partner teams. That way, newcomers never fear they will be out of their depth. Third, each team of volunteers is given an orientation meeting and two training sessions to boost their skills and confidence.

Finally, volunteers *work together*. For most people, volunteering is a social activity: they seek rewards of fellowship from it. More than that, they need to have their motivation reinforced by working alongside like-minded helpers, so that each sets an example for the others. The pioneers of voluntarism who invented husking bees and barn-raisings knew what they were doing.

Some volunteer managers, attempting to apply the idea that volunteering is sociable, arrange a steady stream of parties, dinners, and award ceremonies. While these efforts can have a positive value, we have to note that they do not create situations where volunteers are *working* together. Most people volunteer in assistance programs to accomplish something, and sociability devoid of accomplishment leaves them unfulfilled. This is why most volunteers hate meetings. The ideal, then, is to have volunteers working jointly on the assistance activity. In Step-Up, this happens on both the co-partner teams that supervise each family and is further reinforced by having all the teams work together at the same place and time in the Tuesday night meetings.

As the Step-Up Ministry illustrates so well, helping the needy is fundamentally a personal challenge. Certain kinds of paid staff workers—social workers, therapists—are in a position to make some of the constructive personal contacts that uplift requires. But the needy also need friends, human beings with no professional or monetary interest in them. The nineteenth-century charity workers discovered this principle and made it effective in the practice of "friendly visiting." Today we are rediscovering it through the many volunteers who play an active role in assistance programs.

12

Friends Who Inspire

In a materialistic age, we assume that money can buy anything, including uplift of the needy. After many trillions spent, we are beginning to sense the inadequacy of this assumption. Material support may have a role to play in certain types of assistance, but it is not an engine of uplift. For most people who are deemed needy, the main barrier to economic and social success is not a lack of dollar bills; it is a lack of healthy values and motives. How, then, do we impart healthy values? How do we teach children—and adults—to work hard, to be honest, to defer gratification, to stay away from drugs and alcohol? A system that can accomplish this kind of instruction deserves to be considered a first-rate social assistance program.

The process of guiding others to better habits and greater understanding is generally known as mentoring. The word refers to a character in Homer's *Odyssey* named Mentor, an adviser whom Odysseus assigned to his son when he left for the Trojan War. Although Mentor took the appearance of an Ithacan noble, he was actually Athena, the goddess of wisdom, in disguise. Therefore, in the spirit of the tale, a mentor is not merely an adviser but a divinely gifted one.

Mentoring was first recognized as a method of social assistance by the nineteenth-century charity theorists. Indeed, many of them considered it to be *the* method for uplifting the poor. One notable proponent was Octavia Hill, whose system of tenements directed by befriending managers was described in chapter 4. She explained her theory of mentoring in an 1880 letter to fellow charity workers in Philadelphia:

> I am satisfied that visiting, such as I gather you have established, which brings those of different classes into real friendly relations, must in time help to raise those who are fallen low in any sense of the word; from wealth, little can be hoped; from intercourse, everything. That is to say, everything we have to give seems to communicate itself to those we love and know; if we are true, we make them truthful, if faithful, full of faith, if earnest and energetic, earnest and energetic. . . . Human intercourse in God's own mercy seems appointed to be the influence strongest of all for molding character.[1]

To see how mentoring works and what it requires, it is useful to begin with the most important form that it takes: the parental guidance of children.

From Ditchdigger to Doctors

▼

If parenting were an Olympic event, surely Donald and Tass Thornton would be gold medal winners. They raised six daughters, all with outstanding values, and launched them into successful professional careers: two doctors, a lawyer, a dentist, a nurse, and a court stenographer. What would be a notable achievement even for well-placed white parents was nothing short of heroic for the Thorntons, working-class blacks in Long Branch, New Jersey, who faced prejudice and poverty every step of the way.

The story of this remarkable family is told by their daughter Yvonne in *The Ditchdigger's Daughters: A Black Family's Astonishing Success Story*. Early on, Thornton conceived the idea that his daughters, though poor and black, should grow up to be doctors. To reinforce it, he spent a lot of time explaining the values necessary to succeed in life. "That's why teenagers get pregnant," he would say, in a typical lecture to his daughters, "because somebody says, 'Oh, this one time's not gonna hurt.' Or somebody says, 'Oh, one drink isn't gonna hurt you.' If you listen to that, you're weak-minded, and weak-minded people end up in trouble. You have a mind. You got to use it."[2]

But it takes more than vision to raise children. Many fathers and mothers have high hopes for their children, and, goodness knows, they urge values like working hard at school, good manners, and all the rest. The trouble is, too often the advice goes in one ear and out the other. Thornton's children were different: they listened to his lectures and took them to heart.

What gave Thornton his position of authority? The answer, according to Yvonne's account, is that Thornton won respect through his sacrifice. He didn't just sit on the couch and lecture about right and wrong. He worked his fingers to the bone for his children. In the early years, he worked as a ditchdigger and heating oil deliveryman during the day, a janitor at night, and a hod carrier for a bricklayer on weekends. When he was denied a loan to build a house, he began building it himself in spare moments left over from other jobs. His wife, Tass, followed his example, working as a full-time maid.

Urgent needs meant additional sacrifices. "Jeanette and I inherited Daddy's jaw structure," writes Yvonne, "and since he was determined for us not to be dentally crippled as he was, he managed to materialize money enough for us to have teeth pulled and teeth added to align our bites." When the girls showed an aptitude for music, "Daddy cobbled together two more odd jobs he could do on weekends to pay for the music lessons. Once I asked him why he worked on Sundays instead of going to church with us. 'Cookie,' he said, 'you eat on Sundays just like any other day, so I work on Sundays just like any other day.'"[3]

Thornton often pointed to his breadwinning to back his claims of authority.

Sometimes Jeanette would buck whatever it was Daddy was trying to teach us by quoting a friend or teacher. . . . He would say, "You look in the mailbox on your way to school and see if there's a certified check in there to pay for your food and the nap you're wearin' off the carpets in this house. If there is, you bring it to me and I'll listen to the person who's got his name on that check about how to raise my kids."[4]

This episode illustrates the devastating effect of a welfare check on parental authority: when someone else *is* paying the bills, it undercuts the parent's ability to gain respect and obedience. A welfare check also undermines the parents' motivation and self-confidence. One day, when his wife asked him whether he was disappointed that he had only daughters and no son, Thornton told her, "Tass, for me to work hard for myself is no purpose. But for me to work hard for my wife and my children who need me, that has come to be my purpose and that's all I need."[5] Imagine what would have happened to this family if a welfare check had made Donald Thornton's hard work unnecessary.

Thornton's teachings were especially effective because he set an example himself. He lived out his lessons about hard work, self-discipline, and planning ahead. When he began to build his house with his own hands in his spare time, an electrician and a plumber volunteered to donate wiring and plumbing work. Thornton used the episode to teach initiative. "'You see how it is, kids,' Daddy said to us. 'People aren't gonna throw their time or money away on somebody who gets a bottle of Thunderbird wine and lies down on the sidewalk, but if you show people you're tryin', they're gonna want to help.'"[6]

It may at first seem odd to include mentoring as a type of expectant giving, but a closer look reveals that it is a real exchange—not an exchange of anything material, but a trading of effort and commitment. The parents give their love and make sacrifices, and in return, the children obey and emulate the parents. Thornton was fully aware of this system when he discussed his child-rearing philosophy with Yvonne many years later:

Girls are very determined to win and keep the love of their daddy. For me to smile was like Santa Claus coming to a child on Christmas. When I was frownin', they begged me, "Daddy . . . please tell us what's the matter." I'd say, "You've been bad girls." "Daddy, we'll be good. Just talk to us. Just smile. . . . "

A beating only matters to a child when you're beating them. So then I told them, "You want me to be a good daddy, you got to be a good daughter. . . . In other words, if you expect me to be nice and give you the things you want, you got to be nice and give me what I want. I want you to study. I want you to do good by your music lessons."[7]

If parents are respected and admired, the impulse to please them will extend far in time. Yvonne Thornton writes that, now in her forties and a doctor on the staff of Rockefeller University Hospital in New York, she still doesn't feel comfortable going against her parents' early teachings, even on small points. Waiting at a restaurant for a taxi one day, she found herself avoiding sitting on a bar stool because her mother had taught her that ladies don't do that.

Mentoring depends on the commitment of the mentor. This commitment includes an emotional investment—the mentor personally cares about the success of the learner—and an investment of time and attention. Successful mentors also establish personal ties with learners, because influence is partly a function of the personal relationship. A parent who sacrifices to support his children will probably not have much influence if he doesn't talk with them and find out about their interests and problems. Finally, the Thornton case points up the importance of setting an example, of living out the principles we teach. The strongest advice is not what we say, but what we do.

Tears and Hugs

▼

After parenting, the next most common mentoring situation is probably the student-teacher relationship in school. Naturally, the degree to which teachers become effective mentors depends on the personal commitment they can make. Many teachers—perhaps understandably—lack the time and emotional energy to take the mentoring process very far. A few, however, make a big investment in their students and have a corresponding impact on their lives and character. LouAnne Johnson is an example of a high-investing teacher. She worked in a California high school where she taught at-risk teens. She describes her techniques of inspiring unmotivated students in her books *My Posse Don't Do Homework* and *Girls at the Back of the Class*. The key to her success is to give students almost endless attention and affection.

She would begin the school year by memorizing students' names beforehand, so that she knew each pupil by name, right away. "How'd you do that?" asked one boy. "I hesitated for a few seconds," writes Johnson,

> to underscore the importance of what I was about to say. "I know your names because you are important people to me," I said, as I looked around the classroom, making eye contact with each student. "When I look at you, I see you. I like you. And I care about you. That's why I'm here."[8]

Throughout the year, she was indefatigable in keeping in touch with students: having heart-to-heart conversations with students after school, telephoning them to find out about problems, going to their homes to meet parents, hounding the school bureaucracy and law enforcement agencies on their behalf. She kept track of everyone's birthday. When it came, she gave each student "a big hug and a goofy little gift." All this attention motivated students to work hard, attend class, and raise their grades. The end result was a nearly perfect graduation rate for these troubled youngsters.

Her sacrifice wasn't mechanical; it came from the heart. Johnson's affection for her students and her desire to see them excel led to many wrenching disappointments. One day, thinking to surprise her students, she brought in a $63 triple-layer chocolate mousse cake—only to find that half of them had cut her class. "I cried and stamped my feet, ripped all the test papers to shreds, smashed the erasers against the chalkboard. . . . I thought I had instilled in these kids a love of literature, of learning, of intellectual exploration." Her involvement with her students left her without a personal life. Her psychiatrist told her she needed to separate her work from her private life. "I can't close my door and forget about the kids," she replied. "Sometimes I think I may be the only person who thinks about them at all."[9]

Some teachers and coaches succeed in mentoring students by focusing on extracurricular activities. The math teacher Tom Larson found a way to break through the apathy of Chicago inner-city youngsters at Orr High School by introducing chess. As they mastered the game and competed among themselves and against other schools, the boys learned they could be winners. Larson lavished attention on them, taking them out for pizza, taking them to chess clinics, phoning them in the evenings to give encouragement, even hiring a private chess tutor for them. Larson's commitment pulled the school team to a citywide championship. More important, he kept a number of at-risk youngsters motivated enough to stay in school and graduate.[10]

One remarkable educational institution based on an extracurricular activity is the Harlem Boys Choir. It was founded in 1974 by Walter Turnbull, a black singer who had grown up in Mississippi. In his autobiography, *Lift Every Voice*, Turnbull recounts the importance of mentors in his own life, especially his high school and college music teachers. Their example has led him to think deeply about methods of inspiring young people. He points to the importance of establishing personal contact, a two-way relationship:

> Establishing trust between teacher and student is paramount to success. Trust is established by demonstrating a genuine concern for a child's well-being. That means talking with a child and actually listening to him or her. Most children have something that they do of which they are proud. Sometimes it's coloring or working with clay. All it takes is a simple question from a teacher: "What do you like doing?" If the child answers he likes to draw, ask him to bring his work in. It's amazing to see what children are proud of, and praise usually comes naturally.
>
> From that point on, a bond has been established. The student sees that the teacher is interested in him as a person, not just as a body sitting in a class. The teacher sees that the child is capable of a variety of skills—attention to detail, ability to complete a task, and courage to share a secret with an adult. It's the little things that count.[11]

From his work with the boys in the choir, Turnbull found himself taking up parental and teaching roles. Gradually, the choir expanded, taking on other teachers and staff; finally, it became a full-scale teaching and mentoring organization for at-risk youngsters. The Harlem Choir Academy, founded in 1987, is now a major New York private school, enrolling 300 boys and 118 girls. The choir and academy have built an impressive record of motivating at-risk youngsters to complete school and go on to college.

Turnbull makes it clear that this success is not achieved by a gushing, one-sided giving of affection. His system of mentoring demands discipline and achievement from the boys and girls in exchange for the commitment of the teachers. If a student arrives late to a rehearsal, he thunders, "You are early for tomorrow's rehearsal. I know you are not coming into my class at this hour of the day."

"Public humiliation," he writes, "was a great motivator, and nothing was too small to launch into a larger lesson on life. If a child asked to be excused to use the bathroom only ten minutes after rehearsal had begun, I would tell the boy and the class about the word 'preparation' and how they had to plan things in their lives."[12] It is important to realize that this "humiliation" is administered in a larger context of affection and trust. One of the choir graduates explained:

> [At first], I never really understood why Dr. Turnbull would scream and yell at us. At times I thought he hated us, but as time went on and I began to realize my situation as a black boy growing into a man in America, I began to see he cared, because if he didn't care he wouldn't stay on us.[13]

Mentoring occurs naturally in the home and at school, but there is no reason to limit it to these situations. Reformers have noted its potential for personal growth and rehabilitation, and they have devised many kinds of organizations to bring its powers to bear. One of the first to put the mentoring idea to deliberate use was Alcoholics Anonymous, the self-help organization that works with alcohol abusers. Founded in the United States in 1939, it now has more than 40,000 chapters in 110 countries. Its founders were moved to begin the organization after they experienced the therapeutic value of friendship with other ex-alcoholics who cared deeply about them. Today, other mentoring organizations that follow the Alcoholics Anonymous format assist people with a wide variety of problems, including drug addiction, gambling, and overeating.

Another type of mentoring situation being widely encouraged today is that between an adult and a child from a single-parent or at-risk background. These matchups were first popularized by the Big Brothers/Big Sisters movement, which began in 1904 and now has some five hundred local agencies serving eighty thousand Big-Little pairs. Many other organizations and local programs have sprung up in recent years to facilitate adult-child contacts. A regional example is Partners, which has sixteen branches in Denver and other western cities. In Michigan, a church-based mentoring program called Kids Hope was started in 1995; it now has branches at seventeen churches.

Successful adult-child mentoring involves mutual responsibilities; it is not one-sided giving. James Russell, executive director of the Big Brothers/Big Sisters agency in Newark, Ohio, made this point when I asked him about children seeking gifts:

> Sometimes, their mothers put them up to that. It's birthday time, Christmas time, give me, give me, give me. Part of our orientation program to the Big as well as the Little is that we're not interested in the Big's money. We're not interested in satisfying birthday or Christmas needs. We're interested in sharing quality, one-on-one time.
>
> Obviously, you get wrapped up in a youngster. . . . There isn't a one of us that's had a long-term match, probably, that didn't help with a scholarship or something in school.
>
> Q. But that's after you really feel comfortable in the friendship?
>
> A. Right. And after they've proven they want to do better and succeed in life.

Another point that has to be kept in mind about mentoring is the importance of example. The adult must have high standards: reliability, self-discipline, good personal habits. Otherwise, the child will learn the wrong thing; indeed, having poor role models has been the problem for many children growing up in poverty. The Big Brothers/Big Sisters agencies stress the importance of finding adult mentors of good character. (As we note later in the chapter, however, this aim is applied in an overly bureaucratic way.)

Also critical for success in mentoring is the commitment given to it. In the typical mentoring program, the adult spends about three hours a week with the child. Though valuable, of course, this amount of time limits the bonding and influence that can be achieved. Most mentoring organizations try to devise ways to increase the contact. Summit County (Colorado) Mountain Mentors, for example, organizes overnight activities and weeklong camping trips for the adult-child pairs. The challenge of these outings, and the prolonged contact between adults and children, enhance the bonding that can occur.

How to Encourage Mentors

▼

Given the importance of mentoring and its potential for turning lives around, the question naturally arises, are there ways to foster this activity? What can society do to have more LouAnne Johnsons, more Walter Turnbulls, more Octavia Hills?

Outstanding mentors are born, not made. Driven by their own concerns and commitment and gifted with a firm sense of right and wrong, they adopt highly idiosyncratic tactics for eliciting excellence and showing love. Walter Turnbull gives an account of his remarkable high school music teacher in Mississippi, Herticene Jones, who inspired him and influenced his own approach to mentoring:

> I liked music but Miss Jones was tough. She would do anything for you, but she was not afraid to ridicule you or your family if you messed up. She didn't care who was around to hear either. If you came in late to a rehearsal, she embarrassed you. "I know you are not coming into my class late," she would snap. She was tall and dark-skinned and carried herself with a regal air. She was a member of the Alpha Kappa Alpha sorority, and she was not about fun and games. She was about perfection. Whatever she believed in, she was right. . . .
>
> She had a lot of influence over our lives and used a combination of tools to motivate us. She kept a box of tissues atop her piano. If you were talkative and within arm's reach, rest assured she'd

smack your head with the box. . . . One time, the whole group was not singing to her satisfaction. She lined everyone up. "Okay, tenors over there, altos over there, and take your belts off," she ordered. She then asked each of us to sing our parts aloud, and if we messed up, we had to walk through the belt line, taking hits from the swinging belts. Nowadays, she would probably be sued for such behavior. But beating children was not her point. She wanted everyone to know that their part was vital to the whole.[14]

Turnbull's comment that today such practices wouldn't be permitted in a government school makes a critical point: bureaucracy can't do much to assist mentoring, but it can certainly hurt it. Because outstanding mentors are usually unorthodox and opinionated, they are particularly likely to run afoul of rules and regulations drawn up by far-off authorities who overlook the subtleties of the mentoring relationship. Today what Miss Jones did would probably be officially described as "striking students" and "inciting students to physical violence against each other." Of course, any such activity would be prohibited, and Miss Jones would have been dismissed—or she would have had her fiery, inspiring personality quenched into bureaucratic grayness.

It's no accident that Turnbull turned his back on the New York City public schools, where he had taught, to found a private school. He saw that the schools' politics, bureaucracy, and trade unionism were killing the possibility for unorthodox, highly demanding teachers and creating teachers who were "cynical and unmotivated."[15]

LouAnne Johnson found herself constantly fighting the bureaucracy at her public school in East Palo Alto—and finally resigned. Instead of supporting her, administrators would take refuge in rules to undermine what she was trying to accomplish. Her unorthodox style also got her into trouble. It fit her personality to rely a great deal on physical affection, hugging and so forth. Once she kissed a sleeping teenager to wake him. "That single kiss had effectively stopped sleeping in my class for more than three years but had also caused more concern among the administration than the sorry statistics of our increasing dropout rate."[16]

Johnson also points out how destructive another bureaucratic rule—lifetime tenure for teachers—can be. She came up against a particularly bad teacher, a man who specialized in vicious personal vendettas against students. When she went to the principal to complain, she was surprised to find that he agreed. "I've got a file this thick on Ken," said the principal, measuring four inches with his fingers. "But the man's been here for thirty-five years. He has tenure."

The principal went on to point out that "Ken" was an energetic and idealistic mentor himself when he first started teaching: "He helped a lot of kids before he burned out. Took kids into his own house, fed them, bought them clothes, paid for their glasses, found them jobs after school."[17] The implication is significant: because mentoring relies on high levels of enthusiasm and commitment, it is not guaranteed to last a lifetime. Mentors can lose their touch or lose their conviction, and when this happens, they should withdraw from the activity. It's a point that mentors and the institutions that recruit them should keep in mind.

Not only local bureaucracies undermine school mentors. Both the federal and state governments have a flood of regulation that, whatever its positive value, almost invariably harms mentoring. In Prince George's County in Maryland, teachers and volunteers had developed a number of successful mentoring clubs—some for girls, such as the Ladies Club in Bowie, and some for boys, such as Men of Madison in Upper Marlboro. Organizers had found that morale and closeness—essential for mentoring—were enhanced by the single-sex clubs. Unfortunately, the Office of Civil Rights of the federal Department of Education found them to be discriminatory and banned single-sex mentoring organizations. Mentors were thoroughly demoralized by the edict. "The whole thing is bull," said Yvonne Payne, a parent volunteer in a girls' mentoring program in Fort Washington. "What they've basically done is destroy the program. A few of us are very upset about it because our hands are tied in terms of what we can do."[18]

Commentators have pointed to many shortcomings in public schools, but the way they undermine mentors may be their greatest failing. There are millions of children today who, in an age of family breakdown, desperately need demanding, self-confident mentors. At the same time, we have millions of idealistic adults who are eager to inspire them. Yet instead of allowing these two groups to come together freely and work their magic, the govern-

ment education system interposes a web of soul-destroying com-
plications and restrictions: mandated education coursework, certi-
fication requirements, mandated textbooks, union work rules, nig-
gling lawyers, and pussyfooting administrators. Some dedicated
mentors manage to struggle against this mountain of obstruction,
but how many scores of thousands have been driven away?

What can society do to have more mentors? Stay out of their
way. Trust them. Give them the freedom to apply their drive, their
instincts, and their unorthodox approaches. The schools are not
the only institutions where this principle applies. In many other
areas where mentors could play a role in helping the needy, they
have been trammeled by government rules and restrictions. A
prime example is drug and alcohol rehabilitation.

Government is spending large sums on drug and alcohol rehabilitation programs staffed by highly trained, state-licensed medical
and counseling personnel. The success rate of these programs has
been disappointingly low. A number of private programs actually
have a much higher success rate and cost much less than government treatments centers. They include Denver's Step-13 shelter,
Chicago's House of Hope, Gospel Mission in Washington, D.C.,
Clean and Sober Streets, also in Washington, and the Austin Street
Shelter in Dallas, Texas.[19]

While several factors account for the success of the private programs, one of the most important seems to be their reliance on
committed mentors. The staff in these organizations are not nine-
to-five clock-punchers, but idealists with special talents and an
unusual commitment. In many programs, the staff are recovered
substance abusers. This experience gives them an ability to
empathize with addicts and the self-confidence to make demands
on them when the occasion requires. In other private mentoring
programs, the leaders' firm convictions are based on religious faith
and sharing their beliefs is a part of their befriending strategy.

Government rules and regulations discriminate against both
kinds of dedicated mentors. Rules about training and licensing of
personnel tend to exclude ex-addicts—as well as anyone else whose
heart is in the right place but who has not jumped through the necessary bureaucratic and academic hoops. And government rules
about religion exclude a whole class of the most inspired mentors.

Sometimes an organization can't protect its mentors even when it refuses government funding. In San Antonio, Texas, Victory Fellowship, a faith-based rehabilitation program founded thirty years by an ex-drug addict, was almost closed down in 1993 by state regulators. The organization relies heavily on volunteers and focuses on providing Christian leadership to addicts. State officials demanded that the facility obtain a state license, which would have meant that it could be staffed only be state-certified personnel. Enough political pull was mustered to hold the regulators at bay.[20] But the threat of government-imposed grayness still hangs over the organization—and over any other group that depends on unorthodox mentors.

Private Bureaucracy

▼

Government regulations aren't the only threat to mentoring. Private bureaucracies can also have a stultifying effect. The Big Brothers/Big Sisters organization illustrates some of the problems. As it has evolved over its ninety-two-year history, BB/BS has become a staff-oriented organization. Each local agency is operated not by volunteers but by paid staff who closely screen and supervise the volunteer mentors. These staff members, and the national office (Big Brothers/Big Sisters of America), which reflects their views, believe that successful mentoring cannot take place unless it is controlled by professionals—usually academically trained social workers.

One consequence of this staff-oriented approach is that BB/BS has become an expensive program, one that can cost more than $1,500 yearly for each mentored youngster. These high costs have driven the organization to seek increased government funding. An even more serious problem is that the paid staff puts obstacles in the way of idealistic volunteers. BB/BS agencies have evolved a cumbersome application procedure for prospective mentors that takes many months to finish. In addition to completing the twenty-two-page application form and orientation sessions, applicants must also provide four or five letters of recommendation and undergo tape-recorded interviews with staff, home visits by staff, and a personality profile test. In states that permit it, the procedure can also include a police record check, traffic violation check, and fingerprint check. All this data collection is burdensome and demeaning to potential volunteers—who are, after all, the heart of the program.

In Los Angeles, an idealistic young black professional went to the Big Brothers office to volunteer. After seeing all the red tape, he commented, "Why is it when you try to do good, they put obstacles in your path?" This made the BB/BS employee defensive, and the young man was rejected as a Big Brother on his "application manners" alone. A rare breed, this volunteer didn't take no for an answer. He appealed his case to the agency's board of directors (who were volunteers), was accepted, and now the staff has only praise for his work. "We wish we had ten more of him," said one of the officers. (To its credit, BB/BS of America carried this story in its own magazine.)[21]

BB/BS leaders are aware of the importance of being user-friendly to volunteers, but the staff-centered orientation impedes radical reform. A measure of what is possible is illustrated by the progress made at the Newark, Ohio, branch after volunteer James Russell joined the paid staff. Russell, one of the founders of the Newark program in the 1970s, has had five Little Brothers over the last twenty-six years. After he retired from his work at Ohio State University, he stepped in to fill the executive director's job. He was appalled by the long waiting period between the time a mentor applied and when he was approved. He saw the problem through the eyes of the volunteer: "When I first came on here, there was a four-month waiting period for an adult. Quite frankly, an adult says, 'Hey, I want to volunteer now. I don't want a bunch of this Mickey Mouse stuff.'" Russell has reduced the waiting time to twenty-one days and plans to get it down to two weeks. One of his key reforms has been to get references over the telephone instead of waiting for a written letter of recommendation.

This episode illustrates the vital role that volunteers play in keeping social assistance organizations on a healthy path. Paid staff are often necessary for many functions, and paid staff members are often dedicated and idealistic. Nevertheless, they have a material interest in the organization, and this connection can cloud their judgment about what is best for the clients. Volunteers—and here we speak of volunteers fully involved in the task of the organization—are vital to counteract this bias. They maintain its idealistic service orientation in a way that no one else can.

The Kids Hope organization in Michigan illustrates the difference that volunteer management can make. Each chapter of this mentoring organization is based in a particular church. The congregation supplies volunteers who teach reading to, and mentor, at-risk children in local schools. The church also supplies additional volunteers to serve as substitutes in the event of the regular mentor's absence and assigns a set of "prayer partners" to each child. The program has minimal screening costs because it is run by people who know and trust each other; overall, the program costs about $300–400 per year for each mentored child—less than one-quarter the cost of the staff-centered Big Brothers/Big Sisters program.

The differences in the programs also show up in the supply of volunteers. BB/BS chapters have long waiting lists of youngsters who need adult mentors because, with its imposing recruitment barriers and red tape, it has an acute shortage of volunteers. At volunteer-friendly Kids Hope, this isn't a problem. The director, Virgil Gulker, reports that his organization faces an opposite kind of challenge. Local coordinators call him asking, "What should we do with the volunteers we can't use yet?"

PART IV

Paths for the Future

The Key to Reforming
Government Welfare Programs

The theme of this book is that sympathetic giving—something-for-nothing giving—is an unsound approach to social assistance. The way to help those in need is expectant giving—asking them to make some positive, constructive step in response to aid. Unfortunately, government has difficulty accomplishing this kind of giving. In chapters 5 and 6, we examined the powerful, built-in bias toward giveaways found in government welfare programs. Two hundred years of experience with government programs of relief, doles, and subsidies confirms the pattern.

In the face of this failure, the sensible conclusion would seem to be that government welfare programs are inherently unsound. Although we are edging toward this view, the country is not yet ready to embrace it. The feeling today is that government welfare programs are necessary, but that they must be reformed to demand steps of self-help from recipients.

History tells us, however, that whenever policy makers have thought they were reforming welfare and adopting policies of "helping people help themselves," they ended up creating more handouts. Is there any way to avoid this fatal pattern? Is there a way to reform government welfare programs to reverse their tendency toward harmful, costly handouts? I believe there is, but it is a measure that does not look like any welfare reform currently being suggested.

To explain it, we will review one welfare policy area—disability. Disability policy is a laboratory of welfare reform failure. For decades, Congress has been trying to correct the handout character of this program and limit its alarming growth, but with no success. A close look shows what it would really take to accomplish these goals.

The federal disability benefit system, which evolved from a number of smaller, preexisting programs, has three main components: a federal program for claimants with some registered work experience (the disability insurance program—DI); another federal program for claimants without adequate registered work experience (supplemental security income—SSI); and state supplemental payments to these claimants. This package of programs is administered by the federal Social Security Administration with a single application process. It is one of the country's fastest-growing welfare programs—and also one of the most costly. In 1997 the disability system had 11.9 million beneficiaries and cost $78 billion per year.[1]

This massive program is an example of pure sympathetic giving. It gives money to claimants who can persuade officials that their disability is serious, and it keeps giving them money as long as the disability seems to render them distressed and unemployable. The problem with this approach, of course, is that it undermines the recipient's motivation to overcome his handicap. He is tempted to magnify his disability instead of striving to overcome it. He is inclined to avoid doing what will make him better, such as following a difficult diet, exercise, or training regimen. He is encouraged not to find work, since that would cause a loss of disability payments. Furthermore, he is encouraged to suffer! We know how suggestible human beings often are. People can walk on hot coals or stick pins in themselves and not feel a thing if they are determined not to. Surely the process works in reverse for some people: attaching a financial reward to subjective conditions like pain, stress, and fatigue can exacerbate these symptoms, causing victims to feel more pain than they otherwise would.

The correct approach to disability should be expectant giving: rewarding steps of recovery, reinforcing efforts to function in spite of the disability. In other words, what is needed is a program that pays people for getting better. How did the U.S. government reject this sound approach and end up with a system that pays people to be sick? As it turns out, the handout approach was never anyone's intention. In setting up the disability system, Congress was aware of the need to incorporate healthy incentives. It attempted to include restrictions and requirements that would give it features of expectant giving. Yet, in practice, these requirements have been ignored or stripped away. To illustrate how good intentions fall by the wayside, let us look at what has happened with the rehabilitation requirement.

Administrators Ignore the Law

▼

Many people who are unable to work because of a disability can recover from it, or they can do other jobs even with the disability. What they need is retraining, technical support, and medical assistance—and plenty of motivation. Therefore, said Congress, the disability program should *require* recipients to participate in vocational rehabilitation in order to get benefits. The chief counsel of the House Committee on Ways and Means summarized the policy:

> The Social Security Act requires that persons applying for a determination of disability be promptly referred to State vocational rehabilitation agencies for necessary rehabilitation services. The act provides for withholding of benefits for refusal, without good cause, to accept rehabilitation services.[2]

In fact, nothing of the sort happens. Almost no one leaves the disability system to engage in self-supporting work. The number is so low that the Social Security Administration doesn't even keep systematic records of such persons. Summarizing the indications from several studies and calculations, the General Accounting Office puts the proportion who leave the disability rolls by returning to work at "less than half of 1 percent" of all beneficiaries.[3]

Obviously, the rehabilitation "requirement" has become a dead letter. To find out how this happened, I interviewed a number of officials and administrators in the field. An administrator in the SSI/DI program in California explained how he viewed the referral requirement:

We have the ability to make referrals to voc rehab [state agency for vocational rehabilitation]. We used to do that a lot more in the earlier years. When we would complete the forms, one of those copies we could send to the voc rehab office, and we would attach the most pertinent medical records and say, "We think you ought to look at this as a potential client."

Quite frankly, the feedback we were getting from rehab was, "Why are you sending these over here? We don't have the funds to handle them."

But money isn't the real problem. The Social Security Administration is authorized to pay public or private agencies to retrain people and get them to work—and off the program. This doesn't help because recipients are not motivated to learn new jobs: remember, they are being *paid* to be unable to work. "When we made referrals," this administrator continued, "the rehab agencies would make a certain commitment to a claimant and expect a certain commitment back. They didn't get paid until they had a successful completion or a successful placement." Naturally, the rehabilitation agencies objected to being sent clients who sat on their hands. "Our rehab agencies have let us know that if they have somebody who is not highly motivated, it is a waste of their time. They have let us know that to send a nonmotivated person there is a waste of everybody's time and effort."

Surprisingly, the branch chief quoted above *didn't even know* about the rehabilitation requirement Congress wrote into the law. When I asked him, "Can people who are on SSI be forced to participate in a rehab program?" he replied, "No, that's not part of the deal."

But the language requiring referral to, and participation in, rehabilitation is quite emphatic: section 222 of the Social Security Act states that claimants "shall be promptly referred," and deductions from benefits for refusing to cooperate with rehabilitation "shall be made." Why have administrators ignored this language and allowed the program to degenerate into a pure giveaway?

The answer can be traced to the political forces that shape government welfare programs—the pressures of institutional self-interest. Except at moments of crisis and high media attention, welfare programs are of little interest to the public and to most politicians. On a day-to-day basis, policy is shaped by those actively involved in the programs—that is, the participants with a personal financial interest in the programs, who are sometimes called "stakeholders": agency personnel, program beneficiaries, and the lawyers, lobbyists, and other professionals paid directly or indirectly by program benefits.

Stakeholders have a common interest in program growth. The beneficiaries naturally want more money rather than less, and they want it with as few strings attached as possible. Their lawyers and the advocacy groups that agitate on their behalf naturally support the same idea. And as we explained in chapter 6, the pressures of "task commitment" lead administrators and employees to want larger programs as a way to validate their importance.

These pressures to expand explain why rehabilitation in the disability program has become a dead letter: to implement this requirement would shrink the program. Requiring recipients to participate in rehabilitation would make the program less attractive and discourage some claimants. And if they did participate in genuine rehabilitation, many would leave the rolls through recovery.

The bureaucratic pressure to expand accounts for many other flaws in the program as well. The desire to preserve the caseload makes the Social Security Administration reluctant to find and punish recipients who are receiving benefits fraudulently or to correct erroneous payments. For example, the Social Security Administration has been sending SSI checks to thousands of prison inmates, directly violating the law prohibiting these payments.[4] Of course, there are always administrative reasons why this kind of error isn't corrected, but in the end it comes down to a balance of priorities. Administrators are naturally more interested in initiatives that add to the grandness of their program than in steps that expose its flaws and shrink caseloads.

The thought emerges then: to preserve meaningful requirements in a welfare program, one has to look beyond current stakeholders and introduce another participant, an entity, independent of stakeholders, that defines its success as *reduced* caseloads. Let us keep this idea in mind as we consider some other failures of the disability system.

Heads I Win, Tails We Flip Again

▼

In the federal DI/SSI disability system, the flaws in theory and policy are matched by strikingly perverse administrative practices. One illustration is the disability appeals process. To get a disability benefit, the claimant makes an application and files medical documentation of the disability, which is then reviewed by a team of doctors and rehabilitation experts. If they make a favorable decision, the claimant gets the money. If this team of experts makes an unfavorable decision, a reasonable person might suppose that would be the end of the process.

Well, it isn't. If a claimant is found not to be disabled, he can demand a reexamination before a second team of experts. If they turn him down, he has the right to a hearing before an administrative law judge (ALJ). If turned down at that level, he can go to an appeals council. And if he is still without his benefit, he can appeal to a federal court. This multi-stage appeals process is heavily used: about 30 percent of those who eventually obtained benefits were turned down at the first stage but managed to score at a later appeals step.[5]

At first glance, this complex system might seem justifiable on the grounds that, although cumbersome and costly, it prevents errors. But notice that it corrects only one kind of error: *not giving money to those who should get it*. There is no corresponding structure to correct the opposite error, of giving money to those who shouldn't be given it. There are bound to be many cases in which the disability award is incorrect: those that involve fraud, for example, or that harm the recipient by undermining his motivation. But there is no appealing when benefits are awarded—only when they are denied. The result is a system of "heads I win, tails I try again." In neither policy nor logic does the disability appeals process make any sense. Its only virtue is that it is structured to increase the number of beneficiaries—obviously the result that stakeholders want.[6]

Again, speculate about what might happen if an entity with an interest in lower spending were included in the process. Might it not campaign against this biased appeals process within the Social Security Administration, and also before Congress and the public?

A Mockery of Judicial Procedure

▼

If there were a body seeking to counter the bias toward giveaways in the disability program, one of its first targets would be the third stage of appeal, the hearing before the administrative law judge. The popularity of this appeals step has grown by leaps and bounds. Each year around half a million disappointed claimants make use of it; they and their lawyers love it because more than two-thirds of the claimants using it are awarded benefits.[7] Over the years, ALJs have added several million individuals with questionable disability claims to the SSI/DI rolls.

To an objective observer, the ALJ appeal stage is clearly superfluous.[8] Before they reach this level, claims have already been exhaustively considered and rejected by two independent teams of disability experts, teams that include doctors and vocational experts. It should be remembered that the experts who determine disability work for the program: their bias, if any, is to *find* disability and thus validate the program that employs them. Furthermore, the administrative law judge who hears the appeals has no expertise on disability. The judge is neither a doctor nor a vocational rehabilitation specialist; he is simply a lawyer who has had four weeks of training in administrative procedures.

The only thing the ALJ hearing provides is its worst feature: a personal, one-sided hearing.

In nineteenth-century England, there was a peculiar charity known as the benevolent association. The needy person would go to the house of a board member, describe his suffering, and get the member to write a letter asking the association to make a payment to him. The nineteenth-century charity theorists deplored this practice because it was rife with misrepresentation and fraud. It trained the poor to become adept at whining about their problems instead of facing and overcoming them. With the ALJ appeal stage in the disability determination process, the Social Security Administration has re-created this discredited practice.

In an ALJ hearing, the claimant's objective is to appear as pathetic as possible. Most claimants are represented by attorneys who specialize in this work—charging a part (up to $4,000) of the eventual award—and they know how to guide their clients into the well-trodden paths of pathos and medically unprovable disabilities. They prompt the claimant to dramatize his pain, his insomnia, stress, fatigue, and troubling flashbacks. In one hearing I attended, the middle-aged female claimant held her shoulder in apparent pain throughout the hearing. She also stood up several times. Her lawyer prompted her to explain that back pain made it impossible for her to sit for any length of time. The ALJs are supposed to be neutral, but of course they cannot be. They are swayed, as we all would be, by empathy for the sufferer and by a desire not to disappoint the claimant and his attorney.

It should be remembered that the suffering on display has, in most cases, been cultivated for years by a claimant who sees this courtroom appearance as his or her ticket to permanent financial security. The ALJ has neither the time nor inclination to make an independent investigation of each claimant in order to establish his or her motives and character; he handles some thirty to sixty cases a month. "Am I confident I'm not being fooled?" asked one ALJ when I queried him about his ability to detect misrepresentation. "I know I'm being fooled some of the time. But I just do my job."

As if the cards weren't already stacked in favor of the claimant, in the ALJ hearing there is no opposing side! The claimant appears with his lawyer, period. The result is a mockery of the judicial process, a hearing in which the attorney and his client have a clear field to sway the judge. At the hearing I attended, the lawyer for the claimant submitted some documents for inclusion in the record. "Are there any objections?" the judge asked the court. "No objection," said the lawyer who had just given him the documents. Neither the lawyer nor the judge understood why I laughed.

The Social Security Administration used to have a halfhearted policy of attempting to represent the opposing side in hearings. Naturally this angered client attorneys, since it interfered with their ability to fleece the system. They sued, and the agency ran for cover, having no interest in anything—such as fair hearings—that might check the growth of the caseload. I asked an administrative law judge whether having only one side represented bothered him:

Does it bother me? As a taxpayer, yes. But the agency has made a decision that they will not be represented at the hearing. For a variety of reasons, they don't want it to be an adversarial proceeding. ... Before I came here, I worked in Washington for twelve years, and this system confounds me. There's got to be something wrong with a system where 65 to 75 percent of the decisions get reversed.

Why does this flawed hearing system continue, adding its hundreds of thousands of questionable giveaways to the disability program each year? We come back to the now-familiar answer: it serves the self-interest of the stakeholders.

Blind Policy from the Courts

▼

As it currently operates, the judicial system is the natural enemy of expectant giving; that is, the courts tend to destroy assistance arrangements that require something of recipients. The reason is that the only cases coming into the courts are those brought by welfare recipients and their lawyers who object to some requirement that has led to lower benefits. No citizen ever brings a case against a welfare recipient, asking that he be required to do something in order to receive his welfare benefits. Hence, judges are never in a position to decide cases that add restrictions and requirements to welfare programs; they can only take them away.

The result is another game of "heads we win, tails we flip again." In the disability program, more than six thousand claimants take their cases to federal court each year.[9] This one-sided legal roulette has resulted in vast expansions of giveaways not legislated by Congress. One example is the 1990 Supreme Court decision in *Sullivan* v. *Zebley*, which decreed a major expansion of benefits for children. The number of children on SSI benefits increased from 300,000 in 1989 (pre-*Zebley*) to 900,000 in 1994. About half of these 900,000 recipients are attributable to the *Zebley* decision and the resulting liberalization in eligibility rules.[10] In other words, the Supreme Court increased welfare spending in this program by $2.6 billion a year. (In the 1996 welfare reform, Congress attempted to reverse some of the consequences of the *Zebley* decision; it remains to be seen whether administrators or the courts pay attention.)

What would it take to keep the courts from stripping away welfare program requirements and multiplying giveaways? A close look at the lineup of participants in the *Zebley* case, as it was argued before the Supreme Court, suggests an answer. Representing Zebley, on the side of those who wanted to expand SSI benefits to children, were five lawyers from two (federally funded) legal assistance organizations. Also supporting that position were forty-eight other entities represented in six supporting (*amicus curiae*) briefs. Virtually all of these organizations represented people with a personal financial interest in expanding childhood disability cases. They included groups representing doctors, pediatricians, and psychiatrists (who earn healthy, tax-funded fees for making evaluations and testifying), and organizations of parents who wanted taxpayers to shoulder the costs of dealing with their children's problems. Also filing a brief was the National Organization of Social Security Claimants' Representatives, the pressure group of lawyers whose lucrative practices rely on assisting clients to extract money from the disability system.

Who was on the other side, against expanding benefits? Only the Justice Department, which handles all government litigation. No other person or organization supported the case against expanding SSI benefits to children.

The Justice Department was a puny knight in this battle. The Zebley forces had made it seem they were asking for a slight improvement in "fairness," so that a certain number of suffering children could be "helped." The Justice Department allowed this definition of the case to stand and tried to argue the case on legal quibbles, ignoring all major issues of policy and morality. Among other things, the *Zebley* decision had the effect of rewarding irresponsible parents, youth misbehavior and violence, and deliberate failure in school.[11] Judges were given no inkling that they were about to mandate a vast welfare policy change, one that portended billions in new spending. Nothing was ever mentioned about perverse incentives, the weakening of families, the morale of teachers in the public schools, or fairness to taxpayers whose children had worse disabilities and who were being forced to pay for the new benefits.

It's not surprising that the Justice Department argued the case ineptly. Justice Department lawyers have no interest or expertise in welfare policy. They also have no particular interest in restraining government spending, and no natural impulse to uphold the interest of taxpayers; indeed, they spend a lot of their time prosecuting them on behalf of the IRS.

Taxpayer Representatives

▼

As the foregoing review indicates, the American welfare system is the product of a deeply irrational decision-making process. It is a system dominated by those with a vested interest in maximizing handouts. Anyone who wishes to reform welfare in a permanent way must come to grips with this bias. It's not enough to have legislation demanding personal responsibility and effort on the part of welfare recipients. Someone or some entity must be there to uphold the spirit of these reforms, decade after decade.

Reformers therefore need to add a new participant to the welfare policy context, a participant with a vested interest in limiting handouts and blocking caseload increases. There are a number of ways to establish this kind of interest. Perhaps the simplest is to attach a "taxpayer representative" to every welfare program and agency. This entity would be given the formal mission of representing the taxpayers' natural interest in restraining welfare giveaways and maintaining program requirements. Automatically funded by a fixed proportion—say, one-half of 1 percent—of the program budget, it would be independent of the agency it oversees. Thus, if a taxpayer representative were created for the disability program, it would obtain $388 million.

The taxpayer representative would have no operational role in the programs. Instead, it would collect data, make reports, and publicize its findings to Congress and the public. In certain respects, it would resemble the General Accounting Office, which produces studies of government programs, including welfare programs. The

GAO, however, has no mission to represent the taxpayer or defend the cause of lower spending. And it is not supposed to question the overall effect of policies. In contrast, the taxpayer representative would be expected to delve thoroughly into the social, economic, and moral consequences of welfare policies and publish searching critiques of destructive and wasteful programs.

Since we are putting forth the taxpayer representative as an illustrative suggestion rather than a finished proposal, we do not need to go into great detail about its actual structure. It should have safeguards against being "captured" by the program it supervises. For example, it would be best if the officials appointed to the taxpayer representative were people who had not worked for government prior to their appointment. To keep employees from becoming financially and professionally dependent on the program they oversee, their term of service should be limited.

Fighting Fallacies, Not Grandmothers

▼

One objection to the idea of taxpayer representatives is that these units would prove to be "toothless," since they would have no control of programs. This view reflects a misunderstanding about how welfare policy is made. Opponents of programs make the mistake of assuming that the way to rein in welfare spending is to gain political control of the purse strings. Their theory is that to cut welfare, all you have to do is cut welfare.

Several decades of failure on this front should have revealed the flaw in this approach. Welfare handout programs exist because there is a powerful, if shallow, sentiment in favor of them. The public's natural sympathy for the needy is mobilized by administrators and special interest leaders who present these programs as compassionate and who suppress their unfair and dysfunctional aspects. When attempts are made to limit welfare spending, these forces swing into action, accusing budget-cutters of trying to starve Grandma. The press and much of the public accept this interpretation because rarely does anyone make an opposing case.

Cutting programs does nothing to correct this imbalance in

information and perception. Hence, welfare programs start growing back even before one has finished trying to cut them. Every welfare reform, including the 1996 legislation, has abundantly documented this pattern: we always end up with a larger welfare establishment as a result of trying to cut it.

The only effective way to limit programs is to expose their flaws and faulty premises. The taxpayer representative would perform this function, and would do so without provoking an emotional backlash because it would have no operational responsibility. It would starve no grandmothers. All it could do would be to inform. Supporters of welfare programs, if they believe their policies can stand scrutiny, should welcome its creation, for it would make possible, for the first time in the history of the welfare state, a balanced, open debate on the merits of assistance programs.

To see the imbalance of information on the welfare debate, pick up a copy of any congressional hearing on a welfare program and peruse the list of witnesses. I took the 626-page volume of the 1995 hearings of the House Ways and Means Committee on the SSA disability program. Out of 29 witnesses, 24 either were employees of the disability program itself or represented entities with a direct financial interest in it. The five witnesses who were not financially dependent on the program had no mission to criticize the program. They included a former social security commissioner, a staffer from the Congressional Research Service, and three GAO researchers. Not one of the 29 witnesses suggested that the disability program had any major flaw or deficiency.

In the system of communication and persuasion on welfare programs that prevails today, only a handful of individuals speak for taxpayers or express society's long-run interest in cultivating self-reliant individuals. On the other side is massed the full weight of government-funded advocacy: more than four hundred schools of social work; the hundreds of thousands of government-employed social workers; the additional thousands of program administrators; the hundreds of private companies that contract to deliver services to welfare departments; the scores of government-funded consulting firms paid to produce flattering evaluations of programs; and the thousands of advocacy organizations representing beneficiaries.

In creating taxpayer-funded units to oppose the expansion of government welfare programs, Congress would be partly redressing a problem it has already created in the other direction. For decades, taxpayer funding has gone to organizations that lobby for larger welfare programs. Indeed, most of the "demand" for welfare programs comes not from ordinary citizens, nor even from welfare recipients, but from the tax-funded welfare lobbying organizations. Catholic Charities is a typical example. This alliance of 1,400 local welfare organizations affiliated with the Catholic Church routinely lobbies for more welfare spending and opposes efforts to limit welfare spending. No doubt its leaders are sincere in believing that larger government programs are desirable, but to what extent have their opinions been shaped by the fact that Catholic Charities gets $1.2 billion— more than 60 percent of its income—from tax sources?[12]

On June 1, 1996, some 426 groups organized a "Stand for Children" march in Washington to agitate for higher welfare spending. Scores of the participating organizations were tax-funded lobbies, including the American Academy of Pediatrics, the American Association of Retired Persons, the American Medical Women's Association, the American Nurses Association, the American Psychiatric Association, the American Psychological Association, the American Rehabilitation Association, the American Speech Language Hearing Association, and the Association for Gerontology and Human Development in Historically Black Colleges and Universities (the reader will notice we are still on "A"). By one tabulation, these lobbying organizations received more than $392 million a year in federal tax funds.[13] Even labor unions of government employees are tax-funded. At the Social Security Administration, taxpayers are paying the salaries and fringe benefits of 145 full-time union leaders.[14]

Anyone who feels sympathy for the disabled would endorse a taxpayer representative. The Census Bureau reports that there are 51.5 million Americans with significant disabilities.[15] Since only 11.9 million get DI/SSI benefits, there are 40 million disabled taxpayers being forced to fund benefits for people who, in many cases, are less disabled than they are. They include workers who are blind or have lost limbs or have serious problems with stress or depression, and who, without handouts, struggle to support themselves.

They need their earnings to cope with their disability, yet the federal government's "program" for them is to tax away their income. With so much tax money being spent to fund lobbies that aim to extract subsidies from taxpayers, simple justice would suggest that there ought to be a tax-funded entity to defend these beleaguered taxpayers.

A New Political Theory for a New Political Age

▼

Why, the reader might ask, should taxpayer representatives be confined to welfare programs? Aren't all government agencies run by self-serving bureaucracies that distort information in their favor and cover up the flaws of their programs? Indeed they are, and in a well-ordered government, there would be taxpayer representatives attached to every program. The Defense Department needs one to provide an independent, critical evaluation of its programs, and so do the Forest Service and all the rest. We live in an age of special interest representation gone mad, when countless organizations struggle to extract wealth from the public till. Yet strangely, modern political theory hasn't noticed the need to represent taxpayers too. The system we are left with resembles a lobotomized sow being sucked to death by its piglets.

Neither Congress nor the public understands the tremendous power of self-justification that all government agencies inherently possess. When Congress creates any program, it automatically creates an apparatus of persuasion that produces a biased national view of that program. When it creates a widget agency, it creates scores of administrators and public affairs officers whose main job is to justify the widget program and to cover up unfavorable information about it; it creates legions of widget employees whose support of the program is literally bought and paid for; it creates beneficiary groups who will form widget lobbying groups to ensure the flow of cash; it creates agency-hired researchers who are paid to produce one-sided studies asserting the value and importance of widgets. If government is not to become an ever-expanding universe of wasteful and unexamined programs, Congress must establish critics alongside each program. Every widget agency needs to have its widget taxpayer representative.

The degree to which an opposing voice is necessary varies from program to program. In some cases, a government program injures an interest or industry so directly that the industry will fund a certain amount of countervailing lobbying. But in many other cases, there is little incentive for anyone to criticize the government program. This is clearly the case with welfare programs, and that is why taxpayer representatives are so important in this sector. For these programs, the task of opposing agency stakeholders is especially difficult and particularly thankless. There is no natural lobby to oppose welfare giveaways that seem, from a distance, compassionate toward those deserving of pity. Though many people privately feel that these programs do great harm, few want to take the superficially hardhearted stance of opposing them. This leaves only a handful of idealists to oppose the massive propoganda generated by stakeholders using taxpayer dollars.

Real welfare reform would create an opposing interest. It would establish taxpayer representatives, also funded with taxpayer dollars, who would serve to balance the flow of information about welfare programs. This is the only dependable way to limit the drift of government welfare programs toward ever-expanding handouts.

The Brave New World of Voluntary Charity

It is beginning to appear that government programs of relief are on the wane. They still have enormous political and budgetary power, but they are losing their intellectual and moral support. Politicians sense this change in direction. Announcing a national summit on volunteerism in April 1997, President Clinton declared, "Much of the work of America cannot be done by government. The solution must be the American people through voluntary service to others."[1] The future of social assistance, it appears, will be in the hands of nonprofits, churches, and volunteer groups.

If voluntarism is upon us, however, it is coming most hesitantly. There is nothing of the firm enthusiasm that characterizes most social and political movements, no masses of committed idealists surging in the streets to demand control of the future. For most people, even for leaders in the voluntary sector itself, voluntarism seems flimsy and incomplete, an arrangement too weak to do the heavy lifting of social assistance in a nation of three hundred million people. They concede that it's a pretty ideal, but worry that it seems unrealistic. "How could it possibly work in practice?" they ask.

At first glance, the objections to voluntarism appear to be empirical. As we explore the arguments, however, we discover that they are based not on facts but often on misunderstandings. To make the case for voluntarism, therefore, we need to expose and rebut the prejudices that get in the way of it.

Some time ago, I gave a talk to graduate students in economics about how a voluntary organization can perform a social service task more efficiently than a government agency. To make my points, I was using the example of a soup kitchen that volunteers at my own church had organized. When I finished, a young man's hand went up. "But how would you get people to participate in such a group?"

It was a revealing use of the conditional tense. Even though I had spent twenty minutes describing this actual, functioning volunteer soup kitchen, the young man still couldn't believe in it. He did not ask, "How *do* you get people to participate?" In his mind, a volunteer soup kitchen was a hypothetical, visionary proposal, something that looks nice on the drawing board but couldn't work in practice. Imagine an observer at Kitty Hawk making this same error. He watches the Wright brothers' plane take off and land and then asks, "But how would a heavier-than-air machine fly?" The use of *would* reveals that the speaker cannot believe the evidence of his senses.

The student couldn't believe in the voluntary soup kitchen because he couldn't understand the motives involved. Economics students are trained to assume that human beings are perfectly selfish, that they will never do anything unless motivated by a personal financial reward. While the rest of us are perhaps not so indoctrinated, we still tend to underrate the power of generosity and idealism in human affairs. We say—thinking ourselves hardheaded and realistic—that fear and greed make the world go round. This mindset leads to the conclusion that voluntarism is unnatural and unworkable.

But it is a flawed mindset. Human beings are moved by a parliament of motives, and among them are kindness, community spirit, idealism, and generosity. The empirical, measurable result of these altruistic motives are the hundreds of thousands of voluntary groups that we see all across the land.

Most critics of voluntarism concede that some, or even many, voluntary groups provide useful assistance programs, but they point to the relatively small size of the voluntary sector today. "How," they ask, "could voluntary groups take over the vast sweep of governmental assistance functions?" Once again, this is not a logical objection. All useful systems start small. Once their viability and desirability are proven, we are drawn to using them, and as a result, they grow. After conceding that the Wright brothers' plane flies, we visualize two such planes, then ten such planes, and so forth, until we have created fleets of Boeing 747s. If critics agree that voluntarism works, and that it is more sensitive and more efficient than government, the logical response would be to work to expand it.

We don't have to stretch our imaginations to visualize a charity system based on voluntary groups; that is what existed in the nineteenth century, before the country succumbed to the fatal illusion that government could do it better. So it takes no great leap of faith to suppose that voluntarism could again take over social assistance—if we decide this is the best way to do it.

Are We Too Busy to Volunteer?

▼

Mention of the nineteenth-century experience often provokes the following objection to voluntarism. "Volunteering may have been possible in the nineteenth century, when life went at a slower pace. But today everyone's working at two jobs. They don't have time to volunteer to help their neighbors."

This view embodies two misconceptions. The first is a confusion of volunteering with voluntarism. Voluntarism is the use of voluntary means to address social problems. To put it another way, voluntarism means *not* relying on the coercion of the tax system or on the coercion of government regulation to accomplish social aims. It is perfectly possible to have voluntarism without volunteers, that is, to have a voluntary system where no one donates unpaid labor services. It is philanthropic voluntarism: citizens donate some of the money they earn in their productive, busy jobs to charities, which in turn hire paid staff to do whatever needs to be done.

Philanthropic voluntarism appears to be the main form of voluntarism today. All around the country there are foster homes, camps, drug rehabilitation clinics, hospitals, retirement homes, and adoption agencies that are supported by voluntary donations and staffed almost entirely by paid personnel. They receive funds through direct fund-raising as well as through intermediaries like the United Way, and they are also supported by millionaires, billionaires, and foundations. The main limit on philanthropic voluntarism does not appear to be a lack of resources. We now see billionaires happily subsidizing the most questionable ventures, from sports teams to the United Nations; if more social service agencies had effective programs, more billions of voluntary donations would flow to them.

So even a shortage of volunteers would not preclude turning social assistance over to the voluntary sector. We could donate a small fraction of our wealth to staff-based agencies that, in our judgment, help the poor, then retire to our castles and BMWs, never even seeing a needy person again. The result might be a rather impersonal, bureaucratic system, but one certainly no worse than the present impersonal, bureaucratic government systems, which are based entirely on paid staff. In fact, philanthropic voluntarism has several advantages over government. Since funds are raised on a voluntary basis, potential donors have the option to decline to give to wasteful, corrupt, and harmful programs—a freedom they do not have with tax-funded programs. So failing programs could be eliminated more promptly than they are under the government system. Philanthropic voluntarism also leads to decentralization; donors support local charities they are likely to know something about. With tax-based systems, of course, donors seldom have any knowledge about the programs they are supporting.

While philanthropic voluntarism represents an improvement over government, it is not the highest form of social assistance. Volunteers are needed in welfare programs to supply the personal relationships that are so vital to providing comfort and uplift. So it is quite true that if not enough volunteers can be attracted, we are not likely to have a high-quality voluntary assistance system. But is it correct to say that the demands of modern life now make it impossible to recruit an adequate number of committed volunteers? Remember, the nineteenth century was the age of large families, twelve-hour work shifts, and hand laundry. The idea that either men or women a century ago had more leisure time to volunteer to help their neighbors is implausible.

To be sure, certain social changes have left some groups with less free time. The rise of single parenting has obviously increased the burdens for some individuals. And the increase in mobility has weakened neighborhood ties. But overall, technology has reduced the time we must devote to the struggle for physical survival—and that means we have more leisure time today. Consider all the people who have benefited from golden parachutes, buyouts, and early retirement. What about the millions of senior citizens lounging poolside in Florida and Arizona? Look at the growth of tourism and sightseeing. Consider the growth of the recreation industry, with its powerboats, golf courses, and tennis courts. Consider the fact that the average American watches twenty-eight hours of television per week!

We also have a great advantage over nineteenth-century volunteers in health and comfort. Modern surgery, dentistry, and optometry have addressed all sorts of physical problems that debilitated volunteers of yesteryear. We eat more, and more nutritious, foods than people did in the nineteenth century. All this adds to our energy and alertness. We have air conditioning, heating that really heats, hot showers, and adequate lighting for our work and study. The telephone makes it easy to contact other people.

In terms of physical comforts, material goods, and leisure time, volunteering is easier than ever before in history. If the nineteenth century was able to have a good social assistance system based on volunteers, the twenty-first century could have a fabulous one. *If* we wanted it. That's the problem. The seniors sitting around pools and the juniors watching TV could be volunteering. They could easily spare the time, and most of them would find it challenging and rewarding. But in order for them to volunteer, they would have to believe that it is the natural system for helping the poor. And today almost no one believes that. So we return to our original point: the real objection to voluntarism isn't that it can't work, or doesn't work. What's wrong is that we just don't believe in it.

The Dream of Banishing Want

▼

Of all the mental blocks against voluntarism, the most significant is a simple fact that looms over all aspects of life and culture in the twentieth century: we believe in government. In spite of all the complaining and cynicism, Americans still look to government to solve problems. And in spite of government's many follies, failures, and disasters, and in spite of its corruption, red tape, and waste, people still believe that government has special powers that no other institution has. This belief, at bottom, is why most people resist the idea of looking to voluntarism to handle social assistance.

The mystique of government appears to rest on two plausible but misguided impressions. The first is the idea that government has absolute power and can therefore fix anything absolutely. While superficially convincing, this proposition breaks down under careful examination. It is certainly true that government has tremendous resources of certain kinds. As the agency marshaling physical force in society, it has vast powers of destruction. If necessary, its policemen and soldiers can collect billions of dollars or kill millions of people to make its will effective. This vision of frightful power easily leads to the conclusion that government can accomplish whatever it wants.

For millennia, mankind has dreamed of banishing want and suffering from the world. Socialism promised the fulfillment of that ambition: the vast power of government would be harnessed to the purpose of eliminating poverty. Here's the picture of life in the socialist utopia that the nineteenth-century writer Edward Bellamy envisioned for the United States in his highly popular novel *Looking Backward*: "No man any more has any care for the morrow, either for himself or his children, for the nation guarantees the nurture, education, and comfortable maintenance of every citizen from the cradle to the grave."[2]

We now know that this hope of governmentally imposed perfection is an illusion. For a century, antipoverty reformers around the globe have tried every variant of governmental power, from terror and mass murder to ponderous legislation. No utopia has been created; in most places, poverty has continued to grow. The lesson we must take from this century of failure is that force—government's basis of power—may be effective in destroying things, but it is a poor tool with which to accomplish growth and renewal.

In spite of all the historical lessons in government's shortcomings, the supposition still lingers that government can succeed absolutely. "In a system of independent private charities," says the critic, "won't people fall through the cracks? Who is to make sure that everyone gets the help they need?"

Notice the underlying assumption: under a governmental system of care, no one falls through the cracks! Obviously, this idea did not come from empirical observation, from walking the streets and alleys of our cities and seeing nothing but happy, well-adjusted people. It springs from this primitive belief that government has the power to put everything right, if it would just try hard enough.

All systems of charity have cracks. Suffering, tragedy, and injustice will always be part of the human condition. Under a system of voluntary charity, millions will go without proper assistance—just as they do today under a half-trillion-dollar system of government care. The more important questions are: which system shows more promise of long-run improvement, and which treats individuals with the dignity they are due—a bureaucratic system based ultimately on force, or a personalized system based on generosity and persuasion?

Who Tells Us What to Do?

▼

The second great appeal of government stems from a natural human desire for a higher authority. The world is a confusing, challenging place, often posing problems we cannot understand or solve, and it is reassuring to suppose that some higher, wiser person or entity does have all the answers. By looking to this entity, we can believe that a world that may be outside our control is at least not out of control. For thousands of years, government has filled this yearning for a supreme entity. Men have looked to pharaohs, emperors, and kings to organize the world and to tell them what to do.

This primitive impulse has been dressed up in intellectual garments by theorists who claim that central control is necessary for a just, efficient society. Plato, writing in the fourth century B.C., was perhaps the first to make this highly plausible argument. He likened society to a ship at sea: it could not be sailed by just anybody, it had to be under the command of a well-trained navigator. This (false) analogy led him to propound a system of totalitarian rule by philosopher-kings.

While hardly anyone these days wants a dictatorship, the appeal of central control remains, and it keeps leading back to government. When someone proposes a system of private, voluntary charity, the impulse is to ask, "But who will control it? Who will make it work?" The picture of thousands of independent entities each doing what it wants is unsettling. We call it "chaos," or "anarchy," and yearn to see an authority put over it, to coordinate and supervise and license and certify.

This was the sentiment expressed by the socialist Michael Harrington in his 1962 book *The Other America*, a volume that profoundly influenced the war on poverty and subsequent welfare programs. After reviewing the problems of the needy, Harrington asked, who could carry out an effective campaign against poverty? Without even examining the issue, he dismissed voluntary organizations as a possibility. "Only the Federal Government has the power to abolish poverty," he said. Washington had to run the effort "because of the need for a comprehensive program and for national planning."[3] Many from the other side of the political spectrum succumb to the same impulse. "American purpose," writes David Brooks, editor of the conservative *Weekly Standard*, "can find its voice only in Washington."[4]

The impulse to look for a higher power is particularly strong in welfare because the problems of the needy are so intractable. How do you restore energy to the listless? How do you inspire the defeated? How do you motivate the addicted to overcome their self-destructive habits? When we have personally tried to address these problems, we have realized that we don't have any clear or simple answers, even in attempting to treat the case of one troubled human being. The idea of correcting millions of dysfunctional lives is absolutely daunting. Out of our frustration and sense of inadequacy comes the yearning to believe that government has the solution.

The world has had a century of experience with government's centralized systems, and we now know that they do not deliver the answers and advantages originally promised. In fact, the evidence is that they are markedly inefficient, and often appallingly destructive. Common sense could have told us why. Government officials are not gods with superior mental powers, capable of discerning solutions that evade the rest of us. Government is made up of ordinary people who are just as confused and misinformed as the rest of us can be.

When you put ordinary people in charge of large domains, you are almost bound to get a disappointing result because the successful operation of a centralized system requires more information than they can possibly collect and digest. This point is now well understood as it concerns the economic system of production and distribution. For generations, economists have been familiar with the analyses of Ludwig Von Mises and Friedrich Hayek, which show that a centrally planned economy is bound to be inefficient because planners can never know enough to regulate wisely.[5]

It's time to apply this same wisdom to social service programs. The complexity of social problems is not the reason government should deal with them, but the reason it should not. Government is a rigid, low-information system that can operate only in simplistic, sweeping terms. An effective system to address the moral, psychological, and physical needs of millions of people requires vast amounts of intricate information. Only a system of many small, independent assistance efforts is capable of adjusting to the individual conditions of each needy person.

The old, primitive impulse to put charity under the control of government authority to ensure an intelligent and comprehensive program is therefore profoundly misguided. When we hear about the growth and proliferation of private charities, we should not ask, "But who will coordinate it?" Instead, we should be saying, "Thank goodness, here's something no one will control." The coming system of voluntary charity will rely on the imagination and intelligence of vast numbers of people. All these individuals acting in their own sphere are smarter than any pharaoh, king, or senator could ever be. Over time, this multitude of independent reformers will create a system of social assistance that will quite surprise us.

How to Help the Poor

Wealth is not always an advantage. For modern nations, it brings new and perplexing problems in welfare policy, particularly the problem of dependency. The advance of industry and technology generates greater wealth, and this wealth makes it progressively easier to give handouts to those we pity. In this way, we reinforce the very misfortunes we deplore.

Participants in the welfare policy debate may dispute many points of policy, but there is wide agreement on the pitfalls of handouts and the danger of continually expanding them. No one wants a country in which large masses of people are perpetually maintained by a system of giveaways. Nevertheless, our growing wealth makes possible this unwanted situation. We are approaching the day when it will be possible for the productive members of society to maintain vast segments of the populace in idleness. The cost of meeting minimal food and shelter requirements would be easily absorbed in a country of such wealth, and one could add free TVs and refrigerators and still hardly notice the financial burden.

The question is, could we live with the moral and social consequences of such dependency? Would we like to be a part of a community that had written off a group of neighbors as useless? This situation would be, it seems, a formula for resentment and bitterness, on the part of givers as well as receivers. And what about the social behavior of this supported class? We don't need exhaustive sociological research to discern the effects of dependency. Idle and futile human beings have low morale, and from low morale sprouts every civilization-destroying vice.

The welfare problem is not an economic challenge but a social and moral challenge. Increasingly, we can afford large giveaway programs. Although most of them are governmental, we should not suppose that private-sector programs are immune to this tendency. Our fatter wallets make it increasingly easy to give blindly to charitable causes, and private charity managers may be tempted, just like the politicians, to operate programs of sympathetic giving that look compassionate from a distance.

The danger of too much giving has not been properly appreciated. In the current discussions about replacing government programs with private ones, the dominant anxiety seems to be that private dollars won't make up for lost government dollars. This concern is misplaced: the real danger is that they will! Nongovernmental systems of sympathetic giving can support millions of people in dependency too.

With or without government programs, prosperity portends a disaster in welfare policy. Our problems of dependency and cultural disintegration today will seem small compared to those we'll have in thirty or forty years if we do not change our assumptions and policies. Modern society urgently needs a reformulated view of social assistance. We need to understand that giving is a complex, double-sided force, like nuclear energy: useful under certain conditions, but capable of lasting harm if used wrongly. To prepare ourselves to manage aid programs wisely, we need to master some basic principles.

Heart and Mind

▼

Unexamined giving leads to defective charity. Modern charity workers need a comprehensive theory of giving to replace the flawed doctrine of give, give, give. Fortunately, we do not need to invent it. The nineteenth-century charity theorists covered this ground thoroughly, and they have left us a clear account of their conclusions.

These reformers insisted that sound policy requires more than a concern for the needy. It has to include tough-minded analysis as well. Octavia Hill, the nineteenth-century English charity leader who enunciated so many sound principles, put the point this way:

> The form that charity takes in this age or that must be decided by the requirements of the time. . . . Only never let us excuse ourselves from seeking the best form in the indolent belief that no good form is possible, and things are better left alone; nor, on the other hand, weakly plead that what we do is *benevolent*. We must ascertain that it is really *beneficient* too.[1]

The American preacher and sociologist Charles Ames made the same point in a paper he gave at the 1876 meeting of the Philadelphia Social Science Association, entitled "Wisdom in Charity":

> The open hand must be guided by the open eye. The impulse of pity, or compassion for suffering, belongs to every well-ordered mind; but like every other impulse, taken by itself alone, it is blind and idiotic. Unable to protect itself against imposition, unable also to discriminate and adapt its relief to the various conditions of actual helplessness, it flings its resources abroad at haphazard, and gushes itself to death.[2]

In many private charities around the country, this advice is disregarded. Charity managers too often operate on the assumption that only good intentions are required. For instance, perhaps someone has the idea of feeding the hungry. She finds friends and fellow church members who endorse the idea, and soon a soup kitchen is functioning. There has been no discussion of what anyone wants to achieve with this activity. Do volunteers want clients to depend permanently on the soup kitchen? Do they want recipients to get jobs? To learn good nutrition? To learn how to cook? To learn manners? To help run the kitchen? To experience spiritual growth? Until such issues are carefully addressed, it is not possible to know how to operate a truly constructive program.

Several traditions underlie the failure to explore purposes. For one thing, government welfare programs have given us a century-long example of thoughtless giving. Professional social workers have participated in and endorsed this vast system of handouts; who are we, say the ladies of the soup kitchen, to question the practice of blind giving, of giving without expecting anything in return?

A misguided religious tradition also encourages thoughtlessness in giving. In ancient times, giving was a way to prove faith in God. Scriptures demanded sacrificing animals and giving tithes as evidence of obedience and as acts of worship. The giver of a tithe wasn't expected to know or care whether the priests getting the tithe deserved the money, or whether they used it wisely. All that mattered was that he had made the sacrifice that proved his obedience to God.

This view lives on. Sharon M. Daly, the deputy director for social policy at Catholic Charities USA, declares that "in the Catholic tradition, the primary purpose of charity is not to reform the poor, but to bring us closer to God—to save our *own* souls."[3] This is a self-centered view of giving, one that downplays the importance of finding out whether our gifts to the poor are really beneficial.

At my church in Sandpoint, Idaho, I came upon a volunteer, a kind and worthy woman, distributing plastic bags to all parishioners for an upcoming food drive. I asked her whether she knew that the food actually helped the people who would get it. She frankly confessed to having made no effort to find out who received the food, or why, or how it might affect their lives for good or ill. "That's not my job," she said. "All I know is I tried. My conscience is clear." Religiously based self-sacrifice may be admirable, but it should not be carried on at the expense of the poor. If we say we care about the poor, then it is our duty to help *them*. Attention must shift from ourselves, as givers, to those we try to help.

Every social assistance program, therefore, needs an analytical component. Staff, board members, volunteers, and donors need to meet frequently to analyze goals and methods. Groups should have at least a one-hour meeting a month devoted exclusively to this function. Questions to be discussed should include the following:

- Who are our recipients, and how should our program help them?

- How do we know we are helping them?

- In what way might our program be harming recipients (or others)?

- How can we bring about more direct personal contact between helpers and helped?

A suburban Washington church runs an assistance program for the needy of the District of Columbia, giving them food, clothing, travel vouchers, and small amounts of cash. I asked one staff member, a social worker of wide experience with street people, what percentage of the clients of this program were either alcoholic or drug-addicted. "Ninety-eight percent," she replied, then explained that these clients were in need of counseling, befriending, and inspiring—if indeed anything could reach them—and that food and clothing were essentially irrelevant to their real needs.

Toward the end of the interview, an elderly, middle-class volunteer came into the room bearing a carton of juice packets that she was donating to the program. I asked her to estimate the percentage of clients who were drug- or alcohol-addicted. "Oh, I would say 10 percent" was her reply. Clearly, someone is seriously misinformed about the clientele being served by this program. Perhaps it is the volunteer, perhaps it is the social worker. The important point is that issues like this must be raised before any program can supply effective assistance.

No Excuse for Sympathetic Giving

▼

A program should never involve something-for-nothing giving to strangers. This counsel may seem unduly strict, but there's a good reason to be firm. Almost everyone agrees that giveaways are not a high-quality form of assistance. Volunteers operating a free soup kitchen, for example, will not assert that this aid is rescuing the homeless or transforming their lives. They will say, rather apologetically, that it is "the best we can do," or that "at least it's better than nothing."

Neither of these claims should be conceded. Giveaways are never the "best we can do." Even with slender resources, it is possible to create constructive programs of expectant giving, programs that staff, volunteers, and donors will feel enthusiastic about. Give-away programs are a warning sign, pointing toward lack of imagi-nation, a burnt-out staff, volunteers who hold the people they serve at arm's length, or an agency comfortably ensconced in a govern-ment subsidy. The leaders of such a program are almost certainly not holding monthly brainstorming meetings about the purpose of the program and whether it is helping its clients.

It is also rarely true that giveaways are "better than nothing." The general effect of sympathetic giving is to enhance the viability of a dysfunctional—and therefore *suffering*—lifestyle. There will be exceptions, of course: managers of giveaway programs find that from time to time a client returns to thank them for the assistance and reports having gained self-sufficiency. Even if this case is taken at face value, it does not establish the value of the program; left out are all those clients whose suffering was prolonged by the enabling effect of the giveaway.

On the average, sympathetic giving is harmful to recipients. This is the general principle that all the nineteenth-century charity theorists discovered. It may disturb us to confront this old truth, but the path to sound policy requires that we grasp it. The rou-tinized giving of material assistance to strangers must be seen as a vice, not as a praiseworthy activity.

For those who operate programs of sympathetic giving, recogniz-ing that they have drifted into vice can have a healthy galvanizing effect. Many reformers will see that they can fix this defect by instituting some features of exchange. A soup kitchen might make a small charge, for example, or require some kind of work.

Time and again, reformers have to depart from the bad lesson taught by government. For example, government subsidy systems of medical care for the poor have established the tradition that health services should be free, an entitlement requiring no quid pro quo. The principle is unsound, of course. Medical care is a service requiring labor and effort, and this sacrifice needs to be honored by clients.

Private charitable clinics have developed sensitive ways to ask for appropriate payment. The East Liberty Family Health Care Center in Pittsburgh, for example, practices "fee counseling." The bookkeeper meets with the client, explains the full cost of the service, and points out that the client has a responsibility to repay as much as he can; then a payment plan is worked out. No proof of income or assets is required. Clinic staff report an extremely high level of compliance with these voluntary payment plans.

The clinic of the Lawndale urban ministry in Chicago has a minimum fee of eight dollars per visit and a sliding scale of payment based on family size and income. For clients with no money, says cofounder Wayne Gordon, "we have a long list of jobs that need to be done." This is healthier all around. "The truth is that most people want to work. They want to give something in return for what they have received."[4]

In some giveaway programs, discussion among the leaders will reveal that there is no useful way to implement the exchange idea. That's an important piece of information. It suggests that, given its resources, expertise, and clientele, the group is operating in unpromising territory. It should shift to a helping program through which it can effect an exchange. For example, a group of middle-class women running a food bank for inner-city drug addicts may find that charging for the food, or requiring work in exchange, makes the clients disappear. The conclusion should not be that giving the food away is "the best we can do." It should be, "We're out of our depth." They should turn their energies to an activity better suited to their talents and resources—organizing a baby-sitting club for low-income mothers, let us say.

The Personal Touch

▼

Mentoring is the foundation of uplift. Personal relationships between helpers and helped are invaluable in a social assistance system. They are a source of information about what the poor really need, and they lead to the friendships that can motivate and guide real change.

Octavia Hill was a master at developing assistance programs that provided for natural, friendly contacts with the poor. The housing system she set up is an excellent example. Middle-class women became managers and rent collectors in housing units for the poor. This brought them into continuous contact with tenants, and from this businesslike connection, personal ties of trust and friendship naturally grew.

Modern-day Octavia Hills have come forth in recent years to apply this old idea of putting helpers and helped into personal contact. In Holland, Michigan, in 1976, Virgil Gulker developed a program to put church members in contact with people who needed their skills and support. Gulker was led to the system after he discovered that church members were being cut off from the needy. In his book *Help Is Just Around the Corner*, Gulker explains the problem:

> The usual arrangements for helping the needy remove opportunities from church members, reserving those opportunities for a corps of professionals and a small number of others. Church members are deprived of their privilege, their birthright, to minister "to the least of these."[5]

He found that existing assistance programs, by giving away material goods, were cultivating unhealthy attitudes. For example, a number of churches gave away clothing so recklessly that some recipients never did laundry. "When clothes got dirty, they threw them away and went back for more."

> It was incredibly frustrating to realize that our way of doing things unintentionally kept people focused exclusively on their physical needs. We made it virtually impossible for them to achieve any level of self-esteem, because the helping experience was not designed to give them the help they really needed to become self-sufficient.[6]

Gulker's system for involving people in a direct personal way with those who need assistance—called Love, Inc.—has since spread to 102 towns in 39 states.

Another group that stresses personal contact is the Christian community development movement that has grown out of the work of the Black Christian leader John Perkins. In 1960 Perkins began a ministry of social activism in Mendenhall, Mississippi; twelve years later, he began another in Jackson, Mississippi, and another in Pasadena, California, in 1982. In his book *Beyond Charity*, he notes the failure of giveaway programs and the need for a new approach: "As Christians, we need to rethink the way we do charity. If the past thirty years have taught us anything about the poverty mentality it is that undisciplined giving can be just as destructive as the poverty it was meant to alleviate."[7]

Perkins's approach is for community leaders to move into the distressed community to build up personal relationships:

> Instead of coming with a quick-fix solution, more suburban people of all races need to hear and answer the call of God to put themselves in direct, personal relationship to the urban community in order to discover the felt needs of the people. The most effective way to do this is by living among the very people that we have been called to serve.[8]

Following Perkins's lead, reformers have settled in many urban areas to pursue their ministries. They establish friendships, find out what residents need, and work with them to organize day-care centers, health clinics, Bible study groups, thrift stores, and so on. The "urban ministry" idea has been spreading rapidly in recent years. The Christian Community Development Association was founded in 1989 with 37 member organizations; it now has more than 400.

"All They Do Is Take and Take"

▼

Helpers should feel proud of their clients. All too often, social assistance is seen as a "sacrificing" activity, something unpleasant done out of a sense of obligation. Duty has its place in charity, but mainly as a spark plug, a motive for getting involved initially. In the long run, it is not a healthy drive, and it will not lead to a successful social assistance program. Octavia Hill again illustrates the ideal. As her writings make clear, she took enormous delight in her activities as a volunteer apartment manager and was extremely proud of her tenants. If helpers don't feel rewarded and enthusiastic about their clients, it is a sign that those clients are not being uplifted.

One of the most common causes of staff and volunteer discouragement is being involved in a program of sympathetic giving. Helpers sense that they are treating only symptoms and not providing lasting help. And since clients aren't being uplifted, helpers find little to admire about them.

This point comes out clearly in Elliot Liebow's in-depth account of several homeless shelters in the Washington, D.C., area. These shelters were run on the giveaway principle, with no significant effort expected from clients. Liebow was distressed to discover that many volunteers and staff members privately resented recipients. When men at a soup kitchen complained that their soup wasn't hot, Liebow took the bowls back to the volunteer serving the soup, but she refused to reheat it. He brought the matter to the attention of the assistant manager, who also refused to do anything about it. "I don't know what they're complaining about," said the assistant manager. "This ain't the Waldorf Astoria, and they're getting it for free."[9]

When, at a women's shelter, a client refused a tuna casserole and asked for something different, a volunteer privately shared her frustration with Liebow: "Those seven people who were killed last week [the *Challenger* astronauts]—they gave so much to the world, and they died giving more. But these people, they give nothing. All they do is take and take and ask for more."[10]

Although staff and volunteers thought they were covering up their resentment, Liebow found that clients often sensed it, and of course they were hurt. The overall result was tragically ironic. Volunteers and staff wanted to help the homeless, but because their giveaway programs put clients in a bad light, the volunteers disparaged them and unintentionally impaired the clients' already fragile self-esteem. The situation parallels the case of children whose parents don't demand a contribution to the household. The parents' growing resentment of them for being lazy and selfish makes the children insecure.

The solution is painfully obvious: expect an exchange, expect performance in return for help. A volunteer who complains about clients who "take and take" is like a parent deploring her lazy children. Who made them lazy? Who operates the handout system that cultivates a dependent, grasping orientation?

In visiting charities around the country, I have been struck by the correlation between the type of giving and the enthusiasm of workers and volunteers. In charities that operate giveaway programs, participants tend to be weary and frustrated—and also rather secretive, reluctant to talk about the program and unwilling to supply information about it. On the other hand, in programs that demand a great deal from clients, morale is high. Staff members are so enthusiastic about their program that they won't let the interview end. They are like parents who are proud of their children's accomplishments.

The strongest social assistance programs—those that are most helpful to clients and most attractive to donors and volunteers—are the ones that expect the most from clients.

Higher Types of Giving

▼

Assistance programs should emphasize creating opportunities and changing attitudes, not meeting material needs. In considering the problems of the poor, the first impulse is to assume that the needy require material goods, and that supplying these goods will cure the neediness. As we build up personal relationships with needy individuals and gain a chance to look more deeply into the nature of their problems, we see ever more clearly that their real needs are not material. They need guidance, motivation, and opportunities. The point was axiomatic for the nineteenth-century charity theorists; modern charity workers like Virgil Gulker and John Perkins have seen it too.

Unfortunately, many charity groups are still bogged down in a materialistic approach. One is struck, for example, by the widespread giving of food practiced by churches and civic groups. These food programs are not the product of any careful analysis of what the poor really need. Enormous amounts of free food have long been available all around the nation, as those who work with the needy will confirm. John Woods, former director of the Gospel Mission of Washington, D.C., calls the proposition that "the homeless are hungry" the number-one myth about street people. There is, in fact, so much free food available that a program to demand even a tiny amount of work in exchange for food would probably fail: recipients would simply turn to giveaways elsewhere.

When charity reformers gather to discuss strategies and purposes, they should avoid focusing on the *things* needy people may lack. The plan they come up with may involve material assistance, but the focus should be on creating opportunities that let people fill their own needs. As Woods puts it, "I believe we can solve the problem of homelessness. But we need to stop asking what we can do for the homeless. The success of a homeless program hinges on what it enables the homeless to accomplish on their own."[11]

The needy require programs that challenge them and motivate them. In such programs, mere hand-wringing compassion is no help and often gets in the way. We need insight, imagination, and confidence that the needy will live up to their potential as human beings.

Notes

Introduction: Managing a Policy
Beyond Our Comprehension

1. Christopher Georges, "Many States, Overwhelmed, Delay the Moment When Food-Stamp Ax Comes Crashing Down," *Wall Street Journal*, March 11, 1997.

Chapter One:
The Policy Nobody Wants

1. Steve Farkas, *The Values We Live By: What Americans Want from Welfare Reform* (New York: Public Agenda, 1996), pp. 12, 14.
2. R. Kent Weaver and William T. Dickens, *Looking Before We Leap: Social Science and Welfare Reform* (Washington, D.C.: Brookings Institution, 1995), p. 113.
3. Henry Goldstein, "We've Lost Our Will to Help America's Poor," *Chronicle of Philanthropy* (September 19, 1996): 57.
4. Johnson quote from "President Johnson's Message on Poverty" (March 16, 1964), reproduced in U.S. Congress, Senate Committee on Labor and Public Welfare, *The War on Poverty: The Economic Opportunity Act of 1964 (A Compilation of Materials Relevant to S.2642)* (Washington, D.C.: Government Printing Office, 1964), pp. 1, 2. Shriver quote from U.S. Congress, House of Representatives, Economic Opportunity Act of 1964 (Hearings Before the Subcommittee on the War on Poverty Program of the Committee on Education and Labor) (Washington, D.C.: Government Printing Office, 1964), p. 20.

5. William Lock, statement at the regional meeting of the Philanthropy Roundtable, Grand Rapids, Michigan; published in *Philanthropy* (Summer 1996): 11.

6. Fred L. Israel, ed., *State of the Union Messages of the Presidents 1790–1966*, vol. 3 (New York: Chelsea House, 1966), pp. 2814–15.

7. Lyndon Johnson, message on poverty to the U.S. Congress, March 16, 1964.

8. Richard Nixon, special message on welfare reform to the U.S. Congress, March 27, 1972.

Chapter Two:
Helping Those in Need: Basic Principles

1. Peter Edelman, "The Worst Thing Bill Clinton Has Done," *Atlantic* (March 1997): 58.

Chapter Three:
Buying Trouble: The Problems with Sympathetic Giving

1. U.S. House Committee on Agriculture, *Food Stamp Plan: Hearings,* 88th Cong., 1st sess., June 10, 1963, p. 17.

2. For example, five years later, in 1968, Secretary Freeman was back testifying on the food stamp program before the House Committee on Agriculture, asking for an appropriation of $245 million—more than twice what he had earlier predicted would be necessary for the permanent program. A congressman pressed him to project how much the program would eventually cost. "To improve this program and to begin to move it towards an adequate nutritional level—we are still below where we ought to be—will take considerably more," said Freeman. "In the long run, to reach all of the counties, to reach all of the people, to have a mature and efficient-working program, the total program would run—and, again, a horseback opinion—about $1.5 billion." U.S. House Committee on Agriculture, *Amend. to the Food Stamp Act of 1964: Hearings,* 90th Cong., 2d sess., June 11, 1968, p. 76.

3. This episode is discussed in James L. Payne, *The Culture of Spending: Why Congress Lives Beyond Our Means* (San Francisco: ICS Press, 1991), pp. 72–73. Data on the food stamp program from U.S.

Department of Agriculture, Food and Nutrition Service, *Food Stamp Program Information for FY 1980 Through 1995* (April 1996), pp. 3, 5. Estimates for Puerto Rico have been added to participation totals.

4. Barbara Howell and Lynette Engelhardt, "Elect to End Childhood Hunger," *Bread* (Bread for the World newsletter) (February 1996): 5.

5. Quoted in James T. Patterson, *America's Struggle Against Poverty 1900–1985* (Cambridge, Mass.: Harvard University Press, 1986), p. 89.

6. Quoted in Samuel Mencher, *Poor Law to Poverty Program: Economic Security Policy in Britain and the United States* (Pittsburgh: University of Pittsburgh Press, 1967), p. 96.

7. The reader should be aware that the Reform Act of 1834 is in the eye of the modern left-right ideological storm, and therefore the study of this period has been severely affected by modern biases. The poor law system prior to 1834 amounted to a giveaway/income redistribution system of the kind favored by modern left-wing scholars, who are deeply hostile toward the charity theorists who reformed the system. Their bias makes it difficult to get a fair picture of nineteenth-century charity problems and personalities from modern sources.

8. Anonymous, *Essays on the Principles of Charitable Institutions* (London: Longman, 1836), p. 139.

9. Ibid., pp. 139–44.

10. Quoted in Marvin Olasky, *The Tragedy of American Compassion* (Washington, D.C.: Regnery, 1992), p. 55.

11. Ibid., pp. 56, 58.

12. Ibid., p. 72.

13. Quoted in ibid., p. 61.

14. Quoted in ibid., p. 62.

15. Michael Tanner, Stephen Moore, and David Hartman, "The Work Versus Welfare Trade-off: An Analysis of the Total Level of Welfare Benefits by State," *Policy Analysis*, no. 240 (Washington, D.C.: Cato Institute, September 19, 1995), p. 18.

16. Ibid., p. 22.

17. Douglas J. Besharov, "Using Work to Reform Welfare," *Public Welfare* (Summer 1995): 18.

18. George J. Borjas and Lynette Hilton, "Immigration and the Welfare

State: Immigrant Participation in Means-Tested Entitlement Programs," *Quarterly Journal of Economics* (May 1996): 580. This study did not include unemployment benefits or social security as welfare programs.

19. Summarizing the results of several dozen studies, the economist Robert Moffitt reports that "the econometric studies show that labor supply is reduced by the AFDC and Food Stamp programs, [and] that higher potential benefits induce greater participation in these programs." Robert Moffitt, "Incentive Effects of the U.S. Welfare System: A Review," *Journal of Economic Literature* 30, no. 1 (March 1992): 1–61, 56.

20. Philip K. Robins, Robert G. Spiegelman, Samuel Weiner, and Joseph G. Bell, eds., *A Guaranteed Annual Income: Evidence from a Social Experiment* (New York: Academic Press, 1980); Charles Murray, *Losing Ground: American Social Policy 1950–1980* (New York: Basic Books, 1984), pp. 148–53.

21. For a comprehensive review of the studies on this issue, see Michael Tanner, *The End of Welfare: Fighting Poverty in the Civil Society* (Washington, D.C.: Cato Institute, 1996), pp. 69–85.

22. See Kay S. Hymowitz, "The Teen Mommy Track," *City Journal* (Autumn 1964): 19–29; Elijah Anderson, *StreetWise: Race, Class, and Change in an Urban Community* (Chicago: University of Chicago Press, 1990), ch. 4.

23. John B. O'Donnell and Jim Haner, "Welfare Gone Haywire," *Reader's Digest* (May 1995): 96.

24. Social Security Administration, "Fast Facts and Figures," in *Annual Statistical Supplement, 1995 to the Social Security Bulletin* (Washington, D.C.: U.S. GPO, 1995), cover III.

25. Council of Economic Advisers, *Economic Report of the President* (Washington, D.C.: U.S. GPO, January 1964), p. 77.

26. Sheila Zedlewski, Sandra Clark, Eric Meier, and Keith Watson, "Potential Effects of Congressional Welfare Reform Legislation on Family Incomes" (Washington, D.C.: Urban Institute, July 26, 1996), p. 6.

Chapter Four:
"A More Excellent Way of Charity"

1. Gertrude Himmelfarb, *Poverty and Compassion: The Moral Imagination of the Late Victorians* (New York: Random House, 1992), pp. 186, 202.

2. E. Moberly Bell, *Octavia Hill* (London: Constable, 1942), p. 26.

3. Ibid.

4. Ibid., p. 28

5. Ibid., p. 29.

6. Ibid., p. 27

7. Octavia Hill, *Our Common Land and Other Short Essays* (London: Macmillan, 1877), p. 74.

8. Bell, *Octavia Hill*, p. 202.

9. Joseph Marie de Generando, *The Visitor of the Poor* (Boston: Hilliard, Grey, Little, and Wilkins, 1832), pp. 10, 15.

10. Ibid., p. 11.

11. Josephine Shaw Lowell, *Public Relief and Private Charity* (New York: G. P. Putnam's Sons, 1884; reprint, New York: Arno, 1971), p. 84.

12. Octavia Hill, *The Befriending Leader: Social Assistance Without Dependency: Essays by Octavia Hill*, edited by James L. Payne (Sandpoint, Idaho: Lytton Publishing, 1997), pp. 68–70.

13. De Gerando, *The Visitor of the Poor*, p. 14.

14. Mary E. Richmond, *Friendly Visiting Among the Poor: A Handbook for Charity Workers* (1899; reprint, Montclair, N.J.: Patterson Smith, 1969), pp. 49–52. In portions of the passage, Richmond is quoting the English charity theorist Helen Bosanquet.

15. Edward Thomas Devine, "The Essentials of a Relief Policy," *Annals of the American Academy* (1903): 19.

16. Mary Conyngton, *How to Help: A Manual of Practical Charity* (New York: Macmillan, 1909), p. 10.

17. Charles Richmond Henderson, *Modern Methods of Charity* (New York: Macmillan, 1904), p. 338.

18. Frank Dekker Watson, *The Charity Organization Movement in the United States* (New York: Macmillan, 1922), p. 360.

19. Quoted by Max Siporin, "Mary Richmond: A Founder of Modern Social Work," in Richmond, *Friendly Visiting Among the Poor*, p. x.

20. Hill, *The Befriending Leader*, p. 74.
21. Conyngton, *How to Help*, p. 8.
22. Frederic Almy, *Relief: A Primer for the Family Rehabilitation Work of the Buffalo Charity Organization Society* (New York: Russell Sage, 1910), p. 8. Mary Richmond also criticizes the "worthy/unworthy" distinction in *Friendly Visiting Among the Poor* (p. 154).
23. Helen Dendy Bosanquet (Mrs. Bernard Bosanquet), *Rich and Poor* (London: Macmillan, 1896), pp. v–vi.
24. Lowell, *Public Relief and Private Charity*, p. 111.
25. Hill, *The Befriending Leader*, pp. 47–49.
26. De Gerando, *The Visitor of the Poor*, pp. 74–75.
27. Daniel C. Gilman, "A Panorama of Charitable Work in Many Lands," in *The Organization of Charities* (Baltimore: Johns Hopkins University Press, 1894), p. x.
28. Hill, *The Befriending Leader*, p. 46.
29. Charles Richmond Henderson, *Modern Methods of Charity* (New York: Macmillan, 1904), pp. 554–55.

Chapter Five:
How Government Gives

1. Ellen Nedde, "Welfare Reform in the United States," International Monetary Fund working paper WP/95/124 (November 1995), pp. 1, i.
2. U.S. House of Representatives, Committee on Ways and Means, *1996 Green Book* (Washington, D.C.: U.S. GPO, 1996), pp. 459, 1319.
3. Robert Rector and William F. Lauber, *America's Failed $5.4 Trillion War on Poverty* (Washington, D.C.: Heritage Foundation, 1995), p. 12. The *1996 Green Book* gives $316 billion for 1993 and $345 billion for 1994 (the latest year available) (pp. 1319, 1320).
4. General Accounting Office, "Employment Training: Successful Projects Share Common Strategy," (May 1996), p. 1.
5. House Ways and Means Committee, *1996 Green Book*, p. 854.
6. Christopher Georges and Dana Milbank, "Sweeping Overhaul of Welfare Would Put Onus on the States," *Wall Street Journal*, July 31, 1996.
7. Rector and Lauber, *America's Failed $5.4 Trillion War on Poverty*, p. 76.
8. U.S. Department of Labor, Office of the Inspector General, "Job

Corps: Analysis of Return on Investment for the Job Corps Program, Program Year Ended June 30, 1992," report 12–96–002–03–370, p. 39.

9. James L. Payne, *Costly Returns: The Burdens of the U.S. Tax System* (San Francisco: ICS Press, 1993), p. 150.

10. House Ways and Means Committee, *1996 Green Book*, p. 1319; Rector and Lauber, *America's Failed $5.4 Trillion War on Poverty*, pp. 96–97.

11. Congressional Budget Office, "Federal Budgetary Implications of H.R. 3734" (August 9, 1996), table 1.

12. The *Wall Street Journal* (Dana Milbank, "Clinton Says He Will Sign Welfare Bill," August 1, 1996) told its readers that the welfare reform measure "would make deep cuts in food stamps" when in fact food stamp spending was slated to rise from $26 billion to $35 billion. The *Christian Science Monitor* (Daniel Sneider, "Legal Immigrants Hit Hard by Aid Cutbacks," July 25, 1996) said that "federal spending would drop an estimated $59 billion over the next seven years" when in fact spending on the affected welfare programs was slated to rise by $98 billion. The *New York Times* headline on August 23, 1996, was "Clinton Signs Bill Cutting Welfare." An accurate headline would have said, "Clinton Signs Bill Boosting Welfare."

13. Edward Zigler, Sally J. Styfco, and Elizabeth Gilman, "The National Head Start Program for Disadvantaged Preschoolers," in *Head Start and Beyond: A National Plan for Extended Childhood Intervention*, edited by Edward Zigler and Sally J. Styfco (New Haven: Yale University Press, 1993), p. 4.

14. Lawrence M. Mead, *Beyond Entitlement: The Social Obligations of Citizenship* (New York: Free Press, 1986), p. 1.

15. Quoted in Jason DeParle, "Getting Opal Caples to Work," *New York Times Magazine*, August 24, 1997, p. 59.

16. *Newsweek*, February 17, 1964, p. 38; quoted in Patterson, *America's Struggle Against Poverty*, p. 135.

17. Patterson, *America's Struggle Against Poverty*, p. 66.

18. Nancy E. Rose, *Workfare or Fair Work: Women, Welfare, and Government Work Programs* (New Brunswick, N.J.: Rutgers University Press, 1995), pp. 173–74.

19. Jonathan Riskind, "Bill Requiring Diploma for Welfare Nearing Vote," *Columbus Dispatch*, May 25, 1995.

20. LaDonna Pavetti, et al., "Designing Welfare-to-Work Programs for Families Facing Personal or Family Challenges: Lessons from the Field" (Washington, D.C.: Urban Institute, December 30, 1996), p. 3.
21. Ibid.
22. Randy Kennedy, "Workfare Screening of Homeless Starts, Then Stops," *New York Times*, August 21, 1996.
23. Karen Arenson, "Workfare Rules Cause Enrollment to Fall, CUNY Says," *New York Times*, June 1, 1996; "Making Workfare Work for Students," *New York Times*, June 10, 1996.

Chapter Six:
Paying for Failure

1. The General Accounting Office (*Employment Training* [May 1996], p. 1) summarized the official view in 1996: "Congressional and public confidence in federal employment training efforts has eroded in the face of concern that the myriad federally funded employment training programs are characterized by conflicting requirements, overlapping populations, and questionable outcomes." For a review of studies on the failure of job training programs, see Tanner, *The End of Welfare*, pp. 95–99.
2. Quoted in Ken Auletta, *The Underclass* (New York: Random House, 1983), p. 23.
3. Ibid., pp. 65, 57, 120, 121, 122, 153.
4. Social Security Administration, "A Brief History of Social Security" (July 1995), pp. 1, 19.
5. U.S. Department of Health and Human Services, "Standards of Conduct," Personnel Pamphlet Series No. 6 (March 30, 1989), p. 3 (italics added).
6. House Ways and Means Committee, *1996 Green Book*, pp. 861, 870–71.
7. General Accounting Office, *Food Assistance: Reducing Food Stamp Benefit Overpayments and Trafficking* (June 1995), p. 35.
8. General Accounting Office, *Earned Income Credit: Data on Noncompliance and Illegal Alien Recipients* (October 1994), p. 4.
9. General Accounting Office, "Tax Administration Earned Income Credit Noncompliance," testimony of Lynda D. Willis (May 8, 1997), p. 4.

10. These problems are discussed in John A. Gardiner and Theodore R. Lyman, *The Fraud Control Game: State Responses to Fraud and Abuse in AFDC and Medicaid Programs* (Bloomington: Indiana University Press, 1984), p. 7 and passim.

11. Christopher Jencks and Kathryn Edin, "The Real Welfare Problem," *American Prospect* (Spring 1990): 31–50. The authors' purpose in presenting this data was to show that welfare recipients could not survive on their welfare grants, and that therefore benefits should be raised. The data also support an opposite conclusion: welfare recipients are more resourceful than generally portrayed and are therefore capable of supporting themselves without aid. In a subsequent larger study, Edin has confirmed the finding that virtually all AFDC recipients have unreported income; see Kathryn Edin and Laura Lein, *Making Ends Meet: How Single Mothers Survive Welfare and Low-Wage Work* (New York: Russell Sage Foundation, 1997).

12. Ibid., p. 37.

13. Gardiner and Lyman, *The Fraud Control Game*, p. 123. A fraud control officer in Utah's welfare system reported that his efforts are repeatedly undermined by program officers unwilling to follow up on his findings of fraud. "Those of us involved in the law-enforcement end of welfare are frequently frustrated by the lack of consequence for a violation of the rules," concludes Stephen Hayes in "Welfare Fraud," *Policy Review* (May–June 1997): 5.

14. U.S. House of Representatives, Committee on Ways and Means, Subcommittee on Oversight, *Report on Reforms to Address Supplemental Security Income Fraud and Abuse Involving Middlemen*, May 12, 1994, pp. 5–6.

15. Ibid., pp. 4–5, 6.

16. U.S. Department of Labor, Inspector General, "Job Corps: Analysis of Return on Investment," pp. 22, 108. See also General Accounting Office, "Job Corps: High Costs and Mixed Results Raise Questions About Program's Effectiveness," June 1995, pp. 2, 7. The GAO notes that even the levels of employment claimed for Job Corps graduates, low as they are, are padded by at least 10 percent (p. 16). See also Charles Mallar et al., *Evaluation of the Economic Impact of the Job Corps Program, Third Follow-up Report* (Princeton, N.J.: Mathematica Policy Research, 1982), pp. 134, 136.

17. "Bipartisan Budget Agreement Between the President and the Leadership of Congress," May 15, 1997, p. 8.
18. Richmond, *Friendly Visiting Among the Poor*, pp. 151–52.

Chapter Seven:
Can the Poor Survive Income Redistribution?

1. Sir Thomas More, *Utopia*, translated and edited by Robert M. Adams (New York: Norton, 1995), p. 82.
2. The first treatments were those of Michael J. Boskin in "Efficiency Aspects of the Differential Tax Treatment of Market and Household Economic Activity," *Journal of Public Economics* 4 (1975): 1–25; and Edgar K. Browning in "The Marginal Cost of Public Funds," *Journal of Political Economy* 84 (April 1976): 283–98.
3. Charles L. Ballard, John B. Shoven, and John Whalley, "General Equilibrium Computations of the Marginal Welfare Costs of Taxes in the United States," *American Economic Review* (March 1985): 135.
4. John H. Wicks, "Taxpayer Compliance Costs from Personal Income Taxation," *Iowa Business Digest* (August 1966): 16–21.
5. Arthur D. Little, Inc., *Development of Methodology for Estimating the Taxpayer Paperwork Burden* (Washington, D.C.: Internal Revenue Service, 1988); U.S. House of Representatives, Committee on Ways and Means, *Replacing the Federal Income Tax*, prepared testimony of James L. Payne, 104th Cong., 1st sess., June 6, 7, and 8, 1995, p. 185.
6. Ibid. See also Payne, *Costly Returns*.
7. General Accounting Office, "Tax Administration: Employment Taxes and Small Business" (Testimony before the National Commission on Restructuring the Internal Revenue Service), November 8, 1996, p. 7.
8. U.S. House of Representatives, Committee on Ways and Means, *Where Your Money Goes: America's Entitlements (1994–1995)* (Washington, D.C.: Brassey's, 1994), p. 761.
9. Edgar K. Browning, *Redistribution and the Welfare System* (Washington, D.C.: American Enterprise Institute, 1975), pp. 4, 104.
10. Richard A. Cloward and Frances Fox Piven, *The Politics of Turmoil: Essays on Poverty, Race, and the Urban Crisis* (New York: Pantheon Books, 1974), pp. 89, 91.

11. Ibid., p. 89.

12. Guida West, *The National Welfare Rights Movement: The Social Protest of Poor Women* (New York: Praeger, 1981), p. 380.

13. Browning, *Redistribution and the Welfare System*, p. 4.

14. Cloward and Piven, *The Politics of Turmoil*, p. 92.

15. Ibid., p. 89.

16. Christopher Frenze, "Income Mobility and Economic Opportunity," 2d ed., U.S. Senate, Joint Economic Committee Report, August 1995, p. 3.

17. Cloward and Piven, *The Politics of Turmoil*, p. 92. The authors have misused "coerce" to apply to a voluntary exchange.

18. William Julius Wilson, *When Work Disappears: The World of the New Urban Poor* (New York: Alfred A. Knopf, 1996), pp. 112–13, 128.

19. Assar Lindbeck, "Hazardous Welfare-State Dynamics," *American Economic Review* (May 1995): 9.

Chapter Eight:
What Social Workers Believe

1. Linda Cherrey Reeser and Irwin Epstein, *Professionalization and Activism in Social Work: The Sixties, the Eighties, and the Future* (New York: Columbia University Press, 1990), pp. 21–22.

2. *NASW News* (June 1996): 1.

3. Herbert Bisno, *The Philosophy of Social Work* (Washington, D.C.: Public Affairs Press, 1952), p. 5. The statement is approvingly quoted in *Handbook of Clinical Social Work* (San Francisco: Jossey-Bass, 1983), p. 60.

4. Armando T. Morales and Bradford W. Sheafor, *Social Work: A Profession of Many Faces*, 7th ed. (Boston: Allyn and Bacon, 1995), p. 40.

5. Louise C. Johnson and Charles L. Schwartz, *Social Welfare: A Response to Human Need*, 3d ed. (Boston: Allyn and Bacon, 1994), p. 5.

6. Charles Zastrow, *The Practice of Social Work*, 2d ed. (Chicago: Dorsey Press, 1985), p. 46.

7. Quoted in Brenda Dubois and Karla Krogsrud Miley, *Social Work: An Empowering Profession* (Boston: Allyn and Bacon, 1992), p. 122.

8. Heather Mac Donald, "Compassion Gone Mad," *City Journal* (Winter 1996): 90.

9. Mark Robert Rank, "The Realities of Welfare in America," in *Welfare Reform: Facts, Myths and Consequences*, proceedings of a conference sponsored by University Extension, Department of Economics and The Institute of Governmental Affairs, University of California at Davis, May 5, 1995, p. 58.

10. *Encyclopedia of Social Work*, vol. 1, 18th ed. (Silver Spring, Md.: National Association of Social Workers, 1987), p. 894.

11. "Values and Ethics," in ibid., p. 801.

12. John A. Brown, *Handbook of Social Work Practice* (Springfield, Ill.: Charles C. Thomas, 1992), p. 50.

13. Zastrow, *The Practice of Social Work*, p. 38.

14. National Association of Social Workers, *Social Work Speaks*, 4th ed. (Washington, D.C.: NASW, 1997), p. 9.

15. Octavia Hill, *Homes of the London Poor*, 2d ed. (London: Macmillan, 1883), p. 10.

16. H. Wayne Johnson, *The Social Services: An Introduction*, 4th ed. (Itasca, Ill.: F. A. Peacock, 1995), p. 31.

17. Johnson and Schwartz, *Social Welfare*, p. 65.

18. Rank, "The Realities of Welfare in America," p. 61.

19. Ann Hartman, "Homelessness: Public Issue and Private Trouble," in *Reflection and Controversy: Essays on Social Work* (Washington, D.C.: NASW Press, 1994), pp. 92–93, 95.

20. Harry Specht and Mark E. Courtney, *Unfaithful Angels: How Social Work Has Abandoned Its Mission* (New York: Free Press, 1994), pp. 7, 171.

21. Arthur J. Altmeyer, "Social Security in a Postwar World," *Public Welfare* 4, no. 1 (November 1946): 245.

22. Edelman, "The Worst Thing Bill Clinton Has Done," p. 43.

23. Penelope Clarke, "The Experience of Welfare Reform," in *Welfare Reform: Facts, Myths, and Consequences*, p. 47.

24. NASW, *Social Work Speaks*, p. 27.

25. American Public Welfare Association, *Responsibility, Work, Pride: The Values of Welfare Reform* (Wahington, D.C., January 1994), p. 20.

26. American Public Welfare Association, *Good News from the Grassroots: State Welfare Reforms That Work* (Washington, D.C.: APWA, 1995), p. 21.

27. Judith Havemann, "Welfare Reform for Teens Runs into Harsh Reality," *Washington Post*, June 6, 1996.

28. Heather Mac Donald, "Welfare Reform Discoveries," *City Journal* (Winter 1997): 21.
29. National Association of Social Workers, "Social Workers Urge Scrutiny of Welfare Reform's Impact," press release, August 2, 1996.

Chapter Nine:
The Health of Commerce

1. Thomas Mackay, *The State and Charity* (London: Macmillan, 1898), p. 9.
2. Dick J. Reavis, "A Dirty Job," *Dallas Observer*, July 15–21, 1993, pp. 12, 16.
3. Ibid., p. 20.
4. Ann Zimmerman, "Building up Hopes," *Dallas Observer*, February 18–24, 1993, p. 14.
5. Quoted in *Dallas Morning News*, November 29, 1990.
6. Martin L. Buchanan, "Unintended Consequences: How Government Policies Hurt Oregon's Poor," working paper (Portland, OR: Cascade Policy Institute, May 1966), pp. 6–7.
7. Michael Bernick, *Urban Illusions: New Approaches to Inner City Unemployment* (New York: Praeger, 1987), p. 219.
8. Gayle M. B. Hanson, "A Regulatory Nightmare Haunts the American Dream," *Insight* (February 12, 1996): 14.
9. John Tierney, "Save the Flophouse," *New York Times Magazine*, January 14, 1996, p. 16.
10. Ibid.
11. John Tierney, "At the Intersection of Supply and Demand," *New York Times Magazine*, May 4, 1997, p. 42. For a comprehensive account of New York's massive but futile effort to guarantee quality low-income housing through government regulation, see the series "Barely Four Walls," *New York Times*, October 6–11, 1996.
12. Howard Husock, *Repairing the Ladder: Toward a New Housing Policy Paradigm* (Los Angeles: Reason Foundation, July 1996), pp. 26–30.

Chapter Ten:
Charitable Capitalism

1. David Bornstein, "The Barefoot Bank with Cheek," *Atlantic* (December 1995): 40.
2. Quoted in Weldon Welfling, *Mutual Savings Banks: The Evolution of a Financial Intermediary* (Cleveland: Case Western Reserve University Press, 1968), p. 10.
3. Ibid., p. 8.
4. These groups are discussed in Robin Garr, *Reinvesting in America* (Reading, Mass: Addison-Wesley, 1995), pp. 209–12.
5. Margaret Clark, Tracy Huston, and Barbara Meister, *1994 Directory of U.S. Microenterprise Programs* (Washington, D.C.: Aspen Institute, 1994).
6. Bill Shore, *Revolution of the Heart* (New York: Riverhead Books, 1995), pp. 82–83.
7. Hill, *The Befriending Leader*, pp. 11–12.
8. Menlo F. Smith, "Foreign Aid the Voluntary Way," *The Freeman* (October 1994): 555.
9. Albert Schweitzer, *Out of My Life and Thought* (New York: Henry Holt, 1933), p. 113.

Chapter Twelve:
Friends Who Inspire

1. Hill, *The Befriending Leader*, p. 87.
2. Yvonne S. Thornton, *The Ditchdigger's Daughters: A Black Family's Astonishing Success Story* (New York: Birch Lane, 1995), p. 69.
3. Ibid., p. 33.
4. Ibid., p. 43.
5. Ibid., p. 22.
6. Ibid., p. 27.
7. Ibid., p. 57.
8. LouAnne Johnson, *The Girls in the Back of the Class* (New York: St. Martin's Press, 1995), pp. 53–54.
9. Ibid., pp. 36, 148.
10. Peter Michelmore, "All the Right Moves," *Reader's Digest* (January 1996): 141–46.

11. Walter Turnbull, *Lift Every Voice* (New York: Hyperion, 1995), p. 159.

12. Ibid., p. 161.

13. Ibid., p. 229.

14. Ibid., pp. 48–49.

15. Ibid., p. 99.

16. Johnson, *The Girls in the Back of the Class*, p. 50.

17. Ibid., p. 22.

18. Lisa Frazier, "A New Beginning for Mentoring," *Washington Post*, March 12, 1996.

19. Gregg Vanourek, Scott W. Hamilton, and Chester E. Finn Jr., *Is There Life After Big Government? The Potential of Civil Society* (Indianapolis: Hudson Institute, 1996) pp. 39–57.

20. John P. Walters, "HUD Slaps Drug-Rehab Wonder," *Policy Review* (July–August 1996): 7.

21. "Screening in or Screening Out," *The Correspondent* (Spring 1996): 23–24.

Chapter Thirteen:
The Key to Reforming Government Welfare Programs

1. TABLE 13.1: THE FEDERAL DISABILITY BENEFIT SYSTEM, 1997

PROGRAM	COST *(billions)*	NUMBER OF BENEFICIARIES *(millions)*
Disability payments for those with some past work record (DI)	$44.7	6.0*
Disability payments for those with insufficient work record (SSI)		6.6
federal payments	26.6	
state payments	3.0	
Administrative cost	3.3	
Overlap: recipients in both programs		-0.7
Total	77.6	11.9

* Includes spouse and child beneficiaries.

Source: Social Security Administration, current statistical tables and news releases. Figures for March 1997 or twelve-month period ending March 1997. Administrative cost based on 1997 budget request, estimated at one-half total SSA administrative cost, as reported in SSA, *Plan for a New Disability Claim Process* (September 1994), p. 4. Estimate for overlap taken from General Accounting Office, *SSA Disability—Return-to-Work Strategies from Other Systems May Improve Federal Programs* (July 1996), p. 3.

2. U.S. House of Representatives, Committee on Ways and Means, *Where Your Money Goes: The 1994–1995 Green Book* (Washington, D.C.: Brassey's, 1994), p. 55.

3. General Accounting Office, *SSA Disability: Return-to-Work Strategies* (July 1996), p. 2. This figure pertains to DI recipients, who are more likely to work than SSI disability recipients. For other studies on this point, see General Accounting Office, *SSA Disability Program Redesign Necessary to Encourage Return to Work* (April 1996), p. 18; John C. Hennessey and L. Scott Muller, "Work Efforts of Disabled-Worker Beneficiaries," *Social Security Bulletin* (Fall 1994): 43; study by HHS inspector general cited in Christopher M. Wright, "SSI: The Black Hole of the Welfare State," Policy Analysis No. 224 (Washington, D.C.: Cato Institute, April 27, 1995), p. 30.

4. General Accounting Office, *Supplemental Security Income: SSA Efforts Fall Short in Correcting Erroneous Payments to Prisoners* (August 1996), pp. 9–10.

5. Compiled from data given in the testimony of Jane L. Ross, "Social Security Disability Management Action and Program Redesign Needed to Address Long-standing Problems" (Washington, D.C.: General Accounting Office, August 3, 1995), pp. 6–7.

6. For a good survey of the many practices in the disability system that lead to program expansion, see Deborah A. Stone, *The Disabled State* (Philadelphia: Temple University Press, 1984), pp. 146–55.

7. House Ways and Means Committee, *Where Your Money Goes*, p. 57; Social Security Administration, *Plan for a New Disability Claims Process* (September 1994), p. 5; General Accounting Office, *Social Security Disability* (August 1997), p. 59.

8. The ALJ hearing process was not intentionally created as a desirable or needed feature of the disability system. It evolved quite

accidentally from the SSA old-age assistance program, which used ALJs to deal with claimants who lacked birth certificates; see Social Security Administration, Historian's Office, *Evolution and Leadership of the SSA Headquarters Office of Hearings and Appeals* (September 1991), pp. 1–2.

9. Ibid., p. 2.

10. Wright, "SSI: The Black Hole of the Welfare State," p. 14.

11. For a good summary of the *Zebley* issue, see Heather Mac Donald, "Welfare's Next Vietnam," *City Journal* (Winter 1995): 23–38.

12. Catholic Charities USA, "1995 Survey Summary Catholic Charities USA."

13. Kenneth R. Weinstein, "Stand for Children or Last Stand for Big Government?" (Washington, D.C.: Heritage Foundation, May 31, 1996).

14. General Accounting Office, *Social Security: Union Activity at the Social Security Administration* (October 2, 1996), p. 1.

15. GAO, *SSA Disability Program Redesign*, p. 12.

Chapter Fourteen:
The Brave New World of Voluntary Charity

1. Quoted in Paul Demko, "National Summit on Volunteerism Could Galvanize the Non-Profit World," *Chronicle of Philanthropy* (February 6, 1997): 14.

2. Edward Bellamy, *Looking Backward* (1888; New York: New American Library, 1960), p. 73.

3. Michael Harrington, *The Other America: Poverty in the United States* (New York: Macmillan, 1993), p. 171.

4. David Brooks, "A Return to National Greatness," *The Weekly Standard* (March 3, 1997): 20.

5. See G. R. Steele, *The Economics of Friedrich Hayek* (London: Macmillan, 1996), ch. 5.

Chapter Fifteen:
How to Help the Poor

1. Hill, *The Befriending Leader*, p. 65.

2. Rev. Charles G. Ames, "Wisdom in Charity," paper read at the

sixth annual meeting of the Philadelphia Social Science Association, December 7, 1876, p. 3.

3. John Murawski, "An Influential Plea to End the 'Tragedy' of Compassion," *Chronicle of Philanthropy* (June 15, 1995): 11.

4. Wayne L. Gordon, *Real Hope in Chicago* (Grand Rapids, Mich.: Zondervan, 1995), p. 83.

5. Virgil Gulker, *Help Is Just Around the Corner* (Federal Way, Wash.: World Vision/Love, Inc., 1988), p. 33.

6. Ibid., p. 51.

7. John M. Perkins, *Beyond Charity* (Grand Rapids, Mich.: Baker Books, 1993), p. 24.

8. Ibid., p. 33.

9. Elliot Liebow, *Tell Them Who I Am: The Lives of Homeless Women* (New York: Penguin Books, 1995), p. 127.

10. Ibid.

11. John Woods, "Myths About Helping the Homeless," *Washington Post*, April 14, 1996.

Bibliography:
The Nineteenth-Century Charity Theorists

Almy, Frederic. *Relief: A Primer for the Family Rehabilitation Work of the Buffalo Charity Organization Society*. New York: Russell Sage Foundation, 1910.

[Anonymous]. *Essays on the Principles of Charitable Institutions*. London: Longman, Rees, Orme, Brown, Green and Longman, 1836.

Booth, William. *In Darkest England and the Way Out*. London: International Headquarters of the Salvation Army, 1890; reprint, Montclair, N.J.: Patterson Smith, 1975.

Bosanquet, Helen Dendy. *Rich and Poor*. London: Macmillan and Co., 1896.

Chalmers, Thomas. *Chalmers on Charity*. Edited by N. Masterman. Westminster, Eng.: Archibald Constable and Co., 1900.

Chance, Sir William. *The Better Administration of Poor Laws*. London: Swan Sonnenschein, 1895.

———. *Our Treatment of the Poor*. London: P. S. King and Son, 1899.

Conyngton, Mary Katherine. *How to Help*. New York: Macmillan, 1913.

Devine, Edward Thomas. *The Essentials of a Relief Policy*. New York: Charity Organization Society, 1903.

———. *The Principles of Relief*. New York: Macmillan, 1904.

———. *The Practice of Charity*. New York: Dodd, Mead and Co., 1904.

———. *Misery and Its Causes*. New York: Macmillan, 1909.

Emerson, Forrest Fayette. "Charity Reform." An address delivered November 3, 1878, in the Park Church, Hartford, Conn.

Fields, Annie Adams. *How to Help the Poor*. Boston: Houghton Mifflin, 1883.

Gerando, Baron Joseph Marie de. *Visitor of the Poor*. Translated by "A Lady of Boston." Boston: Marsh, Capen and Lyon, 1832.

Gilman, Daniel C. "A Panorama of Charitable Work in Many Lands." In *The Organization of Charities*, report of the Sixth Section of the International Congress of Charities, Corrections, and Philanthropy, Chicago, June 1893. Baltimore: Johns Hopkins University Press, 1894.

Gurteen, Rev. Stephen Humphreys. *Phases of Charity*. 2d ed. New York: Anson D. F. Randolph, 1878.

———. *A Handbook of Charity Organization*. Buffalo: 1882.

Henderson, Charles Richmond. *Modern Methods of Charity*. New York: Macmillan, 1904.

Hill, Octavia. *Our Common Land*. London: Macmillan and Co., 1877.

———. *Letter to Her Fellow Workers in Philadelphia*. Philadelphia: Starr Centre, 1880.

———. *Homes of the London Poor*. London: Macmillan and Co., 1883.

———. *Letters to Fellow-Workers*. London: Adelphi Book Shop, 1933.

———. *The Befriending Leader: Social Assistance Without Dependency*. Edited by James L. Payne. Sandpoint, Idaho: Lytton Publishing Co., 1997.

Hodges, George. *Efficient Philanthropy*. New York: Exchange Branch of Charity Organization Society, 1911.

Lee, Porter. *Treatment: Methods Employed by Organized Charity in the Rehabilitation of Families*. New York: Russell Sage Foundation, 1910.

Lowell, Josephine (Shaw). *Public Relief of Private Charity*. New York: G. P. Putnam's Sons, 1884. Reprinted in *Poverty USA: The Historical Record*, edited by David J. Rothman. New York: Arno Press/New York Times, 1971.

Mackay, Thomas. *The English Poor*. London: John Murray, 1889; reprint, New York: Garland Publishing, 1984.

———. *The State and Charity*. London: Macmillan and Co., 1898.

———. *Public Relief of the Poor*. London: John Murray, 1901.

Moggridge, Matthew Weston. *Method in Almsgiving: Handbook for Helpers*. London: John Murray, 1882.

Paine, Robert Treat. *How to Repress Pauperism and Street Begging*. New York: Charity Organization Society, 1883.

———. *The Empire of Charity Established by the Revolution*. Boston: Press of George H. Ellis, 1895.

Paterson, Arthur. *Administration of Charity*. City Council for Organization of Charity, Clark's Place, Bishop's Gate Within, E.C., 1908. Reprinted from *The Times* (1907).

Richmond, Mary. *Friendly Visiting Among the Poor.* New York: Macmillan, 1899; reprint, Montclair, N.J.: Patterson Smith, 1969.

Rogers, Clement Francis. *Charitable Relief.* London: Longmans, Green and Co., 1904.

Twining, Louisa. *Poor Relief in Foreign Countries and Out-Door Relief in England.* London: Cassell, 1889.

Watson, Frank Dekker. *The Charity Organization Movement in the United States.* New York: Macmillan, 1922.

Index

MEDIA CENTER
ELIZABETHTOWN COMMUNITY COLLEGE
600 COLLEGE STREET ROAD
ELIZABETHTOWN, KY 42701